FINDING

PEACE,
HAPPINESS,
AND JOY

FINDING
PEACE,
HAPPINESS,
AND JOY

RICHARD G. SCOTT

DESERET BOOK

Salt Lake City, Utah

Library of Congress Cataloging-in-Publication Data

Scott, Richard G., 1928-
  Finding peace, happiness, and joy / Richard G. Scott.
    p. cm.
  Includes bibliographical references and index.
  ISBN-13: 978-1-57008-752-3 (hardback : alk. paper)
  1. Christian life—Mormon authors. 2. Peace—Religious aspects—Mormon Church.
3. Happiness—Religious aspects—Mormon Church. 4. Joy—Religious aspects—Mormon
Church. I. Title.
  BX8656.S37 2007
  248.4'89332—dc22   2006035586

Printed in the United States of America
Publishers Printing, Salt Lake City, UT

10   9   8   7   6   5   4   3   2   1

To Jeanene,

my precious wife, whose love, exuberance for life,

and profound faith have inspired this volume

CONTENTS

CONTENTS

PART 3

TO QUALIFY FOR PEACE, HAPPINESS, AND JOY

PART 4

PEACE, HAPPINESS, AND JOY EVEN WITH THE INEVITABLE TRIALS OF LIFE

PART 5

PEACE, HAPPINESS, AND JOY THROUGH DEVELOPING RIGHTEOUS CHARACTER

CONTENTS

PART 6
ADDITIONAL POWERFUL SOURCES OF PEACE, HAPPINESS, AND JOY

ACKNOWLEDGMENTS

I CAN NEVER ADEQUATELY EXPRESS to my precious wife, Jeanene, the breadth and depth of gratitude I feel for her patience, trust, encouragement, and unwavering support in my every righteous endeavor. Throughout her earthly life she led the way to our peace, happiness, and joy. Beyond the veil, she provides the constant motivation to qualify for the supernal blessings of exaltation together. Our treasured children continue to provide like motivation.

My life has been indelibly molded and enduringly enriched by the patient, personal mentoring of Spencer W. Kimball, Ezra Taft Benson, Howard W. Hunter, and Gordon B. Hinckley as Apostles and Presidents of the Church. Presidents Thomas S. Monson, James E. Faust, and Boyd K. Packer have provided like mentoring. The only way to adequately express gratitude for this priceless heritage is to try in my own struggling way to mentor other individuals, personally or through shared messages.

I am also grateful to Elder Neal A. Maxwell, who provided such an impressive example in his own writings and repeatedly encouraged me to write this book.

I express profound gratitude to an exceptionally devoted secretary, Marye Burris, for her painstaking effort to gather the raw material and to transcribe repeated drafts of the majority of the text over a period of several years. I likewise express sincere thanks to Becki Godfrey for her excellent efforts to complete the project.

I am most grateful for the individuals at Deseret Book Company who have worked unitedly to help this book become a reality. Close friend Sheri Dew has been both an inspiration through her exceptional writing and a source of motivating encouragement at times of need. As product director, Cory Maxwell has been an invaluable support and aid. The precise, competent efforts of Jay Parry as editor and Lisa Mangum as editorial assistant have added clarity and improved the accuracy of this work. I thank the designers, Richard Erickson and Sheryl Smith, for their gifted help and Laurie Cook for typesetting the text.

PREFACE

THE SOLE PURPOSE OF this book is to help you, or one you love, find peace with happiness and joy in an ever more challenging world. It is not a book about theory but truth. The counsel it contains is centered in revealed doctrine according to the best of my understanding. Many of the doctrinal foundations are cited in scriptural references, included in footnotes. The truth shared has been proven to be effective by those who have applied it in their personal lives. Its benefit has been repeatedly confirmed in my own personal life and that of my cherished wife, Jeanene. As you read, you will find that some important concepts are repeated. That is intentional. But I will use different examples to clarify those principles so you can understand and use them more easily.

I have written this book in true humility, having prayed and pondered to carefully prepare its content. I have made the effort to express my thoughts as clearly as I am able. I am also aware that unless you prayerfully seek confirmation of the content through the Holy Spirit, most of its value and meaning will be lost. Worse than that, there could develop some misunderstanding that might result in confusion or your misapplication of the gospel principles reviewed.

This book is written to help widely differing audiences. Should you find yourself in a pattern of life you neither enjoy nor want, these pages give suggestions that will lead to peace and happiness. Should you feel that you have made irreparable mistakes, you will learn how to overcome those challenges. This book will also be helpful to you who are living correct principles and desire to avoid the pitfalls of life. It can also serve as a resource to you who are struggling to help a loved one, perhaps a son or daughter, a companion in marriage, an extended family member or close friend who has wandered into errant paths. It describes how the Lord can aid any who are driven by destructive appetites or addictions, helping them begin to shake themselves free of those debilitating habits.

The chapters discuss doctrines and principles that have proven effective in transforming a life from tragic disappointment to one of peace and abounding joy. I have sought to write these things as though the two of us were alone together in an open and frank discussion of truth. Because of the varying nature of the challenges you may face, it is likely that not all counsel will personally apply to you. But I hope that every doctrine and principle reviewed will be of some benefit to you. Each chapter contains truths that are worthy of pondering, even if the specific circumstances do not apply to you.

I have made a conscious attempt to relate doctrine and its practical applications to differing circumstances. My desire was to increase, where needed, your depth of understanding of principles that will aid in your quest for peace and happiness. I have consciously repeated some important principles and scriptures. My intent is to encourage you to more fully use the direction the Lord has provided so that your earth life can be radiantly beautiful and extremely productive as you grow from the challenges you encounter. What is of value herein comes from the abundance of refreshing, ennobling truth the Lord has provided to His children personally or through His prophets—not from the author. I alone am responsible for what is presented.

At critically important times in my life the Lord has made it possible for me to be oriented, guided, and immensely blessed by exceptional mentors. While I can't help you directly in that capacity, my prayer is that the following chapters may be as close to a mentoring experience as I can make it.

Much of the content of this book has been gleaned from lessons I have learned as I have made sincere efforts to help others find peace and happiness where before they have had lives of sorrow, discouragement, and anguish. As my beloved wife, Jeanene, and I lived together the principles emphasized in these chapters, we were richly blessed. Those principles provide me with even greater peace, happiness, and joy now that she is beyond the veil. May the Lord abundantly reward your obedience to His truth in like manner.

PART 1

The Plan of Peace, Happiness, and Joy of the Father

CHAPTER 1

PURPOSE: TO FIND PEACE WITH HAPPINESS AND JOY

AS EXPLAINED IN MORE DETAIL in the preface, the purpose of this book is to help you and others you love find true peace with enduring happiness and joy regardless of your circumstances in life.

What are peace, happiness, and joy? How can they be obtained in this mortal life? To what extent is it reasonable that one living in today's world of declining values, demoralizing influences, and uncertain future can expect to enjoy the blessings of peace, happiness, and joy?

The Savior taught:

> Peace I leave with you, my peace I give unto you: not as the world giveth, give I unto you. Let not your heart be troubled, neither let it be afraid.[1]

> Learn of me, and listen to my words; walk in the meekness of my Spirit, and you shall have peace in me.[2]

The peace that the Master has promised is much more than the absence of strife, turmoil, conflict, and contention. Its greatest blessing is realized in the life of an individual. Its absence is also felt most profoundly in the human mind and heart.

3

An example will illustrate the meaning of peace. I once had an experience that caused me immense anxiety. I was severely troubled. It had nothing to do with disobedience or transgression but with a vitally important human relationship. I was so overcome with concern that I did something I never do. I left my office early and went home to pray. For some time I poured my heart out to the Lord. Try as I might, I could find no solution, no settling of the powerful stirring within me. I pled for help from that Eternal Father I have come to know and trust completely. I could see no path that would provide the calm that is my blessing to generally enjoy. Sleep overcame me. When I awoke I was totally at peace. I knelt again in solemn prayer and asked, "Lord, how is it done?" In my heart, I knew the answer was His love and His concern for me. That is consummate peace.

Happiness has its roots in obedience to the teachings of the Lord and in faith in His capacity to fulfill His promises. It can be enjoyed in an environment of poverty or wealth, sickness or health, scarcity or abundance, serenity or challenge. Happiness can and should be the general background in which life is lived. It can provide strength and comfort when periods of challenge, sorrow, and disappointment are encountered, though we cannot expect that blessing when we are guilty of premeditated disobedience. Happiness and joy are often used interchangeably and will be repeatedly in this work. However, the scriptures confirm that joy can be so intense as to overcome entirely all other feelings.[3] Such joy is a gift of God when fully merited. That singular joy is not often felt in life, while the happiness that comes through application of truth can be the predominant state in which we live.

No formula can prescribe how every individual can be assured of continual peace with happiness and joy in this mortal life. I am a witness that with patience, some long-suffering, and the help of the Lord, coupled with obedience to His commandments, those blessings can be enjoyed most of the time. You have seen a confirmation of that truth in others' lives. My desire is that your prayers and faith—and hopefully some of the insight and truth shared in this volume—will permit you to have those consummate blessings in your own life.

Many in the world are convinced that wealth, power, influence, sexual pursuit, and the artificial stimulation of the mind and body through alcohol and drugs are the sources of happiness. Seeking that path to happiness is like looking for a pot of gold at the end of the rainbow. Not only will the treasure not be found, but the results will almost always be sadness and disappointment, eventually leading to grief, anguish, and addiction. Such are consequences of yielding to Satan's alluring temptations with their hollow promise of "happiness." Only our Father in Heaven and His Beloved Son, Jesus Christ, have given the pattern to acquire real peace and happiness. That is why the Father's plan is appropriately named the Plan of Happiness.[4]

For enduring peace, it is essential that you understand the relationship between peace of conscience and peace of mind. It is also vital that you live the principles upon which both of these blessings are founded. I will explain.

God wants each of His children to enjoy the transcendent blessing of peace of conscience.[5] A tranquil conscience invites freedom from anguish, sorrow, guilt, shame, and self-condemnation. It provides a foundation for happiness. It is a condition of immense worth, yet few on earth enjoy it. Why? Most often because the principles upon which peace of conscience is founded are not understood or adequately followed. My life has been so richly endowed from peace of conscience that I wish to share insights on how it can be obtained.

Peace of conscience is the essential ingredient to your peace of mind. Without peace of conscience you can have no real peace of mind. Peace of conscience relates to your inner self. Only you can take the action required to obtain it. Peace of conscience comes from

God. Its fundamental requisite is a righteous, obedient life. It cannot exist otherwise. On the other hand, peace of mind is most often affected by external forces, such as concern for a wayward child, economic pressures, real or imagined offenses, world conditions, more to do than sufficient time to do it in, or, most pointedly, the transgressions of others. An unsettled mind should be temporary, transitory. Peace of mind is restored by resolving the external forces that disturb it. Not so with a troubled conscience, for it is unrelenting, ever present, a constant reminder of the need to correct your past mistakes, to resolve an offense to another, or to repent of transgression. Oh, a disturbed conscience can be temporarily masked by physical stimulation of the mind and body, where one yields to the temptations of alcohol, drugs, pornography, and worse. All this comes at the cost of an increased appetite for counterfeit methods to calm an aching conscience, and it brings the risk of incurring unrelenting addictions. Such actions will never restore peace of conscience.

The ability to have an unsettled conscience is a gift of God to help you succeed in this mortal life by being motivated to make needed change. It results principally from the influence of the Light of Christ on your mind and heart.[6] The Light of Christ is that divine power or influence that emanates from God through Jesus Christ.[7] It gives light and life to all things.[8] It prompts all rational individuals throughout the earth to distinguish truth from error, right from wrong.[9] It activates your conscience.[10] Its influence can be weakened through transgression and addiction and restored through proper repentance. The Light of Christ is not a person. It is a power and influence that comes from God. When followed, it can lead a person to qualify for the more definitive guidance and inspiration of the Holy Ghost.[11]

It is well to recognize that even with peace of conscience you can have temporary periods when your peace of mind is interrupted by external concerns. Your understanding of the causes of those concerns can relieve much of the pressure they generate. As your personal life conforms to the teachings of the Lord, you can seek His help in resolving troubling issues. Thus, your faith in the Lord and His teachings will yield peace of mind. Your efforts will be stepping-stones to greater personal growth as Spirit-guided solutions are found. In addition, such challenges, as they are resolved, can often bring blessings to those whose needs have caused the disturbed feelings in your mind.

There is a scriptural basis for what we have reviewed. It is found in the extraordinary experience of the people of King Benjamin:

> And . . . the Spirit of the Lord came upon them, and they were filled with joy, having received a remission of their sins, and having peace of conscience, because of the exceeding faith which they had in Jesus Christ who should come, according to the words which king Benjamin had spoken unto them.[12]

In summary, you can obtain *peace of conscience* by living a righteous life or by repenting of personal transgressions that cause you internal turmoil. Then *peace of mind* can be secured by resolving or understanding the external pressures that cause you temporary anxiety, worry, and distress. Yet if in your life there has been significant violation of commandments, try as you might, you will not find enduring happiness until, through repentance, you satisfy personally broken law to restore peace to a troubled conscience.

In subsequent chapters we will review together principles which form the foundation for a life of peace with happiness and joy for yourself or for a loved one. A variety of circumstances will be covered, with suggestions of what helps and what hinders efforts to live in peace with happiness and joy. The next chapter reveals ways to have more of those blessings in your life.

CHAPTER 2

THE PLAN OF HAPPINESS AND EXALTATION

OUR HOLY FATHER IN HEAVEN has declared, "This is my work and my glory—to bring to pass the immortality and eternal life of man."[1] He has established a way for each of His children to accomplish that glorious objective as they willingly and obediently follow a pattern called the Plan of Happiness. We were taught that plan and what supernal blessings it can provide in our premortal life when we lived in the presence of God the Father and His singular Son, Jesus Christ. We were valiant in obeying that part of the plan that applied there. As a result, we qualified to come to earth to further benefit from obedience to the conditions of our Heavenly Father's plan. If successful here we are promised blessings beyond our mortal ability to fully comprehend.

The plan of happiness requires us to understand and live truths and to receive ordinances that provide great peace and happiness during mortal life. They also assure us of qualifying to receive far greater rewards in our postmortal existence. This chapter contains suggestions to help you understand and benefit more from the plan of happiness in your personal life. The next chapter discusses how that should be done as families.

Our son Michael as a child had a small toy robot. It could walk and perform other simple functions. Should it fall, it could, with some difficulty, right itself. It performed its programmed functions mechanically, without feeling. It had no capacity to grow or to alter its destined course. It responded immediately to any external force that satisfied its needs, and it ceased to function when its internal spring was spent. Satan would have all of the children of Father in Heaven behave like robots.

How different is the plan of happiness of our Father in Heaven. Consider the birth of an infant—an independent spirit created by God,[2] matured in the premortal existence, and tabernacled in a body of flesh and bones. A mother and father participate with God in this sacred experience. Thoughtful parents love, guide, and inspire the growing child. With proper understanding and obedience to the teachings of the Savior, the child learns "precept upon precept."[3] By practicing truth, that child can become a self-reliant, loving, serving son or daughter of God, whose potential for growth and accomplishment is limitless. When fully obedient, the destiny of such an individual is to return to the presence of God to partake of His glory and to share in His exalted work. Moreover, such an individual is assured of great happiness in this life.

You are not able to remember one of the most exhilarating moments of your life, when you were filled with anticipation, excitement, and gratitude. That experience occurred in the premortal life when you were informed that at last your time had come to leave the spirit world to dwell on earth with a mortal body. You knew you could finally learn through personal experience on earth the lessons that would bring greater happiness—lessons that would eventually lead you to exaltation and eternal life as a glorified, celestial being in the presence of your Holy Father and His Beloved Son. You understood that there would be challenges, for you would live in an environment of both righteous and evil influences. Yet surely you resolved that no matter what the cost, no matter what the effort, suffering, and testing, you would return victorious. You had been reserved to come when the fulness of the gospel is on earth. You arrived when His Church and the priesthood authority to perform sacred temple ordinances were in place. You anticipated being born into a home where parents would love, nurture, strengthen, and teach you truths. You knew that in time you would have the opportunity to form your own eternal family as husband or wife, father or mother. Oh, how you must have rejoiced at that prospect!

Ponder for a moment. How are you using that opportunity you were so anxious to receive? Do daily decisions lead you toward those goals you so eagerly anticipated as a spirit in the premortal life? Together let us analyze how to make the most productive use of this mortal probation.

Are there so many fascinating, exciting things to do, or so many challenges pressing upon you, that it is hard to keep focused on that which is essential? When things of the world crowd in, all too often the wrong things are allowed to take highest priority. Then it is easy to forget the fundamental purpose of life. Satan has a powerful tool to use against good people, those who are committed to a worthy, righteous life, who want to do good and intend to make the most of this life. His tool is *distraction*. He has an extensive array of undeniably good things that are used to keep us from doing the essential ones. Have you noticed that when you begin to focus on something truly important, something of eternal significance, there often come thoughts of other good things to distract you? Satan promotes distraction. He would have good people fill life with "good things" so there is no room for the "essential ones." Have you unconsciously been caught in that trap?

Remember that you are here on earth for a divine purpose. The purpose is not to be endlessly entertained or to be constantly in full pursuit of pleasure. You are here to be tried, to prove yourself so that you can receive the additional blessings God has for you.⁴ In His infinite kindness He has given us an understanding of His purpose:

> [And God said:] We will go down, for there is space there, and we will take of these materials, and we will make an earth whereon these may dwell;
>
> And we will prove them herewith, to see if they will do all things whatsoever the Lord their God shall command them;
>
> And they who keep their first estate shall be added upon; and they who keep not their first estate shall not have glory in the same kingdom with those who keep their first estate; and they who keep their second estate shall have glory added upon their heads for ever and ever.⁵

This process will require the tempering effect of patience:

> The natural man is an enemy to God, and has been from the fall of Adam, and will be, forever and ever, unless he yields to the enticings of the Holy Spirit, and putteth off the natural man and becometh a saint through the atonement of Christ the Lord, and becometh as a child, submissive, meek, humble, patient, full of love, willing to submit to all things which the Lord seeth fit to inflict upon him, even as a child doth submit to his father.⁶

> The Lord seeth fit to chasten his people; yea, he trieth their patience and their faith. Nevertheless— whosoever putteth his trust in him the same shall be lifted up at the last day.⁷

> The trying of your faith worketh patience. But let

patience have her perfect work, that ye may be perfect
and entire, wanting nothing.[8]

Mortal life is a proving ground. Our individual proving grounds
vary. Some are born with physical limitations; others are lonely or do
not enjoy good health. Some are challenged by economic conditions,
the lack of good parental example, or a myriad of other things that
test our determination. While much of the pain and sorrow we
endure is the result of our own stubborn acts of disobedience, many
of the things that appear to be obstacles in our path are used by a loving Creator for our own personal growth.[9]

Life never was intended to be continually easy. It is punctuated
with periods of proving and growth. It is interwoven with difficulties, challenges, and burdens, all for your eternal benefit. You are
unavoidably immersed in a sea of persistent, worldly pressures that
could destroy your happiness, if you let them. Yet these very forces, if
squarely faced, provide opportunity for tremendous personal growth
and development. When you conquer adversity, it produces strength
of character, forges self-confidence, engenders self-respect, and
assures success in righteous endeavor.[10] When you master growth
challenges, you are rewarded with satisfying happiness.[11] Through
that means you will confirm that life can be lived on a continuing
foundation of happiness.

One who exercises moral agency by faith grows from challenges,
is purified by sorrow, and lives at peace. In contrast, one who franti-
cally seeks to satisfy appetite and worldly desire is driven in a downward spiral to tragic depths. Lucifer's temptations are the motivating
influence in such a tragic use of moral agency.

Some at one time or another let the pressures of life or the false
teachings of men cloud their vision. But when seen with clarity, the
difference between the plan of God and that of Satan is unmistakable. Satan would convert divinely independent spirits into creatures
bound by habit, restricted by appetite, and shackled by transgression.

He has never deviated from his intent to enslave and destroy. He would persuade you to improperly use the divine gift of agency. Through subtle, tempting influence, he encourages you to succumb to appetite or to gratify desire for personal power and influence. He progressively binds those that follow carnal desire. Unless they repent, they are effectively converted into robots who no longer exercise control over their eternal destiny.

He cleverly confuses some until they depict God as an exacting, harsh judge or as a distant deity, devoted to meticulous scorekeeping. God is none of that. He is a loving, patient, understanding Father, deeply interested in your personal welfare, anxious for your happiness, and totally committed to your eternal progression.

> For God so loved the world, that he gave his only begotten Son, that whosoever believeth in him should not perish, but have everlasting life. For God sent not his Son into the world to condemn the world; but that the world through him might be saved.[12]

Your happiness on earth, as well as your eternal salvation, requires many correct decisions, no one of which is difficult to make. Together those decisions forge a character resistant to the eroding influences that surround you. Noble character is like a treasured porcelain made of select raw materials, formed with faith, carefully crafted by consistent righteous acts, and fired in the furnace of uplifting experience. It is an object of great beauty and priceless worth. Yet it can be damaged in a moment through transgression, requiring painful, prolonged effort to be rebuilt. When protected by self-control, righteous character will endure for eternity.

Why has your moral agency been given to you? Only to live a pleasurable life and to make choices to do the things you want to do? There are more fundamental reasons to make the choices that will lead you to fully implement your purpose for being here on earth—

and also to establish priorities in your life that will assure the development and happiness the Lord wants you to receive.

> Men are free according to the flesh; and all things are given them which are expedient unto man. And they are free to choose liberty and eternal life, through the great Mediator of all men, or to choose captivity and death, . . . for [the devil] seeketh that all men might be miserable like unto himself.[13]

Not long ago I spoke with an intelligent young man with great potential. He was undecided about a mission. He had chosen not to attend a university at that point. In his free time he did only what he liked to do. He didn't work because he didn't have to, and because it would take time from pleasure. He passed seminary classes without much thought of personally applying the knowledge gained. I commented, "You are making choices today that appear to give you what you want: an easy life with abundant enjoyment and not much sacrifice. You can do that for a while, but what you don't realize is that every such decision you make limits your future. You are eliminating possibilities and options. There will come a time, and it won't be too distant, where you are going to spend the rest of your life doing things you don't want to do, in places you don't want to be, because you have not prepared yourself. You are not taking advantage of your opportunities."

I mentioned how everything I treasure today began to mature in the mission field. Missionary service is not something we do for ourselves. Yes, great growth and preparation for the future are gained from a mission. However, true missionaries focus outside of themselves on other people. To do so effectively they draw close to the Lord and really learn His teachings. They find individuals interested in the message but not sure of its worth. Missionaries try with every capacity—prayer, fasting, and testifying—to help others embrace the truth. A mission teaches one to be led by the Spirit, to understand our purpose for being on earth and how to accomplish that purpose. As our conversation ended, I gave him a blessing. Then, as he left, I prayed earnestly that the Lord would help him choose the right priorities. Otherwise he will fail in life's purpose.

In stark contrast, consider the example of another young man. Through the years his parents taught him to unwaveringly live the commandments of God. By example and precept, they nurtured him, together with their other children, in truth. They encouraged the development of discipline and sacrifice to obtain worthy goals. This young man chose swimming to instill in his character those qualities. Early-morning practice sessions required discipline and sacrifice. Over time he excelled in his sport.

Then came challenges. Would he participate in a championship swim meet on Sunday? Would he rationalize an exception to his rule of not swimming on the Sabbath to help his team win the championship? No, he would not yield, even under intense peer pressure. He was peppered with derisive comments, called names, even physically abused. But he would not yield. The rejection of friends, the loneliness, and the pressure brought times of sadness and tears. But he would not yield. He was learning firsthand what each of us must come to know, the reality of Paul's counsel to Timothy: "All that will live godly in Christ Jesus shall suffer persecution."[14]

Over the years this consistent pattern of righteous living, woven from hundreds of correct decisions, some in the face of great challenge, has developed a character of strength and capacity. As a missionary, he was appreciated by his peers for his ability to work, his knowledge of truth, his unwavering devotion, and his determination to share the gospel. One who earlier was rejected by his peers became a respected leader among them. He has been sealed in the temple to a lovely, devoted, spiritually sensitive wife. They will be outstanding parents like they have had. Their children will be strengthened as they have been. They are squarely on the path to peace with happiness and joy. Is there a message for you in these two examples?

While wholesome pleasure results from much we do that is good, pleasure is not our prime purpose for being on earth. Seek to know and do the will of the Lord, not just what is convenient or what makes life easy. You have the scriptures with the fulness of the gospel of Jesus Christ.[15] You know what to do, or you can find out through study and prayer. Do it willingly. The Lord has declared:

> It is not meet that I should command in all things; for he that is compelled in all things, the same is a slothful and not a wise servant; wherefore he receiveth no reward.
>
> . . . Men should be anxiously engaged in a good cause, and do many things of their own free will, and bring to pass much righteousness;
>
> For the power is in them, wherein they are agents unto themselves. And inasmuch as men do good they shall in nowise lose their reward.
>
> But he that doeth not anything until he is commanded, and receiveth a commandment with doubtful heart, and keepeth it with slothfulness, the same is damned [meaning stopped in progress and development].[16]

An axiom we all understand is that you get what you pay for. That is true for spiritual matters as well. You get what you pay for in obedience, in faith in Jesus Christ, in diligent application of the truths you learn. What you get is the molding of character, the growth in capacity, and the successful completion of your mortal purpose to be proven and to have joy.[17]

Some do not seem to understand that principle. They apparently feel that a reasonably good life will assure them the fulness of promised blessings. Sometimes at funerals, speakers declare that the deceased will inherit all the blessings of celestial glory when that individual has in no way qualified by obtaining the necessary ordinances and keeping the required covenants. That simply will not happen. Such blessings can be earned only by meeting the Lord's requirements.[18] His mercy does not overcome the requirements of His law.[19] All such requirements must be met for the promised blessings to be received.[20]

May I share these introspective thoughts of an individual who found the path to happiness? He wrote: "I am truly, deeply loved of the Lord. He will do all that I permit him to do for my happiness. The key to unlock that power is myself. While others will counsel, suggest, exhort, and urge, the Lord has given me the responsibility and the agency to make the basic decisions for my happiness and eternal progress. As I read and ponder the scriptures and with deep faith earnestly seek my Father in prayer, peace envelops my being. With sincere repentance and obedience to the commandments of God, coupled with genuine concern for and service to others, fear is purged from my heart. I am conditioned to receive and to interpret divine aid given to mark my path with clarity. No friend, bishop, stake president, or General Authority can do this for me. It is my divine right to do it for myself. I have learned to be at peace and to be happy. I know I will have a rewarding, productive, meaningful life."

That individual is not a robot enslaved by adversity, nor need you be. You can wisely use your agency to follow the teachings of the Savior.

Each of us needs to periodically check our bearings and confirm that we are on course. Sometime soon you may benefit from taking a personal inventory in a quiet place, noting how well you know and are following the will of the Lord in your life. Some places are sacred and holy, where it seems easier to discern the direction of the Holy

Spirit. The temple is such a place. Find a retreat of peace and quiet where periodically you can ponder and let the Lord establish the direction of your life. It may seem difficult to find time to meditate with the daily pressures of life. Yet a moment of thought will confirm that no matter how fast you move forward, if you are on the wrong path, it will avail you nothing.

As you have read this chapter, you have probably had some thoughts about changes that could improve your life or the life of a loved one. Write them down. That is direction from the Lord to help you. I suggest that you keep paper and pen handy as we proceed, so you can record the good thoughts that will come to you as you ponder the truths we will review.

CHAPTER 3

TO LIVE THE FAMILY-CENTERED
GREAT PLAN OF HAPPINESS

THIS CHAPTER CONTAINS counsel directed to parents. But even if you are not now blessed with children, it contains principles that are worthy of your consideration. "And I, God, created man . . . ; male and female created I them."[1] This was done spiritually in your premortal existence, when you lived in the presence of your Father in Heaven. Your gender was established before you came to earth. You elected to have this earth experience as part of His plan for you. The prophets have called it "the plan of our God,"[2] "the plan of mercy,"[3] the "eternal plan of deliverance,"[4] "the plan of salvation,"[5] and, yes, "the great plan of happiness."[6] You were taught this plan before you came to earth and there rejoiced in the privilege of participating in it.

God first gives knowledge of the plan of happiness and then provides instructions or commandments about how to best live it.[7] Obedience to the plan is a requisite for full happiness in this life and a continuation of eternal joy beyond the veil. The inspired proclamation on the family affirms: "The family is ordained of God. Marriage between man and woman is essential to His eternal plan."[8] The holy privilege of procreation must be employed within the bonds and commitment of legal marriage and in the sacred environment of family.[9] Parents have the responsibility to bear children and to nurture and train them spiritually, emotionally, and physically.[10] Essential to the plan of happiness of God is moral agency or the right of personal choice.[11] This divine gift is so essential that our Holy Father allowed the loss of one-third of His spirit children to protect and preserve it.[12]

Satan knows of the gift of agency. He also has a plan. It is a cunning, evil, subtle plan of destruction.[13] It is his objective to take captive the children of Father in Heaven and with every possible means frustrate "the great plan of happiness."

Our Heavenly Father has endowed His sons and daughters with unique traits especially fitted for their individual responsibilities as they fulfill His plan. The closer you adhere to His plan for you on earth, the greater will be your happiness and progress. You will be more qualified to receive the rewards He has promised for obedience. Following His plan means that you do those things He expects of you as a son or daughter, husband or wife. Those roles are different but entirely compatible. In the plan of the Father, it takes two—a man and a woman—to form a whole. Indeed, a husband and wife are not two identical halves, but a wondrous, divinely determined combination of complementary capacities and characteristics. The covenant of marriage allows these different characteristics to come together in oneness and in unity to bless both husband and wife, as well as their children, grandchildren, and in time even great-grandchildren.

For the greatest happiness and productivity in life, both husband and wife are needed. Their combined efforts interlock and are complementary. Each has individual traits that best fit the role the Lord has defined for happiness as a man or woman. When used as the Lord intends, those capacities allow a married couple to think, act, and rejoice as one, to face challenges together and overcome them as one, as they grow in love and understanding. Through sacred temple ordinances and subsequent faithfulness they are bound together as one whole, eternally. That is the plan.

You can learn what it means to be an effective parent by studying the lives of Adam and Eve. In the premortal life Adam was Michael, who helped create the earth. He was a glorious, superb individual. Eve was his equal and a full, powerfully contributing partner. After they had partaken of the fruit of the tree of knowledge of good and evil, the Lord spoke with them. In their responses they reveal some of the different attributes of a man and woman. To Adam He said, "Hast thou eaten of the tree whereof I commanded thee that thou shouldst not eat?"[14] Adam's response was characteristic of a man who wants to be perceived as being as close to right as possible. Adam responded, "The woman thou gavest me, and commandest that she should remain with me, she gave me of the fruit of the tree and I did eat."[15] And the Lord said unto Eve, "What is this thing which thou hast done?"[16] Eve's response was characteristic of a woman. Her answer was very simple and straightforward: "The serpent beguiled me, and I did eat."[17] Neither response was more correct than the other, yet they reveal different traits.

To further illustrate these gender differences, I have highlighted some words in a subsequent scripture. Later, "Adam blessed God and was filled, and began to prophesy concerning all the families of the earth, saying: Blessed be the name of God, for because of *my* transgression *my* eyes are opened, and in this life *I* shall have joy, and again in the flesh *I* shall see God."[18] Adam was thinking about his responsibilities. He was trying to align his performance with the desires of the Lord. Eve said, "Were it not for *our* transgression *we* never should have had seed, and never should have known good and evil, and the joy of *our* redemption, and the eternal life which God giveth unto *all* the obedient."[19] Eve's response was normal for a woman. She embraced all. Eve wanted to make sure that everyone was considered.

One response was not more appropriate than the other. The two perspectives resulted from the traits inherent in men and women.

The Lord intends that we use these differences to fulfill His plan for happiness, personal growth, and development. Note how Adam and Eve complemented each other and together arrived at a broader, more correct understanding of truth. Also observe how Satan would confuse these distinctions by prompting some men to behave like women and women to be like men.

Adam and Eve worked together.[20] They obeyed the commandment to have children.[21] They knew the plan of happiness and followed it, even though at times it resulted in hardship and difficulty for them. They were counseled to offer sacrifice, and they obeyed even without understanding all of the reasons. Then an angel appeared and asked, "Why dost thou offer sacrifices unto the Lord? And Adam said . . . : I know not, save the Lord commanded me."[22] The angel explained: "This thing is a similitude of the sacrifice of the Only Begotten of the Father. . . . Wherefore, thou shalt do all that thou doest in the name of the Son, and thou shalt repent and call upon God in the name of the Son forevermore."[23] They obeyed. Further, they taught their children the plan of happiness.[24] "[They] ceased not to call upon God."[25]

Because Adam and Eve were obedient, the Holy Ghost came upon them and directed them. You will receive such direction in your own life as you are obedient to the teachings of the Savior, qualify for the gift of the Holy Ghost, and receive all the temple ordinances your circumstances permit you to obtain.

Beware of the subtle and ingenious methods Satan would employ to take you from true happiness gained by obedience to the plan of God. A most effective, diabolical approach of Satan is to demean the role of wife and mother in the home. This is an attack at the very heart of God's plan to foster love between husband and wife and to nurture children in an atmosphere of understanding, peace, appreciation, and support. Much of the violence that is rampant in the world today is the harvest of weakened homes. Government and social plans will not effectively correct that deficiency. The best efforts of schools and churches cannot adequately compensate for the absence of the tender care of a compassionate wife and mother in the home.

As a mother guided by the Lord, you weave a fabric of character in your children using threads of truth given through careful instruction and worthy example. You imbue the traits of honesty, faith in God, duty, respect for others, kindness, self-confidence, and the desire to contribute, to learn, and to give in your trusting children's minds and hearts. No day-care center can do that. It is your sacred right and privilege. It is also your sacred responsibility.

Of course, as a woman you can do exceptionally well in the workplace; but is that the best use of your divinely appointed talents and feminine traits? The prophets have declared that to the extent possible, with the help of the Lord, the husband and wife are to work together to keep mother in the home.[26] That effort will do much to avoid the possibility of weakened self-confidence and emotional challenges in your children. It will help avoid the growing problem of children who lack an understanding of who they are and what they can accomplish as divine children of Father in Heaven. As a husband, if at all possible, please don't encourage your wife to go outside the home to work to help in your divinely defined responsibility to provide resources for the family.

I know that I write of the ideal, and you may be disturbed because your life may not now fit that mold. I promise you that through your obedience and continuing faith in Jesus Christ—along with your understanding of the whole plan of happiness, even if important parts of the plan aren't fulfilled in your life now—a fulness of blessings will be yours in the Lord's due time. I also promise you that you can have significant growth and happiness now. As a daughter or son of God, live whatever portion of the plan is available to you the best you can.

Your desire to be a wife and mother may not have its total fulfillment now, but it will in His time as you live in faith and obedience to merit it.[27] Don't be lured away from the plan of our God[28] to the ways of the world where motherhood is belittled, femininity is decried, and the divinely established roles of wife and mother are mocked. Let the world go its way. You follow the plan of the Lord for the greatest measure of true, eternal achievement and the fullest peace and happiness. The current lack of promised blessings for which you qualify will be fully compensated in this life or in the next.

Live righteously. Make much of your life here on earth, and you will find the companion of your dreams here or beyond the veil, where the potential companions will not be limited to this moment in time or your physical location. Joseph Fielding Smith taught: "You good sisters, who are single and alone, do not fear. . . . If in your hearts you feel that the gospel is true, and would under proper conditions receive [the] sealing blessings in the temple . . . ; and that does not come to you now; the Lord will make it up, . . . for no blessing shall be withheld."[29]

I have the opportunity to interview many priesthood leaders. When these men speak to me of their wives, it is with deep tenderness and obvious appreciation for the blessing of being husbands to extraordinary daughters of Father in Heaven. Often tears flow, and virtually without exception they comment something like: "She is the strength of my life," or "She motivates me to be a better person," or "She is more spiritual, purer, and more committed than I am. I couldn't do it without her." As a woman, please don't judge how worthwhile, needed, and loved you are by our inept male ability to express our true feelings. Your divinely conferred trait of giving of self without counting the cost often leads you to greatly underestimate your own worth.

I humbly thank our Father in Heaven for His daughters, you who were willing to come to earth to live under uncertain circumstances. Most men could not handle the uncertainties you are asked to live with. Social customs require that you wait to be asked for marriage. You are expected to go with your husband wherever his employment or a calling will take him. Your environment and neighborhood are determined by his ability to provide, meager or not. You place your life in the Lord's hands each time you bear a child. A man makes no such sacrifice. The blessing of nurturing children and caring for a husband often is intermingled with many routine tasks. You do all of these things willingly because you are a woman, a daughter of our Father in Heaven. Generally you have no idea of how truly wonderful and capable you are, how very much appreciated and loved, or how desperately needed, for most men don't tell you as completely and as often as needed.

Through His plan, our Father has made it possible for each willing spirit child to come to earth. He desires for that child to be born into a family where preparation for life can occur and where he or she can grow in experience, skill, understanding, and knowledge and, in time, form additional families and invite other spirit children into this earth-life experience.

He did that for a purpose. He did it for your eternal happiness and for your joy. That plan will surely bring you happiness as it is carefully followed.

How can you receive the greatest happiness and blessings from this earth experience?

Learn the doctrinal foundation of the great plan of happiness by studying the scriptures, pondering their content, and praying to understand them. Carefully study and use the proclamation of the

First Presidency and the Twelve on the family.[30] It was inspired of the Lord.

Listen to the voice of current and past prophets. Their declarations are inspired. You may verify that counsel in your own mind and heart by praying about it as it applies to your special circumstances. Ask the Lord to confirm your choices and then accept accountability for them.

Obey the inner feelings that come as promptings from the Holy Ghost. Those feelings are engendered by your righteous thoughts and acts and your determination to seek the will of the Lord and to live it.

When needed, seek counsel and guidance from your parents and priesthood leaders.

A choice mother wrote: "How did the pioneer women . . . respond to the challenges of their day? They listened to their prophet's voice and followed him because they knew he spoke the will of the Lord. They met the challenges and reaped great blessings because of their faith and obedience. Their first priorities were not security, nice homes, or an easy life. . . . No sacrifice was too great for them to make for their precious husbands and children."[31]

I obviously don't know what it feels like to be a woman, but I do know what it is to love one with all of my heart and soul. I constantly express to the Lord overflowing gratitude for the unending blessings that flow to our children, grandchildren, and great-grandchildren and so abundantly to me from the life of one of His precious daughters. I want the happiness we have found together to be yours. The more closely you personally adhere to His plan for you on earth, the greater will be your happiness, fulfillment, and progress, and the more qualified you will be to receive the rewards He has promised for obedience. I so testify, for the Savior lives and He loves you.

CHAPTER 4

FULL CONVERSION BRINGS
PEACE WITH HAPPINESS

Each of us has observed how some individuals go through life consistently doing the right things. They seem happy, even enthusiastic about life. When they face difficult choices, they seem to invariably make the right ones, even though enticing alternatives are available to them. Certainly they are subject to temptation, but they seem oblivious to it. In contrast, we have observed how others are not so valiant in the decisions they make. In a powerfully spiritual environment, they resolve to do better, to change their course of life, to set aside debilitating habits. They are very sincere in their determination to change, yet they are soon back doing the very things they resolved to abandon.

What makes the difference in the lives of these two groups? How can you consistently make the right choices? The scriptures give you insight. Consider enthusiastic, impetuous Peter. For three years he had served as an Apostle beside the Master, observing miracles and hearing transforming teachings and private explanations of parables. With James and John, Peter experienced the glorious Transfiguration of Jesus Christ with the accompanying visitations of Moses and Elijah.[1] Yet with all of this, the Savior could see that Peter still lacked consistency. The Master knew him very well, as He does each of us. In the Bible, we read that Jesus said to Peter:

> Simon, Simon, behold, Satan hath desired to have you . . . : But I have prayed for thee, that thy faith fail not: and when thou art converted, strengthen thy brethren.
>
> And he said unto him, Lord, I am ready to go with thee, both into prison, and to death.[2]

Certainly these were not, from the perspective of Peter, idle words. He sincerely meant what he said, though he would act otherwise.

Later, at the Mount of Olives, Jesus said to His disciples: "All ye shall be offended because of me this night: for it is written, I will smite the shepherd, and the sheep shall be scattered." Peter again responded, "Although all shall be offended, yet will not I." Then the Master soberly foretold, "Verily I say unto thee, That this day, even in this night, before the cock crow twice, thou shalt deny me thrice." To which Peter responded more vehemently, "If I should die with thee, I will not deny thee in any wise."[3]

For me, one of the most poignant passages of scripture describes what then occurred. It is a sobering reminder to each of us that knowing to do right, even ardently desiring to do right, is not enough. It is often very hard to actually do what we clearly know we should do. We read:

> But a certain maid beheld [Peter] . . . and said, This man was also with him. And he denied . . . saying, Woman, I know him not. . . . Another saw him, and said, Thou art also of them. And Peter said, Man, I am not. . . . Another confidently affirmed, . . . Of a truth this fellow also was with him: . . . And Peter said, Man, I know not what thou sayest. And immediately,

> while he yet spake, the cock crew. And the Lord
> turned, and looked upon Peter. And Peter remembered
> the word of the Lord, . . . and . . . went out, and wept
> bitterly.[4]

As painful as that confirmation of prophecy must have been for
Peter, that experience changed his life forever. After the Crucifixion
and Resurrection of the Savior, he became that unwavering, rock-
solid servant essential to the plan of the Father. This tender passage
also illustrates how very much the Savior loved Peter. Although He
was in the midst of an overpowering challenge to His own life, bearing upon His shoulders all of the weight of what was then transpir-
ing, yet He turned and looked at Peter—transmitting, as a teacher
to a beloved student, His love, courage, and enlightenment in time of
great need.

Evidence of the permanent transformation that occurred in Peter
and the other Apostles can be seen in subsequent scriptural passages.
Consider when Peter and John were inspired to perform a miracle
that they knew would bring the strongest confrontation with the
Jewish religious leaders who hated them.

> And a certain man lame from his mother's womb
> . . . seeing Peter and John about to go into the temple
> asked an alms.
>
> And Peter, fastening his eyes upon him with John,
> said, Look on us. . . . Then Peter said, Silver and gold
> have I none; but such as I have give I thee: In the name
> of Jesus Christ of Nazareth rise up and walk. And he
> took him by the right hand, and lifted him up: and
> immediately his feet and ankle bones received strength.
>
> And he leaping up stood, and walked, and entered
> with them into the temple, walking, and leaping, and
> praising God. . . .

. . . And they were filled with wonder and amaze-
ment at that which had happened unto him.[5]

Now came the test. Would Peter and John have the courage to
teach this prepared group the things they had been expressly forbidden to proclaim? Yes. After healing the lame man, Peter gave most
powerful instruction regarding Jesus Christ, with scathing accusations against the chief priests and elders, crowned with Peter's
unshakable testimony. Many believed. Peter and John were not
deterred by imprisonment, beatings, or threats against their lives.
"They were all filled with the Holy Ghost, and they spake the word
of God with boldness."[6]

Peter had finally attained what the Savior had counseled him he
must attain. He was converted. Thereafter, Peter rose to the full
stature of his calling. He taught with power and boldness, bearing an
unconquerable testimony despite every obstacle and confrontation.
He was truly converted and ever remained so.

Sometimes the word *converted* is used to describe preparation a
sincere individual has when he decides to be baptized into The
Church of Jesus Christ of Latter-day Saints. However, when properly used, conversion means far more than that, for the new convert
as well as the long-term member. With his characteristic doctrinal
clarity and precision, President Marion G. Romney explained: "To
become converted means to turn from one belief or course of action
to another. Conversion is a spiritual and moral change. Converted
implies not merely mental acceptance of Jesus and his teachings but
also a motivating faith in him and his gospel. A faith which works a
transformation, an actual change in one's understanding of life's
meaning and in his allegiance to God in interest, in thought, and in
conduct. In one who is really wholly converted, desire for things contrary to the gospel of Jesus Christ has actually died. And substituted
therefore is a love of God, with a fixed and controlling determination to keep his commandments."[7]

To become truly converted, you must apply diligently in your life the key words "a love of God, with a fixed and controlling determination to keep his commandments." Your happiness now and forever is conditioned on your degree of conversion and the transformation it brings to your life. What are the steps to becoming truly converted? We can derive the following pattern of conversion from President Romney's message:

The Holy Ghost gives the earnest seeker of truth a witness of truth.

That testimony is strengthened through study, prayer, and the application of truth. The growing testimony yields faith in Jesus Christ and the plan of happiness.

That faith encourages repentance and obedience to the commandments.

Conversion is the fruit or the reward for consistent repentance and obedience.

Conversion brings divine forgiveness, which remits sins and heals the spirit.

Enduring conversion is a lifelong quest centered in consistent obedience and repentance for errors of omission and commission.

In summary, true conversion is the result of faith, repentance, and consistent obedience. Faith comes by hearing the word of God[8] and responding to it. You will receive from the Holy Ghost a confirming witness of truth when you accept it on faith and willingly live it.[9] You will be led to repent of errors resulting from wrong things done or right things not done. As a consequence, your capacity to consistently obey will be strengthened. This cycle of faith, repentance, and consistent obedience will lead you to greater conversion, with its attendant blessings. True conversion will strengthen your capacity to do what you know you should do, when you should do it, regardless of the circumstances.

The parable of the sower taught by Jesus is generally considered to describe how the word of the Lord is received by different individuals as it is preached. Consider for a moment how the same parable may apply to you in different circumstances in your life, as you face challenges or come under strong influences. The word, or teachings of the Savior, can come to you in many ways: as you observe others, or through your own prayer or pondering the scriptures, or through the guidance of the Holy Ghost. As you read the explanation that Jesus gave His disciples of the parable of the sower, mentally examine your life. See if there are periods when correct teachings find in you conditions unsuitable to receive them and consequently you lose the promised fruits of happiness, peace, and progress.

> The sower soweth the word. . . . [Some are sown]
> by the way side, . . . but when they have heard, Satan
> cometh immediately, and taketh away the word that
> was sown in their hearts.[10]

Could that happen to you, in the wrong environment, with the wrong friendships?

> [Some are] sown on stony ground; who, when they
> have heard the word, immediately receive it with gladness; and have no root in themselves, and so endure
> but for a time: afterward, when . . . persecution ariseth
> . . . immediately they are offended.[11]

Have you ever been in a circumstance when someone proposed something inappropriate and you did nothing to resist it?

> [Some are] sown among thorns; such . . . hear the
> word, and the cares of this world . . . and the lusts of
> other things entering in, choke the word, and it
> becometh unfruitful.[12]

Have there been times when you wanted something so badly that you justified an exception to your standards?

> [Some are] sown on good ground; such . . . hear the word, and receive it, and bring forth fruit, some thirtyfold, some sixty, and some an hundred.[13]

I know this is the way you want to live your life. How completely you willingly embrace the teachings of the Savior determines how much fruit, as blessings, you will harvest in your life. This parable illustrates that the degree to which you willingly obey those things you know you should do will determine how truly converted you are. It will likewise determine how fully the Lord can bless you.

Of a group of individuals in difficult circumstances, the Book of Mormon teaches:

> They did fast and pray oft, and did wax stronger and stronger in their humility, and firmer and firmer in the faith of Christ, unto the filling their souls with joy and consolation, yea, even to the purifying and the sanctification of their hearts, which sanctification cometh because of their yielding their hearts unto God.[14]

Make any changes that you know are needed in your life now to receive the blessings promised from true conversion. The Savior said: "Will ye not now return unto me, and repent of your sins, and be converted, that I may heal you? . . . If ye will come unto me ye shall have eternal life."[15]

I bear testimony that as you pray for guidance, the Holy Ghost will help identify the personal changes you need to make for full conversion. The Lord can then bless you more abundantly. Your faith in Him will be fortified, your capacity to repent will increase, and your power to consistently obey will be reinforced. The Savior lives. He loves you. As you do your best, He will help you.

Enduring happiness, then, is the fruit of true conversion. It can be enjoyed even when the world is in turmoil and most are anything but happy. As with the parable of the seeds, you can determine whether your ground will be fertile and ready when truth is sown. When required, the Lord can help you change to be truly converted so that truth has a more powerful influence throughout your life, producing greater fruits of happiness and peace. If needed, will you do it?

With the foundation we have laid, it is now time to discuss how to increase the guidance of the Holy Ghost in your life, to help you know more clearly how to make the right choices from all the alternatives you face. Spiritual guidance is essential in your quest for peace with happiness and joy. The next section will help you receive and understand that direction.

PART 2

PEACE, HAPPINESS, AND JOY THROUGH SPIRITUAL GUIDANCE

CHAPTER 5

TO UNDERSTAND
SPIRITUAL GUIDANCE

THE MATTER OF BEING guided throughout your life by the gentle promptings of the Holy Spirit—essential to find peace with joy and happiness—is discussed in this and the next chapter. In this chapter we will review what spiritual guidance is and how it is manifest. The next chapter will discuss what you can do to qualify to receive spiritual guidance.

Father in Heaven knew that here on earth you would be required to face challenges and make some decisions that would be beyond your own ability to consistently make correctly. In His plan of happiness for your mortal life, He included a provision for you to receive help with such challenges and decisions. That assistance will come to you through the Holy Ghost as spiritual guidance. It is something like a sixth sense—a power beyond your own capability that a loving Heavenly Father wants you to use consistently for your peace and happiness.

As a youth I was not certain of some gospel principles, nor did I understand many of the things that would bring happiness. However, our kind and loving Father in Heaven helped me learn step by step the principles that truly do yield happiness by giving me spiritual guidance. An essential requirement to peace with happiness is to learn how to recognize such guidance. That truth is what I want to share with you now.

I am convinced that there is no simple formula or technique that I could give you that would immediately facilitate your mastering the ability to be guided by the Holy Spirit. Our Father expects you to learn how to obtain that divine help by exercising faith in Him and His Holy Son. Were you to receive inspired guidance just for the asking, you would become weak and ever more dependent on Him. He knows that essential personal growth will come as you struggle to learn how to be led by the Spirit. That struggle will develop your immortal character as you perfect your capacity to identify His will in your life through the whisperings of the Holy Ghost. What may appear initially to be a daunting task will be much easier to manage over time as you consistently strive to recognize the feelings prompted by the Spirit. Your confidence in the direction you receive through the Holy Ghost will also become stronger. In fact, as you gain experience and success in being guided by the Spirit, your confidence in the impressions you feel can become more certain than what you see or hear.

In this chapter I venture to write of something that I do not completely understand. Yet that limited understanding has repeatedly changed the course of my life. It has brought further knowledge, truth, and motivation that could not have been known in any other way. It has shown me undiscovered truths about myself and reduced unnecessary dependence upon others. It has repeatedly filled my heart, mind, and soul with such overpowering joy and all-pervading peace as to be beyond my power to express. It has directed my thoughts and acts for the benefit of others in desperate need and given me specific information and knowledge unattainable by other means. It has been critical to my efforts to act as an instrument to help unravel others' tangled lives.

Personal communication with God through the Holy Spirit is a reality. To me it is as literally real as life itself and far more precious than all of the treasures of the earth. As you understand and use the eternal principles governing such communication, you can learn that the counsel of others and the programs of the Church are useful aids but not the best source of fundamental direction in your life. That guidance comes from the Lord through the Holy Ghost.

In the next several paragraphs I will use different examples to indicate how spiritual guidance is manifest. You then can see how you can recognize such guidance in your own life.

You can learn much about spiritual guidance by being attentive to the feelings that accompany it. A simple example will illustrate what I mean. No matter how hard I try, it would be very difficult to tell you what the meat of a llama, an animal native to Bolivia and Peru, tastes like. But once you tasted it you would know. Thereafter, if you were to eat it again, you could identify it. You would always remember it. So it is with the guidance of the Spirit. Once you learn what spiritual guidance feels like it will be easier to recognize. The more experience you have with those feelings the more you will trust them.

Another example underscores the clarity of spiritual communication. You may have opened your eyes under water while swimming. Everything looks blurred and difficult to identify. Yet with the aid of a diver's mask, every detail can be seen with absolute clarity. Satan tries to blur reality and confuse you by tempting you to incorporate false principles into your life. Father in Heaven can clarify your life by sharing correct principles through the Holy Ghost. How you exercise your moral agency will determine which of these two influences will be predominant in your life. Your happiness now and for the eternities will unquestionably be determined by whether or not you follow the spiritual guidance of the Lord communicated through the Holy Ghost.

Sometimes the Lord reveals truth to us when we are not actively seeking it, such as when we are in danger and do not know it. I remember that on one occasion I had been driving for long hours alone on high Bolivian mountain roads, a single lane wide. As I approached a sharp turn an impression came into my mind: "If your wife, Jeanene, were here she would tell you to honk the horn." I did, and as I turned the corner I saw a jeep skidding to a halt; the driver had heard the warning sound. Had I not done it I would have been in serious trouble. I continued to honk the horn at every sharp turn. About two hours later the same thing happened again, this time with an approaching ambulance.

The Lord will not force you to learn. You must exercise your agency to authorize the Spirit to teach you. As you make this a practice in your life, you will be more perceptive to the feelings that come with spiritual guidance. Then, when that guidance comes, sometimes when you least expect it, you will recognize it more easily. In the foregoing example, I didn't know that I needed help, but the Lord knew I needed it and He gave it to me.

Spirituality yields two fruits. The first is inspiration, that is, to know what to do. The second is power—the power of God or the capacity to do what one has been instructed to accomplish.[1] Those two capacities come together. That's why Nephi could say, "I will go and do the things which the Lord hath commanded."[2] He knew the spiritual laws upon which inspiration and power were based.

President Kimball taught: "Revelations will probably never come unless they are desired. I think few people receive revelations while lounging on a couch. . . . I believe most revelations would come when a man is on his tip toes, reaching as high as he can for something which he knows he needs, and then there bursts upon him the answer to his problems."[3]

May this simple analogy help you understand more about receiving direction from the Holy Ghost. Suppose we are in a remote area of Africa where the inhabitants have been oblivious to the wonders of modern technology. You and I have decided to perform an experiment to determine how well persons from that background could benefit from an electronic device. We place a small tape recorder with an FM tuner on a path with the unconnected earphones beside it. We find a spot where, undetected, we can observe what happens. A local man picks up the device, examines it, and then begins to play with it. Soon he notices that as he pushes a button a little bright red spot appears. That fascinates him. He continues to probe and finds that by pushing another part of the device, another light goes on and off. He also discovers the earphones. Fascinated and smiling, he heads for home with both objects in his hands. At his village he gives the necklace (earphones) to his wife and invites friends to see his new toy. The men of the village are excited about what he has found, and they each amuse themselves clicking the buttons and watching the lights flash on and off.

We judge that it is about time for us to appear, so we go into the village and ask, "Do you know what you have in your hand? When used properly it can bring back the voices of the dead." Some begin to murmur, "Witchcraft!" and others say, "It can't be; impossible!" Some are even considering putting a hex on you and me.

We study their faces and find someone who seems to be more deeply interested than others. "What I told you is true. That device can let you listen to the voices of people who have died. It can do more. You can speak into it and later listen to your own words. Not only that, but you can listen to messages from far away."

The sincere person asks, "Can that really be so?"

We answer, "Yes, bring us your wife's necklace [earphones]." We plug them in, place them on his head, and press a button to play back a recorded bird call familiar to him.

He listens and responds, "I'm astounded. How can it be?" We then tune in the radio, and surely he hears messages from afar off. More intent now, he wants to know more.

41

"Let me show you how your own voice can be heard. If we just press these two buttons together and you speak, you will be able to hear your own voice." We record and play back his own voice.

"I can't believe it. Can I do that?" And he tries, but doesn't push the buttons right. It doesn't work for him.

We explain, "This is a very special device. You have to use it exactly right or you won't have success." He follows our counsel more carefully and is rewarded by success.

Do you see the similarities in that example and how different individuals react to the thought of being guided by the Holy Ghost? The incredulous are convinced that it can't be done and reject the possibility out of hand. Others think it is some sort of mystical power only a few can use. But some are inquisitive, become trusting, and follow the correct principles. They are rewarded with priceless spiritual guidance.

The Holy Ghost can distill in your mind the truths of prophets who have long since gone. Through study, faith, and prayer, it can bring to memory those things that have been stored. It can confirm that the Lord lives and is aware of each of us individually. Have patience as you are perfecting your ability to be led by the Spirit. If you have not yet gained the confidence you seek, by careful practice, through the application of correct principles, and by being sensitive to the feelings that come, you will gain the capacity you seek. I bear witness that the Lord through the Holy Ghost can speak to your mind and heart. Sometimes the impressions are just general feelings. Sometimes the direction comes so clearly and so unmistakably that it can be written down word for word, like spiritual dictation.[4]

I know that can happen. I bear witness that as you pray with all the fervor of your soul, with humility and gratitude, you can have similar experiences. The guidance of the Spirit is essential to solve the perplexities of your life. The Lord will give you that direction as you live righteously. Consider the following example.

Sometimes spiritual guidance comes in response to an urgent, sincere prayer for help. I remember one night in the mission field, after kneeling in prayer with my lovely wife and having thanked the Lord for the blessings of the day, I had a strong impression that one of our missionaries was in trouble. I tried to think who it could be but could not identify him. I excused myself from my sweet companion. I went to my office below our living quarters, where I could review information concerning each missionary to determine who was in trouble. All night long I labored, reviewing in my mind everything I knew about each missionary and every companionship as I pleaded with the Lord that He might let me know which missionary needed help. That answer did not come. As the dawn began to break, I went up onto the flat part of our mission home roof and continued to pour out my heart for guidance. Finally, I received a slight impression regarding which part of the mission he lived in. That prompting was all I needed. I went there and through appropriate interviews found and helped the individual the Lord wanted to save. That elder was about to do something that would have terminated his mission dishonorably. The Lord, through the guidance of the Spirit, saved him. Yes, God answers prayer and gives us direction when we live obediently and exercise the required faith in Him.

One treasured experience can highlight additional truths of how spiritual communication is manifest. It occurred some time ago, when I had responsibilities in Mexico and Central America that were far beyond my personal capacity to fulfill. I spent much sincere effort in seeking guidance and understanding from the Lord in study, fasting, prayer, and anxious service.

Those assignments kept me traveling, so it was difficult to attend my own home ward with any regularity. One Sunday I had the privilege to attend the priesthood meeting of a Spanish branch that met in our ward building in Mexico City. I recall vividly how a humble Mexican priesthood leader struggled to communicate the truths of the gospel in his lesson material. It was obvious that these truths had touched his life deeply. I noted the intense desire he had to share those principles to his quorum members. He recognized that they were of great worth to the brethren present. In his manner, there was evidence of a pure love of the Savior and love of those he taught.

His sincerity, purity of intent, and love permitted a spiritual strength to envelop the room. I was touched. In addition to receiving again a witness of the truths that he presented, I began to receive some personal impressions as an extension of those principles taught by the humble instructor. These impressions were intended for me personally and were related to my assignments in the area. They came in answer to my prolonged, prayerful efforts to learn.

As each impression came, I faithfully wrote it down. In the process I was given precious truths that I greatly needed in order to be a more effective servant of the Lord. The details of the communication are sacred and, like a patriarchal blessing, were for the benefit of the recipient. The specific counsel began with this paragraph: "You are to continue to build the Church on the foundation of true principles, but with an increased expression of love and appreciation you have been blessed to understand and feel for the great Lamanite people." There followed specific directions, instructions, and conditioned promises that have altered the course of my life.

Subsequently, I visited the Sunday School class in our ward, where a very well-educated visiting professor presented his lesson. That experience was in striking contrast to the one enjoyed in the priesthood meeting. It seemed to me that the instructor had purposely chosen obscure references and unusual examples to illustrate the principles in the lesson. I will confess that I had the distinct impression, perhaps erroneously (although I think not), that this instructor was using the teaching opportunity to impress the class with his vast store of knowledge. At any rate, he certainly did not seem as intent on communicating principles as had the humble priesthood leader.

In that environment, strong impressions began to flow to me again. I wrote them down. Some of the paragraphs began with phrases such as these: "Teach and testify to instruct, edify, and lead others to full obedience, not to demonstrate anything of self. All who are puffed up shall be cut off." Another entry reads, "You are nothing in and of yourself, Richard." That was followed with specific counsel on how to become more effective as an instrument in the hands of the Lord. A later section begins, "Through qualification by obedient self-restraint and the power of faith," followed by further promises conditioned upon those requisites.

This time, I received such an outpouring of impressions that were so personal that I felt it inappropriate to try to record them in the midst of a Sunday School class. I sought a more private location. There I continued to write the feelings that flooded into my mind and heart as accurately and as faithfully as possible. After each powerful impression was recorded, I pondered the feelings I had received to determine if I had accurately expressed them in writing. As a result, I made a few minor changes to what had been written. Then I studied their meaning and application in my own personal life.

Subsequently I prayed, reviewing with the Lord what I thought I had been taught by the Spirit. When a feeling of peace and serenity confirmed what I had sought, I thanked Him for the guidance given. I was then impressed to ask if there was yet more that I could be given to understand. I received further impressions, and the process of writing down the impressions and pondering and praying to know if I had done it properly was repeated. Again I was prompted to ask, "Is there more I should know?" There was. When that last, most sacred experience was concluded, I had received some of the most precious, specific, personal direction one could ever hope to obtain in this life. I am convinced that had I not responded to the first impressions, valued, and recorded them, I would not have received the last, most precious guidance.

What I have described is not an isolated experience. It embodies several principles I know to be true regarding communication from the Lord to His children here on earth. I believe that we often leave the most precious, personal direction of the Spirit unheard because we do not respond to, record, and apply the first promptings that come to us. Impressions of the Spirit can come unsolicited when we are in need or in response to urgent prayer.

What does spiritual communication entail? How does it occur? The Savior has taught us much concerning the principles of spiritual communication:

> Wherefore, I the Lord ask you this question—unto what were ye ordained?
>
> To preach my gospel by the Spirit, even the Comforter which was sent forth to teach the truth.[5]

Thus communication must be by the Spirit, "which was sent forth to teach the truth." The Lord then clarifies:

> Verily I say unto you, he that is ordained of me and sent forth to preach the word of truth by the Comforter, in the Spirit of truth, doth he preach it by the Spirit of truth or some other way?
>
> And if it be by some other way it is not of God.
>
> And again, he that receiveth the word of truth, doth he receive it by the Spirit of truth or some other way?
>
> If it be some other way it is not of God.[6]

Then, by way of summary and further clarification, the Lord adds:

> Therefore, why is it that ye cannot understand and

know, that he that receiveth the word by the Spirit of truth receiveth it as it is preached by the Spirit of truth?

Wherefore, he that preacheth and he that receiveth, *understand* one another, and both are *edified* and rejoice together.[7]

The verb *understand* refers to that which is spoken and heard. It is the same message to all present. *Edified* concerns that which is communicated by the Holy Ghost. *Edified* content will be different and tailored by the Spirit to the needs of each individual prepared to feel it. This verse is one of the evidences in the scriptures that the Lord will personalize a message taught by the Spirit of Truth for the further enlightenment of the sincere, honest, obedient seeker. When you teach others, encourage abundant participation, because their use of agency to take part authorizes the Holy Ghost to instruct them. It also helps your message to be better understood and retained. As truths are verbalized through participation, they can be confirmed in the participant's soul by the Holy Ghost. The result is a strengthened personal testimony of those truths.

In my priesthood meeting experience in the Spanish branch in Mexico City, I *understood* the principles that were taught by a Spirit-guided instructor. I had a witness of their truthfulness. But in addition to that, I was *edified* by precious feelings as I received spiritual guidance from the Holy Ghost. The message taught by a human was powerfully expanded for my own personal benefit by sacred impressions communicated through the Holy Ghost.

Profound doctrine concerning spiritual guidance is found in an account of Nephi, the son of Helaman. It teaches eloquently the effect of obedience to the will of the Lord. It illustrates the consequence of a life devoted to determining the will of the Lord and to resolutely obeying it. Because he declared with power the message given to him by the Lord to a wicked people, he was placed in a very difficult situation. He was accused of being a confederate of the individual who had murdered the chief judge.[8] Yet his understanding of the principles of spiritual communication, coupled with a life devoted to being obedient to sensitive impressions of the Spirit, allowed him to receive through that Spirit the information that saved his life.[9] After that experience, we read:

> Nephi went his way towards his own house, pondering upon the things which the Lord had shown unto him. . . .
>
> And it came to pass as he was thus pondering in his heart, behold, a voice came unto him saying:
>
> Blessed art thou, Nephi, for those things which thou hast done; for I have beheld how thou hast with unwearyingness declared the word, which I have given unto . . . this people. And thou hast not feared them, and hast not sought thine own life, but hast sought my will, and to keep my commandments.
>
> And now, because thou hast done this with such unwearyingness, behold, I will bless thee forever; and I will make thee mighty in word and in deed, in faith and in works; yea, even that all things shall be done unto thee according to thy word.[10]

And then these choice words of testimony from the Lord bear witness to the character of Nephi:

> For thou shalt not ask that which is contrary to my will.[11]

In subsequent verses, Nephi was given the power to seal because of the total trust the Lord had in him. From this experience, we learn that seeking the will of the Lord and complying with it, while obeying the commandments unwearyingly, will produce blessings of incalculable worth.

We learn other lessons of spiritual guidance from the brother of Jared, who had become a powerful servant of the Lord, as evidenced by this statement:

> The Lord did bring Jared and his brethren forth even to that great sea which divideth the lands. And . . . they dwelt in tents . . . upon the seashore for the space of four years.[12]

Then we read:

> And it came to pass at the end of four years that the Lord came again unto the brother of Jared, and stood in a cloud and talked with him. And for the space of three hours did the Lord talk with the brother of Jared, and chastened him because he remembered not to call upon the name of the Lord.[13]

That must have been a crushingly difficult interview for the brother of Jared. He recognized that earlier in his life his closeness to the Lord had permitted him to lead his people to safety. Now the Lord personally chastened him because he had forgotten to pray adequately. As we read further, we see a measure of the character of the brother of Jared, for the very next statement records:

> And the brother of Jared repented of the evil which he had done, and did call upon the name of the Lord for his brethren who were with him. And the Lord said unto him: I will forgive thee and thy brethren of their sins; but thou shalt not sin any more, for ye shall remember that my Spirit will not always strive with man.[14]

It was after this experience that the brother of Jared's obedience, diligence, and resolute determination to know and follow the will of the Lord permitted the Savior to say to him:

> Never has man come before me with such exceeding faith as thou hast; for were it not so ye could not have seen my finger.[15]

And the Lord said unto him:

> Believest thou the words which I shall speak?
> And he answered: Yea, Lord, I know that thou speakest the truth, for thou art a God of truth, and canst not lie.
> And when he had said these words, behold, the Lord showed himself unto him, and said: Because thou knowest these things ye are redeemed from the fall; therefore ye are brought back into my presence; therefore I show myself unto you.[16]

The scriptures promise that the Lord will answer our prayers for guidance, but they do not indicate *when* the Lord will provide those answers. Most often it seems that He gives answers in packets, that is, in pieces of the solution. That way of providing answers requires you to exercise your faith; and by so doing you will increase in character. You do not become improperly dependent upon God.

As mentioned earlier, prayer is fundamental to the doctrine of spiritual guidance. You communicate with God through sincere prayer. He answers you through the Spirit by impressions that come to your mind and heart. How can you learn to pray properly? By speaking openly to a trusted Father you love. The Lord has given you the way to pray for answers to questions in your life. For example, He has done that through recording an experience Oliver Cowdery had when he was not able to translate as he had been encouraged to do. As is often the case, this guidance given to an individual is applicable to us all. He said to Oliver:

> Behold, you have not understood; you have sup-posed that I would give it unto you, when you took no thought save it was to ask me.
>
> But, behold, I say unto you, that you must study it out in your mind; then you must ask me if it be right, and if it is right I will cause that your bosom shall burn within you; therefore, you shall feel that it is right.[17]

Note how the answer comes as a *feeling*. Two separate categories for such feelings are defined by the Lord:

> Yea, behold, I will tell you in your *mind* and in your *heart*, by the Holy Ghost, which shall come upon you and which shall dwell in your heart.
>
> Now, behold, this is the spirit of revelation.[18]

So one form of answer is described as to the mind, the other to the heart. Both are communications from the Holy Spirit to our spirits. I feel the basic difference between the two is that communication to the mind is very specific and can be written down as if dictated, while communication to the heart is more generalized. For example, you could have a feeling such as, "I need to do better in my life" or "I need to study harder." Then the Lord clarifies,

> But [if what you propose to the Lord] be not right you shall have no such feelings, but you shall have a stupor of thought that shall cause you to forget the thing which is wrong.[19]

To me that phrase doesn't mean that you will automatically forget what you are proposing. Instead, the feelings you have will indicate that what you propose is not the will of the Lord, and therefore you should choose to forget it. Thus, if what you have proposed to do is contrary to His will and therefore would be undesirable, you will have the feeling He describes as a "stupor of thought." Sometimes that is a feeling akin to what you sense when someone proposes to do something totally contrary to your righteous, basic principles. You have a feeling of rejection, discomfort, uneasiness, and, in extreme cases, even disgust.

When what you propose is correct, as has been quoted, "I will cause that your bosom shall burn within you; therefore, you shall feel that it is right."[20] I liken those feelings to what is sensed when you are in a testimony meeting and have the impression that it is time for you to bear your witness.

Another way in which positive answers come is described in another revelation to Oliver Cowdery:

> Did I not speak peace to your mind concerning the matter? What greater witness can you have than from God?[21]

The feeling of peace is the most common confirming witness that I personally experience. There have been times when I have been very concerned about an important matter, struggling to resolve it without success. As in faith I continued those efforts, an all-pervading peace has come, settling all concern as He has promised.

A key to increased spiritual guidance is to learn to ask the right questions in prayer. Consider how you can change from asking the Lord so often for the things you want to honestly asking what He wants for you. Then as you find out His will, pray you will be led to have the strength to fulfill it. When you feel that you understand what the Lord wants you to do, you are on the path to achieve it. Whether with your best effort you can fully accomplish it today, tomorrow, next week, or even in this life doesn't make that much difference when you know that what you are consistently doing is what He wants you to do. That understanding will provide the greatest assurance of a satisfying life. You will be on course to receive the rewards promised the righteous. They will be given according to the Lord's plan and in His time.

Spiritual communication cannot be forced. I have heard some say that they "call down the Spirit." That is a false principle. You must qualify yourself and be ready to receive the Lord's guidance and direction when He determines to provide it. No matter how urgent your personal timetable, the Lord responds according to His own timing because He knows that in the long run it will be the best for you.

Consider this example when a prophet taught with conviction a truth he learned from personal experience. President David O. McKay testified:

"It is true that the answers to our prayers may not always come as direct and at the time, nor in the manner, we anticipate; but they do come, and at a time and in a manner best for the interests of him who offers the supplication."[22]

I find great comfort in that statement of a prophet of God. President McKay later confirmed the truth of that principle with an experience from his own life. He related that when he was a boy hunting cattle he stopped to let his horse rest. In his own words:

"An intense desire came over me to receive a manifestation of the truth of the restored gospel. I dismounted, . . . and there, under a serviceberry bush, I prayed that God would declare to me the truth of his revelation to Joseph Smith. I am sure that I prayed fervently and sincerely and with as much faith as a young boy could muster.

"At the conclusion of the prayer, I arose from my knees, . . . and got into the saddle. As I started along the trail again, I remember saying to myself: 'No spiritual manifestation has come to me. If I am true to myself, I must say I am just the same "old boy" that I was before I prayed.' I prayed again when I crossed Spring Creek, near Huntsville, in the evening to milk our cows."[23]

The Lord did answer that prayer much later, when it had more significant meaning. In what would now be called a zone conference his mission president pointed to Elder McKay and, moved by the Spirit, prophesied, saying: "If you will keep the faith, you will yet sit in the leading councils of the Church."[24] At that moment a powerful, unmistakable witness came in answer to his supplication as a sincere youth. It came when he needed it, to confirm a vital prompting of the Spirit.

I testify that this principle of timing is true. Who better than the Lord understands our needs and is better equipped to respond to them in the most appropriate moment, when we qualify by obedience?

Some time ago, in the northern reaches of Japan, with the cold, misty rain settling about a missionary companionship and with the hour soon approaching when tracting would be over, the senior companion said, "Let's go home; we haven't had any success today. We will hit it hard tomorrow when things will be better." His junior companion said, "I feel we should finish this street." The sensitive senior understood the significance of the word *feel*. They continued to labor. As a result a young Japanese boy was baptized. The missionaries became his best friends. They inspired him to be a missionary. He was most effective. His mission president was moved to encourage him to learn English. He did that during the mission. Afterward he bought a transistor radio to listen to English programs as he continued to study the language. He prepared himself professionally and later served as a mission president, a stake president, a regional representative. The membership of the Church has been blessed by Elder Yoshihiko Kikuchi as a General Authority. It all began because a junior companion had confidence in the promptings of the Spirit of the Lord.

I would like to pass on two precautions concerning seeking spiritual guidance. First, an illustration about how easily the best efforts to communicate principles relating to the Spirit can be misunderstood. As a mission president, I observed how one missionary who was unusually gifted in working with people operated. He seemed to be working very hard. He and his companion had convert baptisms. Yet I felt unsettled about what he was doing, although I could not identify what caused the uneasiness.

During a zone meeting where he bore his testimony, I received a strong impression that helped me discover what was wrong. I realized he was an extraordinary mimic. He could speak to workers in the field as though he were one of them, and then to a professional group with such clarity and precision as to deeply impress them. He carefully and perceptively studied each person to find the most effective approach to influence him or her. In a word, he was a skilled technician, but he lacked the Spirit. His testimonies were given as a polished actor who had observed others, memorized their comments, and repeated them with great precision. Sadly, he was very sincere and did not realize what he was doing wrong.

Following up on that impression, I called him for an interview. After laying a foundation, I said "Elder, you have extraordinary skills of persuasion, but you do not work by the Spirit. You are most convincing in what you say, but I don't believe you understand what it means to have a testimony of truth. You are pretending."

He responded strongly. "That's not true, President. I have as strong a testimony as any missionary. I love the Lord, and I'm working hard to bring souls to Him through convert baptisms."

I continued to express the feelings in my heart, "You've memorized what others say and repeat it with great skill. I am not even sure you realize that bearing a witness of truth involves the heart as well as the mind."

"President, how do you know what's in my heart? You're not being fair. We're having success. We're baptizing many people."

"Yes, Elder, you are having convert baptisms in spite of what you are doing wrong. But you would be a much more powerful servant if you would learn to be led by the Spirit. You are teaching with your own capacity and strength, not by the Spirit of the Lord. Some day your battery is going to go dead, and you will fall flat on your face."

"Why do you say that, President?"

"Because I feel it, Elder." As hard as I tried, I could not communicate what I knew to be true. He was disturbed and, like many of us, focused on justifying what he had been doing rather than trying to understand new truths.

Despite my best efforts, he left very upset. I prayed that the Lord would touch his heart so that he could understand. A few days later, he called for another interview. He entered the office so dejected that I think he could have passed through the gap between the bottom of the door and the floor. He said, "President, I want to go home. I am a hypocrite. I manipulate people. I am not worthy to be a missionary."

In my heart, I thanked the Lord for what was happening and asked that I might be blessed to say those things that would open his eyes. I expressed my love, my concern, and my appreciation for him. We spoke of feelings he had begun to have and the change that would allow him to be an instrument in the hands of the Lord. Somehow the Spirit conveyed what was needed, and he began to seek guidance with faith. It was a turning point in his life. He learned to look beyond his own talents and abilities. He began to understand what the guidance of the Holy Ghost means. He became a most outstanding missionary and a dear friend.

The second precaution I would share is to not trifle with spiritual things, even unintentionally. I remember a missionary companionship that reported that they would sit on a bus and concentrate every way they could to try to make the person in front of them turn around. They began to feel that they were gaining spiritual strength when the person would turn around. I cautioned them never to do that. Follow correct principles, and you will avoid being led down inappropriate paths and prevent spiritual guidance from the dark side.

There are two times when you shouldn't talk about a spiritual experience. One is when it is very sacred. If you speak of it without being authorized of the Holy Ghost, you may offend the Lord. You may not be trusted with additional deeply sacred experiences. They can come to you when you are in tune, but they shouldn't be treated lightly. Such experiences should be written in a sacred journal and pondered, but they should not be shared without a feeling of confirmation to do so. Also, you would want to prayerfully thank the Lord that He trusted you with sacred guidance.

The other time you shouldn't talk about a spiritual experience is when you have had a negative experience from an evil source. I do not understand exactly why, but I know it is a spiritual law that when there is conversation about negative things, they seem to spread and grow in influence. They then can affect many others. When they are quietly handled with no discussion, they dissipate. To illustrate, once I was with a mission president planning activities for the mission. His assistant came in excitedly and said, "Elder Scott, we need you immediately. We think that one of the sister missionaries has been possessed of an evil spirit." I turned to him, and I said, "Elder, you have the priesthood. Go take care of it. We're planning the work of the Lord. I don't have time for those things. You have the authority to handle it well." Initially he probably didn't understand what I was doing, until he acted and was strengthened.

Don't talk or think about such negative things, for that causes them to have greater influence. Yes, Satan is real and he has very real agents. That has been confirmed in my life through personal experiences. I also have a testimony that evil beings have no real power over a righteous individual who has faith. They can threaten, confront, even appear to be powerful and menacing, but unless one fears and yields, they have no power. Remember when you exercise faith, live righteously, and do not fear, you are provided secure protection against Satan's efforts to influence your life.

Having discussed spiritual guidance and reviewed examples of how it is manifest, let us now study what you need to do to qualify to receive such direction in your own life.

CHAPTER 6

TO OBTAIN SPIRITUAL GUIDANCE

WHEN I FIRST RECEIVED Church assignments that involved training others, I shared personal experiences I thought would have some application to them. Later, when someone came for help or for counsel, I had a mental list of examples from my own life, or lessons learned from others, to share with the intent to benefit them. This was done with great sincerity and a desire to help. As the years have passed, I find that I am now much less moved to try to help people with the things that I have learned. Rather, I am powerfully motivated to share with them how the lessons were learned. While I have acquired many things from others that have deeply touched and molded my life, I have come to recognize that the guidance, understanding, enlightenment, and experiences I treasure most have come directly from the Lord through the Holy Spirit.

As you seek spiritual guidance, search for principles. Carefully separate them from the detail used to explain them. Principles are concentrated truth, packaged for application to a wide variety of circumstances. A true principle makes decisions clear even under the most confusing or compelling circumstances. It is worth great effort to organize the truth we gather into simple statements of principle. One of the best ways to do that is to combine the applicable content of scriptures from various sources. By doing so, you can crystallize an important statement of principle that does not exist in any single place.

In preparing this chapter I wanted to develop a simple statement of principle concerning how to obtain spiritual guidance. I analyzed several scriptures to provide the necessary doctrinal foundation. Some of the scriptures that I considered helpful are included below. I have emphasized some words to help you more easily identify the doctrinal origin of the statement of principle I was seeking.

> Yea, he that *repenteth* and *exerciseth faith,* and *bringeth forth good works,* and *prayeth continually* without ceasing—unto such it is given to know the mysteries of God; yea, unto such it shall be given to *reveal* things which never have been revealed.[1]

> Verily, thus saith the Lord: It shall come to pass that every soul who *forsaketh his sins* and *cometh unto me,* and *calleth on my name,* and *obeyeth my voice,* and *keepeth my commandments,* shall see my face and know that I am.[2]

> The words which I had often heard my father speak concerning eternal life, and the joy of the saints, sunk deep into my heart. . . . I kneeled down before my Maker, and *I cried unto him in mighty prayer* . . . ; and all the day long did I cry unto him; yea, and when the night came I did still raise my voice. . . . There came a voice. . . . My guilt was swept away. And I said: Lord, how is it done? And he said unto me: *Because of thy faith in Christ,* . . . thy *faith* hath made thee whole.[3]

> *Ask, and it shall be given unto you; seek, and ye shall find; knock, and it shall be opened* unto you. For

every one that asketh, receiveth; and *he that seeketh, findeth; and to him that knocketh, it shall be opened.*[4]

I *will visit thy brethren* according to their *diligence in keeping my commandments.*[5]

The *meek will he guide* in judgment: and *the meek will he teach* his way.[6]

If thou shalt *ask,* thou shalt *receive revelation* upon revelation, *knowledge* upon knowledge, that thou mayest *know . . . that which bringeth joy,* that which *bringeth life eternal.*[7]

For they that are wise and *have received the truth,* and *have taken the Holy Spirit for their guide,* and have not been deceived . . . shall abide the day.[8]

They had waxed strong in the *knowledge of the truth;* for they were men of a sound understanding and they had *searched the scriptures diligently,* that they might *know the word of God.* But this is not all; they had given themselves to much *prayer,* and *fasting;* therefore they had the spirit of prophecy, and the *spirit of revelation.*[9]

And if your *eye be single to my glory,* your *whole bodies* shall be *filled with light,* and there shall be no darkness in you; *and that body which is filled with light comprehendeth all things.*[10]

Behold, I say unto you they are made *known unto me by the Holy Spirit of God.* Behold, I have *fasted* and *prayed* many days that I might know these things of myself. And now *I do know of myself* that they are true;

for the Lord God hath made *them manifest unto me by his Holy Spirit.*[11]

And in that day that they shall *exercise faith in me,* saith the Lord, even as the brother of Jared did, that they may become sanctified in me, then will I *manifest unto them the things* which the brother of Jared saw, *even to the unfolding unto them all my revelations,* saith Jesus Christ.[12]

From a sincere effort over a considerable period of time, I have tried to understand the doctrinal foundation of spiritual guidance. For this book I have attempted to express the important aspects of that guidance briefly. I now share the resulting statement of principle in hope that it will be a beginning place for your study of how to obtain spiritual guidance. Succinctly expressed, that principle is:

To acquire spiritual guidance and to obey it with wisdom, one must:

Seek divine light, in humility
Exercise faith, especially in Jesus Christ
Repent
Strive diligently to keep His commandments
Pray continually
Hearken to spiritual guidance
Express gratitude

I will further explain each element of that statement of principle using examples from the scriptures, the prophets, and the priceless, though difficult, laboratory of personal experience. My desire is that the suggestions given in these pages will help you in your quest for spiritual direction throughout your life. In time, that guidance will lead you to accomplish the objective given by President Joseph F. Smith:

"The greatest achievement mankind can make in this world is to familiarize themselves with divine truth, so thoroughly, so perfectly, that the example or conduct of no creature living in the world can ever turn them away from the knowledge that they have obtained. . . .

"From my boyhood I have desired to learn the principles of the gospel in such a way . . . that it would matter not to me who might fall from the truth, . . . my foundation would be . . . certain in the truths . . . I have learned."[13]

Like President Smith, you and I need that kind of secure anchor to keep our lives centered in righteousness and to avoid being swept away by the ruthless waves of worldliness that surround us.

SEEK DIVINE LIGHT, IN HUMILITY

Why seek divine light? The Lord Himself answers that question: "That which is of God is light; and he that receiveth light, and continueth in God, receiveth more light; and that light groweth brighter and brighter until the perfect day."[14]

The scriptures clarify:

> Thy word is a lamp unto my feet, and a light unto my path.[15]

> Verily, verily, I say unto you, I will impart unto you of my Spirit, which shall enlighten your mind, which shall fill your soul with joy; . . . by this shall you know, all things whatsoever you desire of me, which are pertaining unto things of righteousness, in faith believing in me that you shall receive.[16]

Regarding divine light President Wilford Woodruff recorded: "Now, if you have the Holy Ghost with you—and every one ought to have—I can say unto you that there is no greater gift, there is no greater blessing, there is no greater testimony given to any man on earth. You may have the administration of angels; you may see many miracles; you may see many wonders in the earth; but I claim that the gift of the Holy Ghost is the greatest gift that can be bestowed upon man. It is by this power that we have performed that which we have. It is this that sustains us through all the persecutions, trials and tribulations that come upon us."[17]

After he died, Brigham Young appeared to Wilford Woodruff and said: "'I have come to see you; I have come to watch over you, and to see what the people are doing.' Then, said he, 'I want you to teach the people—and I want you to follow this counsel yourself— that they must labor and so live as to obtain the Holy Spirit, for without this you cannot build up the kingdom.'"[18] President Woodruff testified: "Joseph Smith visited me a great deal after his death, and taught me many important principles. . . . Among other things he told me to get the Spirit of God; that all of us needed it."[19]

Joseph Smith told Brother John Taylor on one occasion: "Now, if you will continue to follow the leadings of that spirit, it will always lead you right. Sometimes it might be contrary to your judgment; never mind that, follow its dictates; and if you be true to its whisperings it will in time become in you a principle of revelation so that you will know all things."[20]

President J. Reuben Clark observed:

"There is spiritual learning just as there is material learning, and the one without the other is not complete; yet, speaking for myself, if I could have only one sort of learning, that which I would take would be the learning of the spirit, because in the hereafter I shall have opportunity in the eternities which are to come to get the other, and without spiritual learning here my handicaps in the hereafter would be all but overwhelming."[21]

Why must one, in humility, earnestly seek divine light? Does it really require that much effort? Elder Henry B. Eyring learned a treasured lesson from his father, Henry Eyring, that has served him well. That father is honored as a world-renowned scientist and educator whose brilliance left a heritage of fundamental scientific principles that remain prized today. At the time Elder Eyring was at a pinnacle of formal education, having received his master's and doctor's degrees from Harvard. He was serving as a professor in the Stanford Graduate School of Business and as a Visiting Sloan Faculty Fellow at MIT. His perceptive father said:

"Hal, you have a problem. You are confused. You think education is where you have been. It is not. It is what you do, not where you go to do it. You can get an education anywhere if you work hard enough at it. You can go into the desert with a good book and blackboard and with diligent work, you can become educated."[22]

That wisdom is abundantly documented in the holy scriptures and in the declarations of the Lord's anointed. For example, speaking of His servants, the Lord said:

And inasmuch as they were humble they might be made strong, and blessed from on high, and receive knowledge from time to time.[23]

Why is humility essential to the acquiring of spiritual knowledge? To be humble is to be teachable. Humility permits you to be tutored by the Holy Spirit and to be taught from sources inspired by the Lord, such as the scriptures, the voice of His servants, or inspired parents. The seeds of personal understanding and growth germinate and flourish in the fertile soil of humility. When cultivated through the exercise of faith, pruned by repentance, and fortified by obedience and good works, such seeds produce the cherished fruit of spirituality.[24] Divine guidance and power then result—guidance to know the will of the Lord, and power to provide the capability to accomplish that inspired will.[25] Such power comes from God after we have done "all we can do."[26]

A proud individual cannot know the things of the Spirit. Paul taught this truth, saying:

> For what man knoweth the things of a man, save the spirit of man which is in him? even so the things of God knoweth no man, but the Spirit of God. . . . But the natural man receiveth not the things of the Spirit of God: for they are foolishness unto him: neither can he know them, because they are spiritually discerned.[27]

Therefore, spiritual guidance must be cultivated in the environment of humility. Pride, overconfidence, selfishness, seeking for position or the honors of men stifle spiritual direction.

We also learn from the Book of Mormon that humility produces strength of character, as attested by the Lord's declaration:

> If men come unto me I will show unto them their weakness. I give unto men weakness that they may be humble; and my grace is sufficient for all men that humble themselves before me; for if they humble themselves before me, and have faith in me, then will I make weak things become strong unto them.[28]

One of my favorite portions of the Book of Mormon is the series of accounts in Alma chapter 17 through chapter 26 that deal with the missionary experiences of those great sons of Mosiah who went forth to teach the Lamanites truth. Those verses contain principles that have molded and refined my life. You will recall that at one point Ammon begins to speak of the exceptional blessings they had received and of the many people who were converted to the Church. Then Aaron, his brother, rebukes him saying, "Ammon, I fear that thy joy doth carry thee away to boasting." There follow these insightful words of Ammon:

> I do not boast in my own strength, nor in my own
> wisdom; but behold, my joy is full, yea, my heart is
> brim with joy, and I will rejoice in my God. Yea, I
> know that I am nothing; as to my strength I am weak;
> therefore I will not boast of myself, but I will boast of
> my God, for in his strength I can do all things; yea,
> behold, many mighty miracles we have wrought in this
> land, for which we will praise his name forever.[29]

What an excellent depiction of a worthy, humble servant of the
Lord, yet one who speaks with boldness when moved by the Holy
Spirit. What a marvelous pattern for us to follow in teaching gospel
truths. Humility, then, is an essential starting point for greater spiritual enlightenment.

Exercise Faith, Especially in Jesus Christ

The following scriptures will help you comprehend the power of
faith in Jesus Christ:

> And Christ hath said: If ye will have faith in me ye
> shall have power to do whatsoever thing is expedient in
> me.[30]

> And it came to pass that . . . the Spirit of the Lord
> came upon them, and they were filled with joy, having
> received a remission of their sins, and having peace of
> conscience, because of the exceeding faith which they
> had in Jesus Christ.[31]

> They did fast and pray oft, and did wax stronger
> and stronger in their humility, and firmer and firmer
> in the faith of Christ, unto the filling their souls with
> joy and consolation.[32]

Profound spiritual truth and the guidance that flows from it cannot simply be poured from one mind and heart to another. It takes faith and diligent effort. Precious truth comes a small piece at a time through faith, often with great exertion and at times with wrenching struggles. The Lord intends it be that way so that we can mature and progress. Moroni said, "Dispute not because ye see not, for ye receive no witness until after the trial of your faith."[33]

President Hugh B. Brown said, "Wherever in life great spiritual values await man's appropriation, only faith can appropriate them. Man cannot live without faith, because in life's adventure the central problem is character-building—which is not a product of logic, but of faith in ideals and sacrificial devotion to them."[34] We exercise faith by doing. Joseph Smith said that "faith [is] the principle of action and of power."[35]

To illustrate: There may be some who read this book who sincerely have not yet developed a powerful testimony of the prophet Joseph Smith. Is it hypocritical to bear witness of something you're not sure of yourself? A missionary asked President Kimball that question once, and he explained that the way to gain a testimony of a principle is to prove your faith by bearing witness of that principle. He invited the elder to lean on his testimony. That is not being hypocritical because what is testified of is true. He clarified that as one demonstrates with faith a willingness to follow that principle of the Lord, He will confirm that Joseph Smith is in very deed a prophet.

I remember being awakened very early one morning by a missionary who applied that counsel. Thrilled, he said, "President, I was with the Juarez family last night. I did as I was taught, and when I bore witness that I know that Joseph Smith was a prophet, from the top of my head to the soles of my feet I felt the answer I have been searching for. President, I know Joseph Smith is a prophet."

The need to exercise faith in Jesus Christ is understood by most of us. We know it is a fundamental requisite of the plan of salvation.

When that exercise of faith is coupled with urgent need, the personal growth and blessings that flow are transcendent. Elder James E. Faust gave this expression of feelings regarding such experiences:

"During the years of my life, and often in my present calling, and especially during a recent Gethsemane, I have gone to my knees with a humble spirit to the only place I could for help. I often went in agony of spirit, earnestly pleading with God to sustain me in the work I have come to appreciate more than life itself. I have, on occasion, felt the terrible aloneness of the wounds of the heart, of the sweet agony, the buffetings of Satan, and the encircling warm comfort of the Spirit of the Master.

"I have also felt the crushing burden, the self-doubts of inadequacy and unworthiness, the fleeting feeling of being forsaken, then of being reinforced an hundredfold. I have climbed a spiritual Mount Sinai dozens of times seeking to communicate and to receive instructions. It has been as though I have struggled up an almost real Mount of Transfiguration and upon occasion felt great strength and power in the presence of the Divine. A special sacred feeling has been a sustaining influence and often a close companion."[36]

Faith is discussed further in the chapters that follow.

REPENT

The third element to gain spiritual direction is repentance. Where there is unworthiness, there is no permanent spiritual communication. I can testify to that. I recall an interview with a choice missionary. He was an outstanding young man, a superior intellect, a graduate from a leading university, and skilled in the presentation of self and effective in communication. In an interview he asked, "President, what's wrong? Why can't I act? Why can't I serve as I want to serve? Why can't I feel guidance in my mission?" He knew what the answer was, but at that time he lacked conviction and faith in the Lord. For some additional time he tried to serve while covering up a serious transgression that occurred prior to his mission. Finally, one day, he came into my office a very humble young man. He had a stack of papers in his hand about an inch thick. He dropped them on my desk and said, "I have really tried, President, but I have confirmed that there is no other way. I need to tell you something." Then he poured forth the feelings of his heart. He said, "President, I know that telling you this will probably destroy the love you have for me, but I cannot go on in the mission field the way I am. If I must go home, I want you to know that I love the Lord, and I would do whatever He asked me to do." I responded, "I love you the more, for I know how difficult it is to do what you have done." A mission president is guided by the Spirit, as are other priesthood leaders who are judges in Israel. The Holy Ghost guided our conversation and his subsequent steps of repentance. Finally the glorious day of the Lord's full forgiveness came, unlocking his mind and heart to spiritual power again. A great man became a marvelous missionary. He has since been a stalwart husband and father, an outstanding professional, and an impressive Church leader.

Chapters 12 and 13 elaborate further on what is required for full repentance to yield the immense blessing of forgiveness.

Strive Diligently to Keep His Commandments

The Lord explained why He was able to give Nephi, the son of Helaman, vital spiritual guidance that saved his life when He made this declaration:

> Blessed art thou, Nephi, for those things which thou hast done; for I have beheld how thou hast with unwearyingness declared the word, which I have given unto thee, unto this people. And thou hast not feared them, and hast not sought thine own life, but hast sought my will, and to keep my commandments.[37]

The basis upon which inspiration and power are granted is clarified in this scripture:

> And ye are to be taught from on high. *Sanctify yourselves* and ye shall be endowed with power, that ye may give even as I have spoken.[38]

President Harold B. Lee stated that in this verse the expression "*sanctify yourselves*" can be better understood by replacing it with an equivalent statement: "Keep my commandments."[39] As the scripture is understood with that inspired clarification, we read:

> And ye are to be taught from on high. [Keep my commandments] and ye shall be endowed with power, that ye may give even as I have spoken.

Thus, faithful obedience to God's commandments is fundamental and a prerequisite that must be met to be assured of divine inspiration and power.

The sacred scriptural declarations included at the beginning of this chapter emphasize how extremely important it is to obey the commandments to qualify to receive guidance of the Spirit of God. In the prior chapter it was noted that the Spirit communicates to our spirit in two ways described as to the mind and to the heart. But to obtain that help you must follow the rules upon which it is based. Consider a simple analogy. Assume that we are in a television studio broadcasting over channel 7 to warn the people of a coming disaster. The inhabitants are in varying stages of readiness to receive the warning. One groups' picture tubes are burned out, another's TV sets are unplugged, a third have their sets tuned to channel 5, and a few have excellent equipment synchronized to channel 7. The last group is the only one that will receive that warning message, which represents spiritual direction. Those with the destroyed picture tube represent individuals with serious unresolved transgressions, who must be healed through repentance to receive help from the Spirit. Those with the plug disconnected are focused on the things of the world and are not seeking spiritual guidance. The individuals tuned to channel 5 have allowed things of lesser importance to distract them.

Let us analyze further a scripture discussed previously, for it contains the Lord's explanation of how the foregoing simple example applies to spiritual communication:

> He that receiveth the word of truth, doth he receive it by the Spirit of truth or some other way? If it be some other way it is not of God. Therefore, why is it that ye cannot understand and know, that he that receiveth the word by the Spirit of truth receiveth it as it is preached by the Spirit of truth?

And now a very important phrase:

> Wherefore, he that preacheth and he that receiveth, *understand one another,* and *both are edified* and rejoice together.[40]

With the above television broadcast example, I have explained how they "*understand one another.*" When individuals teach and listen together, they can understand the teaching and have the truth of it confirmed by the witness of the Spirit. Now let us examine the second half of the verse, the personal part: *"and both are edified."*

Suppose that I were teaching a group of people some principles of spiritual communication. To make a point I have equipped a companion somewhere in the middle of the group with a radio receiver and earphones. He is blindfolded and is listening for directions. So that others cannot hear, I whisper into a small microphone connected to a transmitter. I relay detailed instructions that allow him to maneuver from his position to stand beside me. He is then told to remove the blindfold and reach into my left suit pocket to retrieve a five-dollar bill. I comment: "That is yours. Put it in your pocket. You have been an obedient servant." The whole group is then asked: "Why didn't the rest of you do that?" They respond: "We didn't hear anything."

That example illustrates two principles of spiritual direction. First, we must be ever attentive to the possibility of receiving spiritual guidance. Second, the Lord personalizes His teachings to us. Even when many are carefully prepared to be led by the Spirit, they will not necessarily all receive the same message. The Spirit can communicate a separate, distinctly different message to meet the individual needs of each person prepared to receive it.

Here is another observation concerning how you can be guided spiritually and how prayers are answered. The Lord has said, "I will tell you in your mind and in your heart, by the Holy Ghost, which shall come upon you and which shall dwell in your heart."[41] That is the vehicle through which pure truth is transmitted. When the Lord permits it, every soul in the world can benefit temporarily from the guidance and inspiration of the Holy Ghost. However, only those who are obedient to the gospel, who are baptized, and who receive the gift of the Holy Ghost have that Companion as an eternal right.

Your faith in Jesus Christ and obedience to His teachings are absolutely essential to spiritual guidance. When your exercise of faith is coupled with sincere effort, based upon your willingness to hearken to His counsel, great personal growth and blessings follow. The Savior declared:

> I now give unto you a commandment . . . to give diligent heed to the words of eternal life. For you shall live by every word that proceedeth forth from the mouth of God. For the word of the Lord is truth, and whatsoever is truth is light, and whatsoever is light is Spirit, even the Spirit of Jesus Christ. And the Spirit giveth light to every man that cometh into the world;

and the Spirit enlighteneth every man through the world, that hearkeneth to the voice of the Spirit. And every one that hearkeneth to the voice of the Spirit cometh unto . . . the Father.[42]

The role of obedience in gaining spiritual direction is crucial, as this comment of President Joseph Fielding Smith confirms:

"Now the Lord would give us gifts. He will quicken our minds. He will give us . . . a knowledge that will be so deeply rooted in our souls that [it] can never be rooted out, if we will just seek for the light . . . and the understanding which is promised to us, and which we can receive if we will only be true and faithful to every covenant and obligation pertaining to the gospel of Jesus Christ."[43]

PRAY CONTINUALLY

Our communication with God is through prayer. His communication with us almost always is through inspiration to ourselves or through others. His guidance takes a wide variety of paths.

The entreaty to pray "continually without ceasing"[44] does not mean to always be on our knees. You can maintain the attitude of prayer, have a prayer in your heart, and be ready to respond to an answer in many settings and circumstances throughout your day.

For prayer to be answered, you should first formulate a decision and then present it to the Lord for ratification. Specifically, as has been mentioned, the Lord has told us:

> If it is right I will cause that your bosom shall burn within you; therefore, you shall feel that it is right.
> But if it be not right you shall have no such feelings, but you shall have a stupor of thought that shall cause you to forget the thing which is wrong.[45]

As you study that scripture and others that apply to the

principles of prayer, you will find that nowhere does it say *when* the Lord will answer. Some of us misunderstand the doctrine. We urgently plead for an answer. We pray with sincerity, following the steps outlined, and nothing happens. I will share something found by personal experience. It has been confirmed so repeatedly that I know it is true. When you follow the laws of prayer given you of God, one of *three* things happens. First, you can feel that peace, that comfort, that assurance, that certainty that your decision is right. Or second, you can sense that uncomfortable feeling, that stupor of thought, and you know that what you have chosen is wrong. Or third—and this is the difficult one, you feel nothing.

What do you do when you have prepared yourself, have prayed fervently, waited a reasonable time for a response, and still do not feel an answer? I have come to thank the Lord when that occurs, for it is an evidence of His trust. I positively know that as you apply your decision as though it were confirmed powerfully from on high, one of two things will certainly occur at the appropriate time: either the stupor of thought will come, indicating an incorrect choice; or the peace or the burning in the bosom will be felt confirming that your choice was correct. When you are living righteously and are proceeding in trust, the Lord will not let you go too far without a warning if you have made the wrong decision.

As noted, prophets have indicated that the answer comes when you need it most, not necessarily when you first ask for it. But what happens if the timing is such that you have to make a decision and you're still unsure about what to do? You have prayerfully studied the question and have evaluated it to make sure it's consistent with the principles of the gospel. Then you have determined that it seems to be in harmony with your understanding of what your Father in Heaven would want you to do. Yet when you pray for an answer and none comes, what should you do?

What I say now requires that your life be righteous and that you are willing to obey the direction of the Lord, both of which qualify you to receive His guidance. Under those circumstances, when you diligently seek but receive no answer, you may proceed with conviction.

Remember, the requisites are living the commandments and making sure that what you propose to do is consistent with the Savior's teachings. Then, if you don't receive an answer and can't wait longer, proceed. Again, the Lord won't let you make a mistake. If in trust you have selected a wrong path, He will let you know by the impressions that come before it is too late. But you must be attentive, looking for that direction. If you've chosen the right thing to do, that feeling of peace will come as you carry it out, when He confirms your correct choice. If not, you will be warned before it is too late. I promise you that. I testify that these principles are true. Even when the decisions are the most vital in life, that is the process as I have come to understand it.

I will share two experiences to demonstrate what I mean. One day a very close friend came to my home. He was a bishop very much enjoying his calling. He had an opportunity for employment in another part of the country and was undecided about whether or not to go, yet he had to give an answer the next morning. We discussed the principles just reviewed. He went home and made a decision to move. He felt no confirmation of the correctness of that decision, but moved to the new job anyway. His employment was good and his family doing well, yet he continued to feel uncomfortable, not knowing for sure whether he had made the right decision. A week passed, then a month, then additional months. One day one of the Brethren was assigned to reorganize the stake in the area where he now lived. My friend received his confirmation from the Lord when he was selected to be the new stake president. This clear impression came to him as he was called: "Now you know why you have come here."

An example of the opposite kind of experience came as I followed, as carefully as I knew how, the principles we have discussed. One of the most sacred responsibilities of a mission president is the assignment of companionships, for it must be done through inspiration. On one occasion, having carefully followed the same procedure as always, I invited a missionary into my office and said, "Elder, you're going to be thrilled with your new assignment."

His eyes lit up with enthusiasm. Then, just as I was about to give him his assignment, an impression came to my mind: "No, not there; you can't send him there."

The more he stared wide-eyed, the more uneasy I became. I said, "Just a minute, Elder. I'll be right back." I went to another room and prayed again to find out where he should go. He never knew what had happened, but I had learned an important lesson regarding spiritual guidance. I was acting with trust that his assignment was correct. The Lord knew of circumstances that made that an incorrect choice. Because I was attentive to a feeling of the Spirit, He kept me from innocently making a mistake. He was even kind enough to later let me discover why the first assignment was unwise.

President Marion G. Romney taught: "Now, I tell you that you can make every decision in your life correctly if you can learn to follow the guidance of the Holy Spirit. This you can do if you will discipline yourself to yield your own feelings to the promptings of the Spirit. Study your problems and prayerfully make a decision. Then take that decision and say to him, in a simple, honest supplication, 'Father, I want to make the right decision. I want to do the right thing. This is what I think I should do; let me know if it is the right course.' Doing this, you can get the burning in your bosom, if your decision is right. If you do not get the burning, then change your decision and submit a new one. When you learn to walk by the Spirit, you never need to make a mistake."[46]

Your prayers are answered through the Holy Ghost to you or to another who can help you.

> Draw near unto me and I will draw near unto you; seek me diligently and ye shall find me; ask, and ye shall receive; knock, and it shall be opened unto you. Whatsoever ye ask the Father in my name it shall be given unto you, that is expedient for you.[47]

> And I will pray the Father, and he shall give you another Comforter, that he may abide with you for ever; even the Spirit of truth; whom the world cannot receive, because it seeth him not, neither knoweth him: but ye know him; for he dwelleth with you, and shall be in you. I will not leave you comfortless: I will come to you. . . . These things have I spoken unto you, being yet present with you. But the Comforter, which is the Holy Ghost, whom the Father will send in my name, he shall teach you all things, and bring all things to your remembrance, whatsoever I have said unto you. Peace I leave with you, my peace I give unto you: not as the world giveth, give I unto you. Let not your heart be troubled, neither let it be afraid.[48]

Oh, what a marvelous promise.

God sometimes answers prayer so clearly and concisely that we can write His counsel down as though it were dictated to our mind and heart. I have done that. Again, God answers urgent prayer when there is a need, but He chooses when the answer will come.

Hearken to Spiritual Guidance

Even though we are instructed to pray for the Lord's guidance, we are also asked to do all we are capable of doing first, before asking for divine assistance. In explaining that truth President Lee gave this insightful instruction:

"When we . . . cannot get anything to help ourselves, then we may call upon the Lord and His servants who can do all. But it is our duty to do what we can within our own power.

"That is a tremendous principle. In order to teach young people how to approach the Lord and how to prepare to receive what the Lord has promised for those who are faithful, we must teach them these fundamental steps. After Moroni had read [the] great experience of the brother of Jared, he added: ' . . . wherefore, dispute not because ye see not, for ye receive no witness until after the trial of your faith.' (Ether 12:6.)

"The grandson of Lehi illustrates this principle also. Enos went out in the mountains to pray and to ask forgiveness for his sins. He closed his brief record about this experience by saying:

"'And my soul hungered; and I kneeled down before my Maker, and I cried unto him in mighty prayer and supplication for mine own soul; and all the day long did I cry unto him; yea, and when the night came I did still raise my voice high that it reached the heavens.' (Enos 4.)

"I once read that scripture to a woman who laughed and said, 'Imagine anybody praying all night and all day.' I replied, 'My dear sister, I hope you never have to come to a time where you have a problem so great that you have to so humble yourself. I have; I have prayed all day and all night and all the next day and all the next night, not always on my knees but praying constantly for a blessing that I needed most.'

"Enos continued:

"' . . . while I was thus struggling in the spirit, behold, the voice of the Lord came into my mind again, saying: I will visit thy brethren according to their diligence in keeping my commandments. . . .' (Enos 10.)"

Now President Lee gives a marvelous conclusion to this teaching: "The Savior's blood, His atonement, will save us, but only after we have done all we can to save ourselves by keeping His commandments. All of the principles of the gospel are principles of promise by which the plans of the Almighty are unfolded to us."[49]

President Gordon B. Hinckley also taught: "Listen to the whisperings of the Spirit. Brother Harold B. Lee set me apart, when he was a member of the Twelve, as a stake president. I remember only one thing he said: 'Listen for the whisperings of the Spirit in the middle of the night, and respond to those whisperings.' I don't know why revelation comes sometimes in the night, but it does. It comes in the day as well, of course. But listen to the whisperings of the Spirit, the gift of revelation, to which you are entitled."[50]

While there is much of value to be learned, there is only one arena of study where we may learn absolute truth, and that is centered in the gospel of Jesus Christ. Yet to obtain spiritual direction or to acquire spiritual knowledge are not sufficient—you must find the courage and strength to consistently use them.

> For behold, it is not meet that I should command in all things; for he that is compelled in all things, the same is a slothful and not a wise servant; wherefore he receiveth no reward. Verily I say, men should be anxiously engaged in a good cause, and do many things of their own free will, and bring to pass much righteousness; for the power is in them, wherein they are agents unto themselves. And inasmuch as men do good they shall in nowise lose their reward.[51]

The chastisement the Lord gave Joseph Smith in the following scripture indicates how important it is to Him that we recognize, appreciate, and obey the guidance He provides through the Holy Ghost.

> For although a man may have many revelations,
> and have power to do many mighty works, yet if he
> boasts in his own strength, and sets at naught the coun-
> sels of God, and follows after the dictates of his own
> will and carnal desires, he must fall and incur the
> vengeance of a just God upon him.[52]

Sometimes considering an experience from everyday life awak-
ens our understanding of truth. Consider for a moment a man, heav-
ily overweight, approaching a bakery display. In his mind are these
thoughts: "The doctor told you not to eat any more of that. It's not
good for you. It just gives momentary gratification of appetite. You'll
feel uncomfortable the rest of the day. You've decided not to have any
more." Then he hears himself say: "I'll have two of those almond
twists and a couple of doughnuts and two chocolate brownies."

He succumbed to the temptation: "One more time won't hurt.
Do it just once more and that will be the last time." Ridiculous as
that example may appear, I am afraid we sometimes do even more
crazy things with valid impressions that we don't necessarily want to
receive. Inspiration can be of value in your life only as you determinedly apply it.

We gain the courage and strength to apply truth as we live close
to our Father in Heaven and as we form a personal relationship with
Him. President David O. McKay once said, "The greatest comfort
in this life is . . . having a close relationship with God."[53] Spiritual
knowledge and its consistent application bring peace and satisfaction.
They stimulate self-reliance.

Brigham Young learned truth by carefully listening to Joseph
Smith and striving to understand everything the Prophet taught by
word, example, or the Spirit. Brigham Young diligently obeyed the
lessons taught. The resulting tutoring has blessed generations. It conditioned him to learn additional truths through personal spiritual
guidance from the Holy Ghost. Such guidance equipped him to

share with others far more than he had received personally from Joseph Smith. Follow his example.

Hearkening to the spiritual guidance can include service. Such service often embodies earnest, diligent, hard work. I can think of no more fitting examples of devoted service to the Lord than that of our beloved prophets and their devoted wives.

This example of work was shared by Elder Spencer W. Kimball as an Apostle in a missionary zone conference[54]:

"I was interviewing a missionary once, but he said, 'I don't like to work. I don't like to tract.' And then I said, 'Oh, is that so? I thought every missionary just loved to tract.' He looked at me a little funny, and I said, 'Did you know that the worthwhile things of life are not the things that you just want to do. They are the things you should do. Do you just love to study everything that is assigned in the university? Do you just love to do everything you do, or isn't there anything in the world you do because you ought to do it. You want to do it because you ought to do it.' Well, I smiled at him, and I could see he was thinking a little bit, and I said, 'What do you like to do?' and he answered he liked to play baseball. Neither did I enjoy tracting to the degree that I liked to play baseball, but I went forward in my tracting because it was the thing I needed to do to develop me and to bring souls to Christ.

"I said, 'My goodness, my boy, you are headed for a total loss if you only do the things you like to do.' I said, I wanted to go on a mission. I was scared to death. Me. A little fellow coming from a country district. I wondered if I could do it. I was quite sure I would have difficulty, and then I began to analyze and remember specific friends that had done it, and I could play basketball better than they could. I could make more baskets and do more, so if they all can do it, maybe I can do it."

Now here's the key to President Kimball's success: "I decided."

Once he made a decision in his life he never looked back. He just did it.

"I decided I wanted to go on a mission as I had been taught all my life. When I got to the end of my high school, I went to Globe, Arizona, to get a job, so that I could save money because I wasn't like some missionaries who would only have to say, 'Dad, I need some money' and the money was provided. My father was having a little problem with a large family to support." [What an understatement that was.]

"So I went and earned the money. I had earned the money for my school the last two or three years, and I earned it for my mission."

He talked about a black colt that he had raised and how he sold it and every penny went for his mission. Then he said,

"I'd grown up on a farm so I could milk cows. I could do a lot of things. My father bought me a little pitchfork when I was just a little boy, and I found work in the dairy wasn't easy either. I didn't like it. I would milk the cows and then go in and do the washing of the cans and bottles. We would use scalding water, and our fingers would get somewhat used to it, and then I would go out to milk the cows the next time, and my fingers would crack and bleed.

"I went to the Globe Ward every Sunday night. We would walk about two miles down the railroad to get there. I would hold my hands above my head as we walked, so that the weight of the blood in my fingers wouldn't crucify me. It hurt terribly, so I walked that way. I guess people thought I was giving up, but I wasn't. I wasn't surrendering. I was just on my way, and so my fingers bled every day, but every night I went back and milked the cows, somewhere between twenty and twenty-eight cows I milked every night and every morning with my hands, not with machines. In between, we would go out to turn the cows into the field and take a square-ended shovel. You know what we did with the shovel. We cleaned up after the cows. You know, I never did like to clean manure. It was about the filthiest job I ever had, but I had to do it to keep my job. It was part of my job. So I said to this boy, 'So you don't like to tract. Well, for heaven's sake, what do you like to do that will pay dividends? Think about that, too. If tracting is hard, and other visits are hard and preaching the gospel is hard and study is hard, so what, it pays big dividends."[54]

Regarding service, President David O. McKay said, "Let us make God the center of our lives. . . . To have communion with God, through his Holy Spirit, is one of the noblest aspirations of life. It is when the peace and love of God have entered the soul, when serving him becomes the motivating factor in one's life and existence, that we can touch the lives of others, quickening and inspiring them, even though no word be spoken."[55]

Express Gratitude

One of President N. Eldon Tanner's favorite scriptures, which he often quoted, was this: "In nothing doth man offend God, or against none is his wrath kindled, save those who confess not his hand in all things, and obey not his commandments."[56] I have found that expressing gratitude for specific blessings is an essential step to finding peace with happiness and joy. As the years have passed, I find that the greater part of my prayers has become an expression of gratitude for a host of specific blessings. While that gratitude is not motivated by the desire to receive greater gifts of the Spirit, they often come from a compassionate, generous Father in Heaven, who has heard my prayers.

I am confident that with a few moments of pondering, you can identify many matters for which to pour out your heart in gratitude to your Father in Heaven. I know that when you do this sincerely He will respond with evidence of His love and appreciation. You will also be able to remember many reasons to thank parents, friends, and even those who may have offended you with expressions of gratitude, written or stated, for what they have contributed to your life.

Once I saw a sheet of paper that had thirty-seven suggestions of what a mother should do or should be. I thought, a woman does not need that guilt trip. Tear it up. Just be your best selves. Don't over-program. Enjoy the life you have as mothers and wives. If a man, an important way to show greater gratitude is to consistently express the things of your heart to your wife or mother. When you do there would likely be less of a tendency for a mother who is really doing very well to be overly critical of herself. Unwarranted self-criticism robs a mother of joy and a fulness of life.

For the greatest benefit, as spiritual guidance unfolds, *it must be understood, valued, used, and remembered.*

• **Understood.** As you encounter a significant new element of truth, you should carefully examine it in the light of prior knowledge to determine where it fits. Ponder it; inspect it inside and out. Study it from different vantage points to discover any hidden meaning. View it in perspective to confirm you have not jumped to false con-clusions. Spend time in prayerful reflection to obtain further under-standing. Such evaluation is particularly important when the truth comes as an impression of the Spirit.

When you understand that acquiring and using knowledge with wisdom takes substantial commitment, you will avoid the tragedy that can occur when teaching and learning become mechanical. Taken to an extreme, a process results that Elder Neal A. Maxwell characterized as transferring the professor's notes to the student's notebook without passing through either's mind.[57]

• **Valued.** You show knowledge is valued by expressing apprecia-tion for it, especially in heartfelt prayers of gratitude. The Lord said, "He who receiveth all things with thankfulness shall be made glori-ous; and the things of this earth shall be added unto him, even an hundred fold, yea, more."[58]

• **Used.** Obedient application of truth is the surest way of making it eternally yours. The wise use of knowledge will permeate your life with its precious fruit.

At the conclusion of an inspiring semiannual general conference, President Spencer W. Kimball counseled: "We hope that the leaders and the members of the Church who have attended and listened to the conference have been inspired and uplifted. We hope you have made copious notes of the thoughts that have come to your mind. . . . While sitting here, I have made up my mind that when I go home from this conference this night there are many, many areas in my life that I can perfect. I have made a mental list of them, and I expect to go to work as soon as we get through with conference."[59]

• **Remembered.** In previous chapters I have referred to the importance of writing down impressions. I would now like to expand and state that suggestion as a principle that, if understood and consistently applied, will bring enormous blessings throughout your life. It is not difficult for me to explain nor for you to understand. However, it will require of you significant, determined effort to yield its full potential. With it you can learn vital truths that will bring you greater, enduring happiness and make your life more productive and meaningful. I suggest that you write down this principle and put it in a prominent place where you can ponder and apply it.

Throughout the remainder of my life I will consistently strive to learn by what I hear, see, and feel. I will write down the important things I learn, and I will do them.

If you were to stop reading this book at this point you would have received one of the most meaningful ways to gain peace with happiness that I could impart. If the principle just shared doesn't seem that important, think again. Much of what I treasure I have learned by carefully following it.

You can learn vitally important things by what you *hear* and *see* and, even more so, by what you *feel,* as prompted by the Holy Ghost. Many individuals limit their learning primarily to what they *hear* or what they *read.* Be wise. Develop the skill of learning by what you *see* and particularly by what the Holy Ghost prompts you to *feel.* Consciously and consistently seek to learn by what you see and feel, and your capacity to do so will expand through repeated practice. Significant faith and effort are required to consistently learn by what you see and feel. Ask in faith for such help. Live to be worthy of it. Seek to recognize it. I suggest that you conscientiously practice this principle as you read the remainder of this book.

Write down in a secure place the important things you learn from the Spirit. You will find that as you record precious impressions, often more will come. Also, the spiritual knowledge you gain will be available throughout your life. Always, day or night, wherever you are, whatever you are doing, seek to recognize and respond to the direction of the Spirit. Have available a card or piece of paper to record such guidance.

Express gratitude for the help received and obey it. This practice will reinforce your capacity to learn by the Spirit. It will permit the Lord to guide your life and to enrich the use of every other capacity latent in your being.

Powerful spiritual direction in your life can be overcome or forced into the background unless you provide a way to retain it. Brigham Young declared, "If you love the truth you can remember it."[60] Knowledge carefully recorded is knowledge available in time of need. Spiritually sensitive information should be kept in a sacred place that communicates to the Lord how you treasure it. That practice enhances the likelihood of your receiving further light. I put brackets around recorded spiritual impressions to remember their origin. These notes are transferred to a safe place where their sacred nature can be preserved.

Joseph Smith taught the Twelve the importance of recording

spiritual direction: "Perhaps, for neglecting to write these things [spiritual guidance] when God had revealed them, not esteeming them of sufficient worth, the Spirit may withdraw and God may be angry; . . . a vast knowledge, of infinite importance, . . . is now lost."[61]

That advice is meticulously followed in the presiding counsels of the Church. You will be blessed as you heed it in your own private life.

These last two chapters contain a lot of spiritual meat. You may want to return to them later to ponder them carefully.

CHAPTER 7

TRUST IN THE LORD

I T IS SO HARD WHEN sincere prayer about something we desire very much is not answered the way we want. It is especially difficult when the Lord answers *no* to that which is worthy and would give us great joy and happiness. Whether it be overcoming illness or loneliness, recovery of a wayward child, coping with a handicap, or seeking continuing life for a dear one who is slipping away, it seems so reasonable and so consistent with our happiness to have a favorable answer. It is hard to understand why our exercise of deep and sincere faith from an obedient life does not bring the desired result.

No one wants adversity. Trials, disappointments, sadness, and heartache come to us from basically two different sources. Those who transgress the laws of God will always have those challenges. The other reason for adversity is to accomplish the Lord's own purposes in our lives, that we may receive the refinement that comes from testing. There is a third source of challenge. It is the willful, destructive, abusive acts of others, when we are innocent of the violation of God's laws. It is vitally important for each of us to identify which of these sources our trials and challenges come from, for the corrective action is very different. (Abuse is dealt with in chapter 19.)

If you are suffering the disheartening effects of transgression, please recognize that the only path to permanent relief from sadness is sincere repentance with a broken heart and a contrite spirit.[1]

Recognize your full dependence upon the Lord and your need to align your life with His teachings. There is really no other way to get lasting healing and peace. Postponing humble, sincere repentance will delay or prevent your receiving relief. Admit to yourself your mistakes and seek help. Do it now. Your bishop is a friend with keys of authority to help you find peace of mind and contentment. The way will be opened for you to have strength to repent and be forgiven. Chapters 12 and 13 have been prepared to give you additional help.

Now may I share some suggestions with you who face the second source of adversity? This is the testing that a wise Heavenly Father determines is needed even when you are living a worthy, righteous life and are obedient to His commandments.

Just when all seems to be going right, challenges often come in multiple doses, applied simultaneously. When those trials are not consequences of your disobedience, they are evidence that the Lord feels you are prepared to grow more.[2] He therefore gives you experiences that stimulate growth, understanding, and compassion. Such testing will polish you for your everlasting benefit. To get you from where you are to where He wants you to be requires a lot of stretching, and that generally entails discomfort and pain.

When facing adversity, you can be led to ask many questions. Some questions serve a useful purpose; others do not. To ask, "Why does this have to happen to me? Why do I have to suffer this, now? What have I done to cause this?" will lead you into blind alleys. It really does no good to ask questions that reflect opposition to the will of God. Rather ask, "What am I to do? What am I to learn from this experience? What am I to change? Whom am I to help? How can I remember my many blessings in times of trial?" Willing sacrifice of deeply held personal desires in favor of the will of God is very hard to do. Yet when you pray with real conviction, "Please let me know Thy will" and "May Thy will be done," you are in the strongest position to receive the maximum help from your loving Father.

This life is an experience in profound trust—trust in Jesus Christ, trust in His teachings, and trust in our capacity, as led by the Holy Spirit, to obey those teachings to enjoy happiness now and to attain a purposeful, supremely happy eternal existence.[3] To trust means to obey willingly without knowing the end from the beginning.[4] To produce fruit, your trust in the Lord must be more powerful and enduring than your confidence in your own personal feelings and experience.

To exercise faith is to trust that the Lord knows what He is doing with you and that He can accomplish it for your eternal good even though you cannot understand how He can possibly do it. We are like infants in our understanding of eternal matters and their impact on us here in mortality. Yet at times we act as if we know it all. When you pass through trials for His purposes, as you trust Him and exercise faith in Him, He will help you. That support will generally come step by step, a portion at a time. While you are passing through each phase, the pain and difficulty that comes from being enlarged may continue. If all matters were immediately resolved at your first petition, you could not grow. Your Father in Heaven and His Beloved Son love you perfectly. They would not require you to experience a moment more of difficulty than is absolutely needed for your personal benefit or that of those you love.

As in all things, the Master is our perfect example. No one could have asked with more perfect faith, greater obedience, or more complete understanding than did He when He beseeched His Father in Gethsemane: "O my Father, if it be possible, let this cup pass from me: nevertheless not as I will, but as thou wilt."[5] Later He pled twice again that we are aware of: "O my Father, if this cup may not pass away from me, except I drink it, thy will be done."[6]

How grateful I am personally that our Savior taught we should conclude our most urgent, deeply felt prayers, when we ask for that which is of utmost importance to us, with "Thy will be done."[7] Your willingness to accept the will of the Father will not change what in His wisdom He has chosen to do. However, it will certainly change the effect of those decisions on you personally. That evidence of the proper exercise of agency allows His decisions to produce far greater blessings in your life. I have found that because of our Father's desire for us to grow, He may give us gentle, almost imperceptible promptings which, if we are willing to accept them without complaint, He will enlarge to become a very clear indication of His will. This enlightenment comes because of our faith and our willingness to do what He asks even though we deeply desire something else.

Your Father in Heaven has invited you to express your needs, hopes, and desires unto Him. That should not be done in a spirit of negotiation, but rather in the spirit of a willingness to obey His will no matter what direction that takes. His invitation to "ask, and ye shall receive"[8] does not assure that you will get what you want. It does guarantee that, if worthy, you will get what you need, as judged by an all-knowing Father who loves you perfectly and who wants your eternal happiness even more than you do.

I testify that when the Lord closes one important door in your life, He shows His continuing love and compassion by opening many other compensating doors through your exercise of faith in Him. He will place in your path packets of spiritual sunlight to brighten your way. They often come after the trial has been the greatest, as evidence of the compassion and love of an all-loving Father. They point the way to greater happiness and more understanding, and they strengthen your determination to accept and be obedient to His will.

It is a singularly marvelous blessing to have faith in the Savior and a testimony of His teachings. So few in the world have that brilliant light to guide them. The fulness of the restored gospel gives perspective, purpose, and understanding. It allows us to face what otherwise would appear to be unjust, unfair, or unreasonable challenges in life. Learn those helpful truths by pondering the Book of Mormon and other scriptures. Try to understand those teachings not only with your mind but also with your heart.

True enduring happiness, with the accompanying strength, courage, and capacity to overcome the most challenging difficulties, comes from a life centered in Jesus Christ. Obedience to His teachings provides a sure foundation upon which to build. That takes effort. There is no guarantee of overnight results, but there is absolute assurance that, in the Lord's time, solutions will come, peace will prevail, and emptiness will be filled. Again we note that the Savior has proclaimed:

> But blessed are they who are faithful and endure
> . . . for they shall inherit eternal life.[9]

> For verily I say unto you, blessed is he that keepeth my commandments . . . and he that is faithful in tribulation, the reward of the same is greater in the kingdom of heaven. Ye cannot behold with your natural eyes . . . the design of your God concerning those things which shall come hereafter, and the glory which shall follow after much tribulation. For after much tribulation come the blessings.[10]

A great leader I have come to admire very much, suffering from physical handicaps that come with advancing age, said, "I am glad I have what I have." It is wisdom to open the windows of happiness by recognizing all discernable blessings.

Don't let the workings of adversity totally absorb your life. Try to understand what you can. Act where you are able. Then let the matter rest with the Lord for a period while you give to others in worthy ways before you take on appropriate concern again.

Please learn that as you wrestle with a challenge and feel sadness because of it, you can simultaneously have peace and rejoicing. Yes, pain, disappointment, frustration, and anguish can be temporary scenes played out on the stage of life. Yet behind them there can be a background of peace and the positive assurance that a loving Father will keep His promises. You can qualify for those promises by determining to accept His will, by understanding the plan of happiness, by receiving all of the ordinances you are able to obtain, and by keeping the covenants you have made, to assure their fulfillment.

The Lord's plan is to exalt you to live with Him and to be greatly blessed. The rate at which you qualify is generally set by your capacity to mature, to grow, to love, and to give of yourself. He is preparing you to be exalted. You cannot understand fully what that means, yet He knows. As you trust Him, seeking and following His will, you will receive blessings that your finite mind cannot always recognize or understand here on earth.

Your Father in Heaven and His Holy Son know better than you what brings happiness. They have given you the plan of happiness. As you understand and follow it, happiness will be your blessing. As you willingly obey, receive, and honor the ordinances and covenants of that holy plan, you can have the greatest measure of satisfaction in this life—yes, even times of overpowering joy. You will prepare yourself for an eternity of glorious life with your loved ones who qualify for the highest kingdom.

I know the principles we have discussed are true. They have been tested in the crucible of personal experience. To recognize the hand of the Lord in your life and to accept His will without complaint is a beginning. That decision does not immediately eliminate the struggles that will come for your growth. But I witness that it is the best way for you to find strength and understanding. It will free you from the dead ends of your own reasoning. It will allow your life to become a productive, meaningful experience, when otherwise you may not know how to go on.

I testify that you have a Heavenly Father who loves you. I witness that the Savior gave His life for your happiness. I know Him. He understands your every need. I positively know that as you accept Their will without complaint, They will bless and sustain you no matter what the challenge.

CHAPTER 8

TO MAKE AND KEEP THE
RIGHT DECISIONS

E ACH OF US FACES THE NEED to make critically important decisions in our life. These decisions have a profound influence on
our happiness, on what we will become, and how we will spend eternity. What follows is the result of repeated efforts to be guided to
share with you some of the principles that lead to correct decisions.
The principles are true. They are founded in doctrine and have been
repeatedly proven in the unfolding of my own life. Without divine
guidance you do not have the assurance of making the right choices
in essential matters. I will give suggestions to help you obtain that
guidance. May you somehow feel the love of the Lord for you personally when He conveys a message to your mind and heart, through
the Spirit, tailored to your personal needs.

The spiritual moments in your life will often come in clusters
when you feel so occupied that it seems difficult to record them. As
noted in chapter 6, that special effort is powerfully rewarded when
you take a few moments to make a permanent record of the sacred
impressions of the Holy Spirit. Begin now. If needed, find paper and
pencil to do it.

You may have found that each day the challenges you face are
becoming more numerous and more intensely focused. Yet never was

96

there a more exciting, stimulating, potentially productive time to live on earth. You will continually face important decisions that vitally affect your happiness now and forever. Depending on your circumstances, those decisions could include who will be your eternal companion, what will be your profession, how will you sustain your family, how you can live worthily in a world that is ever more difficult, or how you can get out of the hole dug with bad decisions. I feel deeply the responsibility of sharing truths with you in a way that is acceptable to the Lord and helpful to you personally as you make and keep correct decisions.

If you have been wise, you likely know what to do regarding most important things in life. You have made those decisions, but perhaps you find, as do I, that at times it's hard to follow through on all of the important choices made. I don't mean that you are necessarily doing the wrong things, just not enough of the ones you know to be right.

I will cite two visual aids used with a group of youth to illustrate the two potent influences that constantly surround you. I will also give a third illustration to help you confirm which of the influences you may be following at a given moment in your life.

I asked a small group of students to form a circle. I then explained that I was going to ask them to do something that would appear harmful. But I said, "If you trust me and follow my instructions carefully, I promise you that nothing unpleasant will happen to you. You have my word of honor. But please follow carefully the instructions I give you or I cannot be responsible for what happens." I also invited Elder Henry B. Eyring to join the circle to give the illustration more credibility. A cable with a light bulb was plugged into current. The bulb glowed. I then explained that I was going to cut the socket off the end of the cord, bare the wires, and then ask two persons at each end of the circle to hold the bare wires while all the rest tightly held hands. I invited any that did not trust me to leave the circle. The cord was then carefully plugged into the power source so that all could see. Nothing happened to the students. I quickly cautioned the audience never to try that experiment. Since I did not want to harm the trusting students, I explained that one of the prongs of the plug had been bent so that it would not enter the power source and, therefore, it could not carry the electricity.

I introduced the second demonstration as my effort at mind over matter. A two-foot-long block of wood was placed on its end on a table, and I announced that I would attempt through the sheer force of mental power to cause it to move. After a moment it moved slightly. Encouraged, I said I would try to cause it to fall. After some apparent exertion on my part it fell over. I then clarified that the wood had been moved by trickery, for I had no such mental power. The wood was caused to fall by a radio-controlled device in its interior.

While we had some fun with these examples, I explained that they were not intended for entertainment. They were to provide hooks in the mind to which eternal principles could be securely tied. Such memories can help you identify, choose, and fulfill correct decisions. When kept, such decisions will help you receive the blessings the Lord wants you to obtain.

The first example embodied many of the challenges encountered in life. I had asked a group of trusting youth to do something their own experience would indicate would bring them difficulty. Yet I also had promised, "If you trust me and follow my instructions carefully, I promise you that nothing unpleasant will happen to you. You have my promise. But please follow carefully the instructions I give you or I cannot be responsible for the outcome." They trusted me, and because of that trust we were able to carry out the illustration. The point that I had hoped to make was that when we carefully obey God and trust Him He will answer our righteous prayers, even though we may not understand how it will be done.

In another place in the world, with a small group of youth, I tried this same demonstration. As I explained to the young men and women in the circle that nothing would happen to them, I noticed that one of the girls whom I had asked to hold the bare wire carefully moved her fingers down the cable until it reached the insulation. She did not trust me. I was greatly disappointed, so I excused her from the circle. Yet her example could illustrate how some in the world today meet challenges. They want to have it both ways. They want to appear to be doing the right things, but they are willing to cheat if they feel it will be to their advantage.

Never play games with the commandments of the Lord. When you trust Him fully, He is able to bless you richly. He knows what is best for you. Sometimes a very clever person can deceive a human being, but none of us can do that with the Lord. Trust Him. Live so that He can trust you. He then will guide and bless you more abundantly. I am confident that the Lord expects each of us to do the right things. He expects us to be pillars of strength in His kingdom.

What of the mind-over-matter example? I explained that it was to illustrate deceit. Does that remind you of so many things you see in the world around you? One who follows the pattern of deceit tries to appear to have influence and capabilities that he does not possess. Satan is the epitome of this model. He has absolutely no power over a determined, righteous individual because the Lord protects that person. Be assured that were Satan to have such capacity he would use it. God constantly protects our moral agency and thus assures that Lucifer can have no such power. Satan can gain influence over a normally righteous individual only when that person yields to temptation or allows fear to overcome faith.

The devil has great influence in this world by leading individuals to make the wrong choices. He is the father of lies. Nothing he tempts you to do will have a beneficial outcome—absolutely nothing.[1] The hook may be baited by seemingly attractive promises and outcomes, but he is the master of deceit and his agents are power-fully effective in his cause. I have come to know that Satan is a real personage with devoted, capable assistants. However, as a servant of Jesus Christ, I bear solemn witness that as you trust the Lord, are obedient to His commandments, and follow the directions of the Spirit, Satan cannot have any power over you.

The heavenly light that sheds forth from God has power to over-come the darkness of unwholesome influences around you. That is as certain as the power of brilliant light to disperse the darkness in a room. How can you get the brilliant light of the Lord into your life more abundantly? By prayerfully and consistently making the right choices and fulfilling them.

Now I refer to another visual aid employed in that youth meet-ing. It demonstrated how you can determine when an influence for good or evil is operating in your life.

I asked a student (my granddaughter, Camille Call Cook) to pass her hand over a box that had been equipped to have a strong attract-ing force (a magnet) representing good and a powerful repelling force (a magnet of opposite polarity) representing evil to see if she could detect them. She could not. She was then given a green sensing device that could detect good (a magnet that attracted). She found the device was drawn to the good influence and repelled from the evil one. Given a red sensing device that detects evil (a magnet of opposite polarity), she reported that it was attracted to the force rep-resenting evil and repelled from the good force. Gradually, successive layers of books (containing repelling magnets but no attracting mag-nets) were placed on top of the original box to represent the effect of transgression. She discovered that the good influence decreased and finally could not be detected, while the evil force increased in strength.

When she used the sensing tool representing the Holy Ghost and when there was no barrier in the way, Camille was able to discern invariably, without error, the influence representing good and the influence representing evil. So it is with a righteous person with faith in the guidance of the Holy Ghost. As I added the barriers representing transgression, detection of good was more difficult, while the influence of evil was arranged to get stronger. We also observed that when an evil-seeking tool representing the influence of Satan was used, evil appeared to be good and good evil. That is what occurs when an individual begins to rationalize departures from truth and proper behavior. It may begin with a small thing and then grow and grow into major difficulties.

Have you observed how in the life of someone in sin that serious transgressions become increasingly compelling? Finally, that person is consumed by such appetites. He does things that seem to be totally unreasonable and illogical. It is hard for an observer to understand why the transgressor breaks a growing array of commandments through a pattern of life that cannot bring happiness. The reason is that sin is addictive. Once begun, serious sin is hard to restrain and most difficult to overcome. But it can be conquered with the help of the Lord.

You have the capacity to become an incredibly sensitive instrument to discern righteous and evil influences around you. It is done by cultivating the gift of the Holy Ghost. This is accomplished by consistent, righteous living wherein you make the correct choices and follow them to completion. As you enhance your capacity to sense the direction of the infallible Holy Ghost in your life, you will avoid serious errors. May the simple visual aids I've referred to help you remember to trust the Lord, His servants, and others who are living exemplary lives and have no ulterior motive in the counsel they give.

When you seek inspiration to help you make decisions, the Lord will give gentle promptings that require you to think, to exercise faith, to work, to struggle at times, then to act. It is a step-wise process that enables you to finally reach an inspired conclusion.

Seldom will you receive all at once a complete answer from the Lord. It will come a piece at a time. Inspiration comes in packets so that you will develop and grow and not remain as a child, given everything. Such an approach to divine guidance also helps you to more fully appreciate it, give thanks for it, treasure it, and apply it. Moreover, the answer will seldom come as the prayer is offered; rather, the Lord will speak to you in quiet moments when the Spirit can most effectively touch your mind and heart. Hence the need for periods of quiet time to keep perspective and to be instructed and strengthened. Discover how a clean, neat, quiet place can enhance spiritual direction in your life.

The Lord's pattern allows you to grow. Satan's methods would bind you more to his ways, with the loss of agency.

Do you feel overwhelmed, wondering if you can make the correct choices, uncertain of how to proceed? Does trying your best not seem good enough? I understand what you are going through. Earlier in my life I felt the same way. It took me a long time to figure out that part of the plan for our growth on earth is to have periods in life when we have far more important things to do than we can possibly accomplish. You know that feeling when there is more weight on your shoulders than you think you can possibly bear, far more questions than answers. That is a test to teach the importance of establishing priorities. It emphasizes the wondrous treasure of time. When you encounter more vital things to do than you can possibly accomplish yourself, you will learn how the Lord can, through the guidance of the Spirit, give you help and assurance.

Have you ever had the feeling that the walls are closing in, that you are not in control, and that you simply can't do it? Those feelings of frustration are not from the Lord. They are caused by Satan. He wants you to bolt and run when you encounter a difficult growth challenge. (Chapter 22 relates a personal experience that may help you handle pressure.)

Don't judge yourself by what you understand of your potential. Trust in the Lord and what He can do with your dedicated heart and willing mind.[2] Order your life more effectively; and eliminate trivia and meaningless details and activity; they waste the perishable, fixed, and limited resource of time. Choose to emphasize those matters that have eternal consequence.

No matter how difficult the problems that surround you, the Lord knows how to resolve them. As you exercise faith, doing what you can, He will help you handle those things within your capability. He will bring into your path priesthood leaders who can counsel and advise, friends who can give you support, or parents or others who can provide answers. Through the avenue of prayer and the path of inspiration, He will help you know what to do. It is a process that takes time to master, but knowing that it exists should give you great comfort as you face the difficult decisions you must make in life.

The Lord puts challenges in your path to mold your character. For your own personal growth, He will often let you struggle with a matter for a while, even when you are pleading for help. But as you follow true principles, He will finally see you through. He intends that when you have reached your extremity, you will turn to Him for comfort, peace, and assistance. He will send those blessings through the quiet prompting of the Spirit. He will give reassurance and guidance that are essential to finding solutions for the challenges of your life.

You are learning powerful, eternal lessons. Be sure you understand them. The Lord does not abandon your urgent pleas, nor is He ever, for even a moment, unmindful of your anguish and heartache. He hears every supplication. He invariably answers according to spiritual law. Understanding that law will help you appreciate how the Lord answers your prayers. His silence and seeming absence at times are powerful means of expanding your vision and understanding as you continue in faith to do your best.

Consider this simple example. A race horse may resist efforts to develop his potential to run, preferring to enjoy the beauty and rich, green grass of the pasture. Yet if the horse will train, even at times against his will, he will develop a new excitement, a grander pleasure—the incomparable joy of winning. The pleasure of the pasture is not diminished, but his joy of life is expanded.

Your capacity is greater than you can imagine. Satan will try mightily to discourage you. Initially he may encourage you to do many worthwhile things, but not the essential ones. Then he will try to lead you through rationalization into gray areas and subsequently into dark ones. Beware of rationalization. It is to twist something you know to be true into a pattern that appears to support an exception to truth. Again, rationalization would lead you down blind alleys. It can take you from the path to happiness because it distorts your understanding of truth.

Have you noticed that when you have determined to accomplish a very important task, many good ideas for other things to do seem to come to your mind? If they are allowed to interfere, they will distract you from the more important objective. I have found help by writing down those alternate thoughts as they come, promising myself that as soon as I finish the important task I will attend to them in priority. That practice focuses me on those matters that are essential. I believe that there can come into your life, because of your righteousness and your determination to do what is right, times when Satan will not be able to deflect you into serious transgression. He will switch then to the strategy of placing before you a banquet of good and worthwhile things meant to distract you from those which are the most important and essential to accomplish in your life. Fortunately, as you pray for guidance, the Holy Ghost will help you identify those matters that are vital and necessary to accomplish above others. That guidance means at times you may have to set aside some things that would be worthwhile and enjoyable to pursue those that are most vitally important at that period of your life.

Have you discovered that detailed instructions from someone else on how to make choices or how to best live your life are not nearly as helpful as personal guidance from the Holy Ghost? Such divine guidance comes from pondering and living the doctrines of the Lord, understanding His plan of happiness, and obtaining the ordinances and keeping the covenants central to that plan. Such a foundation allows the Holy Ghost to give you guidance and direction, taking into consideration your personal strengths and needs. The promptings of the Holy Ghost will tell you how you stand before God, if you are progressing or retrogressing, what you need to improve, and how to do it.

I know the principles we have discussed are true. They have blessed my life many times. One vivid example is when I was called to be a mission president, while I worked as a civilian for an admiral in charge of a program essential to the national defense of our country. When I told the admiral of the call, he was most upset because he did not understand how the call had come and what it meant. He concluded a tense conversation with the words, "You are a traitor to your country. I'll see that you never have success in this industry. I will not speak to you again. You are finished here. If that's the way Mormons are, I'm going to get rid of all of them that work for me."

I answered, "Admiral, I will carefully turn my assignment over to a replacement unless you prevent me."

I knew what was right for me to do and was not worried about the outcome. Yet I was very concerned that my decision could cause a loss of work for innocent people who were honorably supporting their families in the program. As I struggled with that thought, there came into my mind the song, "Do what is right, let the consequence follow." I could not see how this circumstance could lead to a positive consequence, but I felt a peace and calmness as I proceeded to do my best to instruct a replacement.

I can see now that the Lord guided me each step of the way in what to do and what to say. My replacement was a very capable, experienced individual who learned rapidly. I was impressed to identify those things that needed to be done and even was able to outline some suggestions for important future improvements in the program. On my last day at work I asked to see the admiral again. The experience was totally different. That conversation ended with a much deeper appreciation for each other and for my beliefs. No other Church member was adversely affected because of my decision. At times, you could think of what the words of the song "Do What Is Right" mean in your life. May the doctrinal message it contains be as helpful to you as it has been to me.

Unless you have already done so, make this fixed decision now: "I will live to have no regrets." I can testify of the incomparable peace that is continually present from being able to say, regarding those serious sins of immorality, "I have no regrets; I have not participated." Yes, through the process of repentance even egregious sins can be forgiven. Yet, for those who have committed serious sin, in quiet moments of deep pondering there must remain a disturbing memory of times when those boundaries have been crossed, even when full forgiveness has been given by the Savior. How much more serenely pleasant it is to live never having done those things. I testify that such a life brings immense joy, peace, and tranquility on earth and throughout eternity. Live to have no regrets.

Have you been writing down the impressions that come as you ponder the doctrines and principles referenced in these pages? If you are doing so, congratulations. If not, please begin to write them down and follow them. The guidance you will receive is personalized direction from the Lord. It is, therefore, vitally important.

CHAPTER 9

DIVINE CURRENTS

ONE OF THE GREAT purposes of mortality is to obtain an understanding of the Lord's specific plan for your own life. He has placed currents of divine influence in your life that will lead you along the individual plan He would have you fulfill here on earth. In the October 1974 Semiannual General Conference, President Spencer W. Kimball gave a message that has repeatedly blessed my life. He spoke of how icebergs are quietly moved through the ocean by immense currents that guide them. He taught that we are more like ships than icebergs, for we have our own motive power and a rudder to give us advantage. He said:

"The icebergs spawned by the Greenland ice sheet followed a highly predictable course. As the silent Labrador Current ceaselessly moves to the south through Baffin Bay and Davis Strait, it takes with it these mountainous icebergs, even against the force of the winds and the waves and the tides. Currents have much more power to control its course than the surface winds. . . .

"Youth . . . are subjected to so many swirling winds that we sometimes wonder if they can survive. The winds of fashion push those about who are insecure and who require the feeling that they are in step with the crowd. The winds of sexual temptation drive some to . . . dash bright prospects or to degrade themselves. Bad companions, addicting drugs, the arrogance of profanity, the slough of pornography—all these and more act as influences pushing us, if we are not being carried forward by a strong, steady current toward the righteous life."[1]

I have come to know that there are currents of divine influence in our life that will lead each of us along the individual plan the Lord would have us follow while on earth. They are identified through the whisperings of the Holy Spirit. Seek through that Spirit to identify that plan and carefully follow the direction the Lord will provide. It will come through answers to prayers and pondering or the counsel of others who are worthy. Align yourself with it. Choose, willingly, to exercise your agency to follow it. Do not be overcome by concentrating solely on today, its challenges, difficulties, and opportunities. Those things are the relatively insignificant surface winds and waves of today. Such preoccupations must not totally capture your interest and attention so as to consume your life.

Oh, how I would encourage you to weave deeply into the fabric of your soul the recognition that your life now is a part of a much bigger plan the Lord has for you. You lived part of it in premortality. You were valiant there and came here because you wanted to grow more and enjoy greater happiness. What you decide to do now will affect how well that divine plan He has for you is fulfilled. More than that, your decisions today can powerfully affect your children and grandchildren. If you are not married, think carefully about the preparation of the parents of your own children. Of course I mean you and the eternal companion you will be or have been sealed to in the temple.

The more closely you follow the current of divine guidance, the greater will be your happiness here and for eternity. Moreover, the more abundant will be your progress and capacity to serve. I do not understand entirely how it is done, but this divine current does not take away your moral agency. However, I do know that as you seek to know the will of the Lord in your life, you will more easily discern that divine current. The right of moral agency is so important to our Father in Heaven that He was willing to lose one-third of His spirit children so that it would be preserved. You can make the decisions you choose to make. But you cannot choose the consequences. They are determined by divine law. Should your choices be wrong, there is a path back through repentance. When the conditions of repentance are fully met, the Atonement of the Savior provides a release from the demands of justice for the errors made. He said, "I the Lord cannot look upon sin with the least degree of allowance; nevertheless, he that repents and does the commandments of the Lord shall be forgiven."[2] A disposition to constantly do right brings peace of mind and heart.

Our Savior, Jesus Christ, can guide you to the help you need to discover that plan and to make the correct choices in your life. He has promised:

> I will tell you in your mind and in your heart, by the Holy Ghost, which shall come upon you and which shall dwell in your heart.[3]

> And the Spirit shall be given unto you by the prayer of faith.[4]

> Pray always, and I will pour out my Spirit upon you, and great shall be your blessing.[5]

> I say unto thee, put your trust in that Spirit which leadeth to do good—yea, to do justly, to walk humbly, to judge righteously; and this is my Spirit.
> . . . I will impart unto you of my Spirit, which shall enlighten your mind, which shall fill your soul with joy. . . . By this shall you know, all things whatsoever you desire of me, which are pertaining unto things

of righteousness, in faith believing in me that you shall receive.[6]

That last scripture confirms the desire of the Savior that you have joy in life and defines how to obtain it.

With the guidance of the Holy Ghost comes the ability to develop a powerfully sensitive capacity to understand the personal plan God has prepared for you. Cultivate that gift. It will guide you to make the right choices. The Lord has said that guidance comes through consistent, righteous living. As you enhance your capacity to sense the direction of the infallible influence of the Holy Ghost, you will attain your goals and avoid disappointment, discouragement, and tragedy. That pattern authorizes the guidance of the Holy Ghost. The results are correct decisions that bring peace with happiness and joy.

It is wondrously simple and so incomparably beautiful. As you continue your resolve to live righteously, you can always know what to do. Sometimes the discovery of that path may require significant effort and trust on your part. Yet you will recognize what to do as you meet the conditions for such divine guidance in your life: obedience to the commandments of the Lord, trust in His plan, and the avoidance of anything that is contrary to it. The more closely you conform your life to the doctrine of the Lord, the more individual capacity you will have to do what the Spirit inspires you to do.[7] The divine current in your life will be made known a segment at a time and, when followed, will bring you greater peace and happiness.

I suggest that you consistently study the scriptures, beginning with the Book of Mormon. You will find it helpful to read often or memorize scriptures that touch your heart and fill your soul with understanding. When scriptures are used as the Lord has caused them to be recorded, they have intrinsic power that is not communicated when paraphrased in your own words. Sometimes when there is a significant need in my life, I mentally review scriptures I have memorized that have given me strength. There is great solace, direction, and power that flow from the scriptures, especially the words of the Lord. These three examples will illustrate:

> Therefore, let your hearts be comforted . . . ; all flesh is in mine hands; be still and know that I am God.[8]

> The works, and the designs, and the purposes of God cannot be frustrated, neither can they come to naught.

> For God doth not walk in crooked paths, neither doth he turn to the right hand nor to the left, neither doth he vary from that which he hath said, therefore his paths are straight, and his course is one eternal round.

> Remember, remember that it is not the work of God that is frustrated, but the work of men.[9]

David rejoiced:

> The Lord is my shepherd; I shall not want.
> He maketh me to lie down in green pastures: he leadeth me beside the still waters.
> He restoreth my soul: he leadeth me in the paths of righteousness for his name's sake.
> Yea, though I walk through the valley of the shadow of death, I will fear no evil: for thou art with me; thy rod and thy staff they comfort me.
> Thou preparest a table before me in the presence of mine enemies: thou anointest my head with oil; my cup runneth over.
> Surely goodness and mercy shall follow me all the

days of my life: and I will dwell in the house of the
Lord for ever.[10]

Sometimes you may feel to complain to the Lord about the challenges that have come into your life. Jacob taught: "Seek not to
counsel the Lord, but to take counsel from his hand. For behold, ye
yourselves know that he counseleth in wisdom, and in justice, and
in great mercy, over all his works."[11] God knows what is best for us.
Although we may not understand why we experience some things
now, in His timetable we will know and be grateful. We are counseled, "Cast thy burden upon the Lord, and he shall sustain thee."[12]
I have been greatly helped by laying a vexing matter at His feet
for a while. When I picked it up again, it was lighter and more
manageable.

All doctrine in scripture can benefit us, even though it may be
given to a specific individual, for God has repeatedly said, "What I
say unto one I say unto all."[13] This principle is confirmed by Nephi,
who recorded, "I did liken all scriptures unto us, that it might be for
our profit and learning."[14]

In that spirit the Savior has said:

> Ye are commanded in all things to ask of God, who
> giveth liberally; and that which the Spirit testifies unto
> you even so I would that ye should do in all holiness of
> heart, walking uprightly before me, considering the
> end of your salvation, doing all things with prayer and
> thanksgiving.[15]

> Look unto me in every thought; doubt not, fear
> not. Behold the wounds which pierced my side, and
> also the prints of the nails in my hands and feet; be
> faithful, keep my commandments, and ye shall inherit
> the kingdom of heaven.[16]

The Lord helped Joseph Smith to accomplish tasks that were completely beyond his personal capacity. At times, he did so through direct guidance and intervention. Yet often he was empowered through the quiet prompting of the Spirit and the accompanying support and strength that came because of his obedience, his faith in the Master, and his unwavering determination to do His will. Why was he so successful? A portion of that answer comes in his personal declaration, "I made this my rule: *When the Lord commands, do it.*"[17]

Trust that within your own personal sphere of activity and framework of responsibilities, the Lord will provide that same help. When needed and earned, you can enjoy divine inspiration to know what to do and, when necessary, power or capacity to accomplish it.[18] Joseph Smith learned how to perfect the ability to follow the guidance of the Lord by practiced, personal discipline. He did not let his own desires, convenience, or the persuasions of men interfere with that compliance as he grew and was schooled by the Lord in how to do the tasks given him. Strive to follow that example.

I encourage you to express gratitude for each blessing, for "in nothing doth man offend God, or against none is his wrath kindled, save those who confess not his hand in all things, and obey not his commandments."[19]

With every capacity, I counsel you to strengthen your testimony that there is, in very deed, a Heavenly Father who is in control. You must come to really know God, through the scriptures, prayer, and the testimonies of His chosen servants. Then He can guide you in the application of His teachings in every circumstance. I emphasize, He has a specific, personalized plan for your life. When needed, He will reveal parts of that plan to you as you seek His guidance with faith and consistent obedience. You may have found portions of it already realized in your life.

His Son has made you free—not from the consequences of your acts, but free to make choices. Your Father's eternal purpose is for you to be successful in this mortal experience. Be attentive to the personal guidance He gives you through the Holy Spirit. Continue to live worthy to receive it. Write it down so you can fulfill it. Then it will be available throughout your life. I am confident that as you pray for that help, some of it will come by gentle guidance of the Spirit as you read these pages. That instruction will be far more important to you than anything you will receive from me.

PART 3

TO QUALIFY FOR PEACE, HAPPINESS, AND JOY

CHAPTER 10

THE ATONEMENT CAN SECURE YOUR PEACE AND HAPPINESS

OUR FATHER IN HEAVEN wants us to enjoy peace and happiness in mortal life. Our Master, Jesus Christ, and His prophets have taught us how to have that peace and happiness, even in a world that is ever more challenging, with increasing conflict and an intense concentration of alluring temptations.

I will illustrate the wrong way to find peace and happiness, and then the proper way, by using an analogy to rock climbing. Some attempt to scale a difficult rock cliff by using a method called "soloing." They ascend alone, without equipment, companions, or any secure protection. They depend on their own skill, capacity, and experience. They do it for the emotional thrill of living on the edge with high risk. It is done despite the probability that in time they will fall and be seriously injured or lose their life. They are like many who face the challenges and temptations of life without the security of following the commandments of God, guided by the Holy Spirit. In today's difficult world they will almost assuredly violate critical laws, with painful, destructive consequences. Do not "solo" in life. You will almost certainly fall into transgression.

There is a safer way to rock climb. When a pair of climbers tackles a difficult ascent, the leader scales a wall, placing anchors a few feet apart. His or her rope is linked to the anchor by a carabiner. Safety is assured by a companion, called the second, who is stationed in a very solid position. The lead is protected as the second belays, that is, carefully controls how the rope is payed out. In this way the lead is assured protection while ascending. Should there be an inadvertent misstep, the anchor will limit the fall, thus avoiding a serious consequence. The second not only secures the lead but gives encouragement with comments and signals as they communicate back and forth. Their goal is to enjoy a safe, exhilarating experience through overcoming a significant challenge. They employ techniques and equipment that are tried and proven. The essential equipment includes a secure harness, a reliable rope, a variety of anchors to be fixed to the rock face, a chalk bag to improve grip, and proper boots or special shoes that each climber can use to grip the surface of the steep wall.

The companionship has studied the rules and techniques of rock climbing. They have received instruction from experienced climbers and have practiced to become comfortable with the proper moves and the use of equipment. They have planned a route and determined how they will work together. When the leader scales far enough and finds a convenient place that is very safe, he or she belays while taking up the rope as the second follows the "pitch" or length of rope that has been extended. When the leader is reached, the process is then repeated. One belays while the other climbs, inserting anchors every few feet as protection should there be an inadvertent fall. While technical rock climbing appears to be risky and dangerous, these precautions assure an exhilarating experience, safely accomplished by following correct principles.

In real life, the anchors are the laws of God, which provide protection under all of the challenges that one could face. The rope and carabiners that secure the rope to the anchors represent obedience to those commandments. When you learn the commandments of God, continue to practice them, and have a plan to avoid danger, you can overcome life's challenges and enjoy peace and happiness. You will have secure means of obtaining protection against Satan's temptations. You will develop strength of character that will fortify you against temptation. Should you make a wrong move, there need be no enduring consequence because of the belaying or help that is available to you through repentance.

Let the Savior be your "lead" in life. He has said, "I am . . . the Rock of Heaven, . . . whoso cometh in at the gate and climbeth up by me shall never fall."[1] The Redeemer will safely lead you through the most difficult challenges of life. His laws are absolutely secure anchors of protection that dispel fear and assure success in an otherwise dangerous world. Such a life will certainly provide you peace and happiness.

True, enduring happiness, with the accompanying strength, courage, and capacity to overcome the most challenging difficulties, will come as you center your life in Jesus Christ. Obedience to His teachings provides a secure ascent in the journey of life. That takes effort. While there is no guarantee of overnight results, there is the assurance that, in the Lord's time, solutions will come, peace will prevail, and happiness will be yours.

The challenges you face, the growth experiences you encounter, are intended to be temporary scenes played out on the stage of a life of continuing peace and happiness. Sadness, heartache, and disappointment are events in life. It is not intended that they be the substance of life. I do not minimize how hard some of these events can be. When the lesson you are to learn is very important, difficulties can extend over a long period of time, but they should not be allowed to become the confining focus of everything you do. Your life can and should be wondrously rewarding. It is your understanding and application of the laws of God that will give your life glorious purpose. That perspective keeps challenges confined to their proper place—stepping-stones to further growth and attainment.

Your happiness in life depends upon your trust in Heavenly Father and His Holy Son, as well as your conviction that the plan of happiness of our Father truly can bring you joy. Pondering Their doctrine will let you enjoy the beauties of this earth and enrich your relationships with others. It will lead you to the comforting, strengthening experiences that flow from prayer to Father in Heaven and the answers He gives in return.[2]

Peace and happiness are the precious fruits of a righteous life. They are possible only because of the Atonement of Jesus Christ. I will explain.

Each of us makes mistakes in life. They result in broken eternal laws. Justice is that part of Father in Heaven's plan of happiness that maintains order. It is like gravity to a rock climber, ever present. It is a friend if eternal laws are observed. It responds to your detriment if they are ignored. Justice guarantees that we will receive the blessings we earn for obeying the laws of God. Justice also requires that every broken law be satisfied. When we obey the laws of God, we are blessed, but we cannot earn additional credit that can be saved to satisfy the laws that we break. If not resolved, broken laws can cause life to be miserable and would keep us from returning to God. Only the life, teachings, and particularly the Atonement of Jesus Christ can release us from this otherwise impossible predicament.

The demands of justice for broken law can be satisfied through mercy. That mercy is attainable by your continual repentance and by obedience to the laws of Jesus Christ. Such repentance and obedience are absolutely essential for the Atonement to work its complete miracle in your life. The Redeemer can settle your individual account with justice and grant forgiveness through the merciful path of your repentance. Through the Atonement you can live in a world where absolute justice reigns in its sphere so the world will have order.

Through His mercy and your faith and obedience, He will lead you to a resolution of your problems.

The Atonement was a selfless act of infinite, eternal consequence, performed by a single glorified personage. It was arduously earned alone, by the Son of God.³ It has eternal impact in the life of every son and daughter of our Father in Heaven—without exception. Through it, the Savior broke the bonds of death. The Atonement justifies our finally being judged by the Redeemer. It can prevent an eternity under the control of Satan. It opens the gates to eternal life and exaltation for all who qualify for forgiveness through repentance and obedience.

Pondering the grandeur of the Atonement evokes in each of us the most profound feelings of awe, immense gratitude, and deep humility. Those impressions, in turn, can provide you powerful motivation to keep His commandments and consistently repent of errors, which will bring greater peace and happiness.

I believe that no matter how diligently we try, we cannot with our human minds fully comprehend the eternal significance of the Atonement of Jesus Christ, nor fully understand how it was accomplished. We can only appreciate in the smallest measure what it cost the Savior in pain, anguish, and suffering. We cannot understand how difficult it was for our Father in Heaven to see His Son experience the incomparable challenge of His Atonement. Even so, with the help of the Holy Ghost you should conscientiously study the Atonement to understand it as well as you can. You can learn what is needful to live His commandments, to enjoy peace and happiness in mortal life. You can qualify, with obedient family members, to live with Him and our Father in Heaven forever.

Lehi taught his son Jacob, "No flesh . . . can dwell in the presence of God, save it be through the *merits,* and *mercy,* and *grace* of the Holy Messiah."⁴

Jesus Christ possessed *merits* that no other being could possibly have. He was a God, Jehovah, before His birth in Bethlehem. His beloved Father not only gave Him His spirit body, but Jesus was His Only Begotten Son in the flesh. Our Master lived a perfect, sinless life and therefore was free from the demands of justice. He is perfect in every attribute including love, compassion, patience, obedience, forgiveness, and humility. His *mercy* pays our debt to justice when we repent and obey Him. Since even with our best efforts to obey His teachings we will still fall short, because of His *grace* we will be "saved, after all we can do."[5]

I testify that, with unimaginable suffering and agony and at an incalculable price, the Savior earned His right to be our Intermediary, our Redeemer, our Final Judge. I know that He lives and that He loves you. Consistently make Him your "lead" in life. The secure anchors of His laws will assure safety and success as you scale the challenges you will face. You will not fall into serious transgression. Yours will be a life of peace and happiness crowned with exaltation in the celestial kingdom.

CHAPTER 11

FORGIVE TO BE FORGIVEN

W HO IS THERE THAT understands to any degree our Father's plan of happiness that is not anxious to be forgiven of mistakes made in life? Those mistakes may be errors of judgment, unintended offense, or violations of the law of God, great or small. When we yield to the gentle promptings of the Holy Spirit that come in moments of serious contemplation, we can enter the portal of repentance that leads to refreshing renewal provided by God's forgiveness. Balance is then restored to our life. Yet it seems that the more serious the offense, the more difficult it is to avail oneself of the relief forgiveness affords through repentance. That is when Satan's pressure is most intense, most vigorous. His intent is to frustrate any effort to abandon a wrong path to return to the narrow but sure way that leads to peace and happiness.

The cleansing and purifying that flow from repentance are made possible through the Atonement of Jesus Christ. Yet no matter how intense and sincere our yearnings for personal forgiveness may be, the Savior has made it clear that an essential condition required to obtain that relief is to forgive others their offenses toward us. "For if ye forgive men their trespasses, your heavenly Father will also forgive you: but if ye forgive not men their trespasses, neither will your Father forgive your trespasses."[1] That is often a most difficult challenge, particularly when one is convinced he has not committed an offense against another.

For his evil purposes Satan will always greatly magnify the impact of a perceived slight or criticism. He tempts us to expand and distort an offense far beyond its true significance. In the early history of the Church, two small matters were expanded into tragic proportions, resulting in great heartache. Because his name was misspelled on a missionary call letter, Symonds Ryder apostatized from the Church. He later was one of the apostate leaders who headed a mob to tar and feather Joseph Smith.

The second example resulted in even more deplorable consequences. The occurrence as related by President Gordon B. Hinckley follows:

"According to the account by Elder [George A.] Smith, while the Saints were in Far West, Missouri, 'the wife of Thomas B. Marsh, who was then President of the Twelve Apostles, and Sister Harris concluded they would exchange milk, in order to make a little larger cheese than they otherwise could. To be sure to have justice done, it was agreed that they should not save the strippings, but that the milk and strippings should all go together.' Now for you who have never been around a cow, I should say that the strippings come at the end of the milking and are richer in cream.

"'Mrs. Harris, it appeared, was faithful to the agreement and carried to Mrs. Marsh the milk and strippings, but Mrs. Marsh, wishing to make some extra good cheese, saved a pint of strippings from each cow and sent Mrs. Harris the milk without the strippings.'

"A quarrel arose, and the matter was referred to the home teachers, . . . 'the bishop, . . . the High Council, . . . and . . . the First Presidency of the Church, and Joseph and his counselors had to sit upon the case, and they approved the decision of the high council.' . . . [All found Mrs. Marsh guilty.]

"'. . . Thomas B. Marsh then declared that he would sustain the character of his wife, even if he had to go to hell for it.

"'The then President of the Twelve Apostles, . . . who should have . . . [caused] reparation to be made . . . , went before a magistrate and swore that the "Mormons" were hostile towards the State of Missouri. That affidavit brought from the government of Missouri an exterminating order, which drove some 15,000 Saints from their homes and habitations, and some thousands perished through suffering the exposure consequent on this state of affairs.'"

President Hinckley counseled: "What a very small and trivial thing—a little cream over which two women quarreled. But it . . . was a factor in Governor Boggs's cruel exterminating order that drove the Saints from the state of Missouri, with all of the terrible suffering and consequent death that followed. The man who should have settled this little quarrel . . . pursued it, . . . [and] lost his standing in the Church. He lost his testimony of the gospel. For nineteen years he walked in poverty and darkness and bitterness, experiencing illness and loneliness. . . . Finally, . . . he recognized his foolishness . . . and [pleaded with Brigham Young] only that he might be ordained a deacon and become a doorkeeper in the house of the Lord."[2]

These incidents not only caused great suffering to the parties involved but were devastating to their posterity. Unwholesome pride severely complicates life. It impedes efforts to resolve differences. Yet the disastrous consequences of Lucifer's snares can be frustrated by the healing act of asking forgiveness, even when one is confident that he intended no offense.

Communication between humans can be very complex. The normal meaning of words can be profoundly altered by inflection, tone, and body language. Even past experiences between individuals can greatly modify the meaning, connotation, and implied intent of phrases used in ordinary conversation.

An example will clarify what is meant. Suppose that I want to communicate message "A" to another, and those factors just mentioned cause him to hear message "B." Then, no matter what my intent, he is assured that I have told him message "B." It is reality to him. Yet I may not even know that there has been a miscommunication that could cause offense. We must be aware that what is innocently said can, under the influence of Satan, become raw material for a quarrel, an acrimonious exchange, a destroyed friendship, or, in an extreme case, even the cause of death. No wonder the Prince of Peace admonishes every soul to show forbearance and quickly and frankly forgive:

> Wherefore, I say unto you, that ye ought to forgive one another; for he that forgiveth not his brother his trespasses standeth condemned before the Lord; for there remaineth in him the greater sin.
>
> I, the Lord, will forgive whom I will forgive, but of you it is required to forgive all men.[3]
>
> Yea, and as often as my people repent will I forgive them their trespasses against me.
>
> And ye shall also forgive one another your trespasses; for verily I say unto you, he that forgiveth not his neighbor's trespasses when he says that he repents, the same hath brought himself under condemnation.[4]

Not only is it important that we say we forgive others their offenses, but it is vital that we forget them. By forget I mean not continue to harbor ill feelings or allow the matter to smolder or fester. We all know some individuals who have superficially acknowledged a willingness to forgive, but in their heart they do not forget. For the Lord, there is no true forgiveness without forgetting.

Offense is a result of perception, which may or may not accurately reflect another's intentions. Hence, when you are accused of offending another even when you are certain that you have not done so, ask for forgiveness. Such an act is an expression of trust in the healing power of the Lord. It will begin a process through which the Holy Spirit can soften hearts and resolve issues while they are in their infancy. Also, being contrite and therefore willing to learn brings great blessings and avoids potentially serious misunderstandings, as this illustration confirms:

Once Joseph Smith publicly, sternly, and vigorously reprimanded Brigham Young for something that appears to have been unwarranted. All present awaited a response. Later President Lorenzo Snow commented, "This was a supreme moment. A rupture between the two greatest men on earth seemed imminent." Brigham stood and without complaint said: "Joseph, what do you want me to do?" Joseph in tears embraced Brigham and said in effect that his loyal friend had passed an onerous test.[5]

Unintended yet real offense can arise from not respecting deeply held traditions or cultural differences. Where possible, one must make every effort to understand and to accommodate them. Failure to do so can seriously complicate communication and can cause unintended severe offense. Consider, for example, the differences between individuals of Anglo-Saxon descent and those born in a Latin culture. The wonderful Latin people are warm and genuine, easily showing love and emotion. They make new friends easily. Where there is love and trust and a perceived need, they are most generous in sharing what they possess. I have seen Latin missionaries share with companions their meager clothing when there was a need. Such acts of kindness are done willingly and without thought of sacrifice. But if there is any perceived pressure to require one of Latin heritage to do something against his or her will, immediately a barrier can arise.

Moreover, an Anglo is often viewed as cold, unfeeling, stern, too regimented, and rigorous. When Anglo-Saxons talk among themselves or with a Latin, they stand at a substantial distance. That creates in one of Latin heritage feelings of aloofness and cold restraint that undermine sincere gestures of friendship. On the other hand, unless that trait is understood, when a Latin friend talks with an Anglo the former seems to stand uncomfortably close, appearing to invade too soon the other's private space.

To illustrate the powerful effects of culture, consider an actual experience between a North American senior companion and his Mexican junior companion. The North American passed by the desk of his companion during study time and observed that he was reading a book on the life of Joseph Smith. It was the hour when the missionary schedule called for that elder to be studying the proselyting lessons. With characteristic Anglo-Saxon brevity, the senior companion shook his finger over the Joseph Smith book and pointed repeatedly to the missionary lessons without saying a word. He then walked off to study himself, innocent of what he had just done.

Always ready to complicate communication, Satan began to prompt the junior companion: "He's offended you. You're not a dog on a leash that he can drag around. You are just as much a missionary as he is. Why does he think he can order you that way?" These thoughts began to ricochet around in the mind of that sweet companion. They grew with the passing hours. When he tried to work or study with his senior companion those thoughts began to tie his stomach in knots. Finally seeking relief, the junior companion asked for an appointment with the mission president. After carefully laying the foundation, the young elder said:

"President, I wonder if I can have an opportunity of serving in another area. I have been in the same place for a long time."

"Is anything wrong, Elder?"

"No. I just feel that a change would be helpful."

"Are you having challenges with your companion?"

"No. He's outstanding. He's wonderful. I just would like another opportunity to serve."

The skillful mission president could sense that something was wrong and patiently he began to untangle the problem. Armed with an understanding of the offense, the president called in the senior, North American companion and said:

"Elder, how are you getting along?"

"Great, President. My companion is going to be an outstanding missionary. He works hard and he is helping me with my Spanish. I really love him."

"Elder, if you love him, why did you offend him?"

"Offend him, President? I've never offended him."

The president then explained what happened. To which the elder responded, "But President, it was the time to study the discussions and he was reading a book. I just want him to be a great missionary, so I showed him what he ought to be doing."

"Well, Elder, whether you meant to or not, you really offended him and you need to ask his forgiveness."

"Me, ask his forgiveness? President, I haven't done anything wrong. If anybody needs to ask forgiveness, it's him. He's come to you and talked about our relationship without mentioning any feelings to me. He ought to be the one to ask forgiveness."

"No, Elder. He did not comment on this experience. I had to carefully extract it from him. He has not criticized you, but feels that it's very difficult to continue this companionship. Will you ask his forgiveness?"

"President, I haven't done anything wrong. I don't know how to do that."

"Pray about it. The Lord will help you."

Now there's a challenge. Will that senior companion simply say, "The president's told me I need to ask your forgiveness. I didn't do anything, but you seem to be upset." Or will he recognize there has been some cultural misunderstanding and, while his intent was to communicate help, will he understand what needs to be done? If, in humility, he recognizes there has been a serious mistake made, innocent or not, and accepts responsibility for it, that misunderstanding can be healed. Otherwise, it will not be.[6]

Here is another example of the effect of differing cultures. Two Latin men leave a meeting together. One says, "I'm going right by your house. Let me give you a ride home."

The other responds: "No. I'm going to take the bus. I wouldn't want to inconvenience you."

"No, really, I'm going right by your home. There is no inconvenience at all."

"I know you. You are so kind that you would go out of your way to help me. I don't want you to do that. I appreciate the offer, but I'll ride the bus."

That conversation continues until there is confirmation that, in fact, there is no additional effort to drop the friend off.

Two North Americans exit together. One says, "Look, I'll give you ride home. It's on my way."

"Are you sure?"

"Yes."

"Okay. Let's do it."

Brief, concise—but in the wrong setting this interchange could be considered rude, unfeeling, and even offensive.

These examples pertain to issues that may arise between two cultures. Realize they are only examples and that they can be applied to many types of interpersonal relationships.

Empathy is an important attribute to help us avoid misunderstandings and offenses, as well as to facilitate forgiveness.[7] Empathy helps compensate for our lack of full understanding of what others are going through in their personal lives, in suffering, in anxiety, in wrestling with problems that they may feel helpless to resolve. Often an individual needs a listening ear, someone who is willing to take the time to be attentive. We sometimes feel we may not be able to help others and don't know how to resolve the challenges they face, yet our kindness in listening may give them courage to continue. In so doing we can help them increase their faith in the healing power of the Savior, just because we were willing to listen attentively.

Sometimes forgiveness needs to be encouraged by a third party. In a classic example worth reading carefully, President Boyd K. Packer described how an unintended act by a harried, overworked doctor caused the death of a mother in labor. The husband was distraught, and his intense grief cankered his soul. He pondered a lawsuit as the agony of his loss festered and wracked him in torment. Through the intervention of a spiritually endowed stake president, he received counsel that he followed, not because he fully comprehended it but because he was obedient. Not until much later did he come to understand why reprisal would have been tragic.[8] Oh, that all who are given inspired counsel to forgive would have the same resolve to obey even where full understanding may be lacking.

There is much joy in the hearts of the forgiven and the forgiver when an onerous offense is reconciled. Consider a demonstration of the tremendous capacity of the Prophet Joseph Smith to love and forgive, as seen in his treatment of William Phelps. In the beginning Brother Phelps was a friend and confidant of Joseph Smith. Later, because of his inappropriate acts, he was properly disciplined and excommunicated from the Church. He turned against the Prophet and made accusations to a judge, which helped bring about the great, prolonged suffering the Prophet and others had to endure while incarcerated in the miserable Liberty Jail.

Later, when William Phelps was destitute and in poverty, he wrote a letter to the Prophet Joseph Smith, asking for forgiveness. He wrote in part: "I am as the prodigal son, though I never doubt or disbelieve the fulness of the Gospel. . . . I will repent and live, and ask my old brethren to forgive me, and though they chasten me to death, yet I will die with them, for their God is my God."[9]

Study this response from Joseph Smith and ponder how you could act in a similar way.

> Dear Brother Phelps:
>
> I must say that it is with no ordinary feelings I endeavor to write a few lines to you in answer to [your recent letter]; at the same time I am rejoiced at the privilege granted me.
>
> You may in some measure realize what my feelings, as well as Elder Rigdon's and Brother Hyrum's were, when we read your letter—truly our hearts were melted into tenderness and compassion when we ascertained your resolves. . . .
>
> It is true, that we have suffered much in consequence of your behavior—the cup of gall, already full enough for mortals to drink, was indeed filled to overflowing when you turned against us. One with whom we had oft taken sweet counsel together, and enjoyed many refreshing seasons from the Lord—"had it been an enemy, we could have borne it." . . .
>
> However, the cup has been drunk, the will of our Father has been done, and we are yet alive, for which we thank the Lord. And having been delivered from the hands of wicked men by the mercy of our God, we say it is your privilege to be delivered from the powers of the adversary, be brought into the liberty of God's dear children, and again take your stand among the Saints of the Most High, and by diligence, humility, and love unfeigned, commend yourself to our God, and your God, and to the Church of Jesus Christ.
>
> Believing your confession to be real, and your repentance genuine, I shall be happy once again to give

you the right hand of fellowship, and rejoice over the returning prodigal.

Your letter was read to the Saints last Sunday, and an expression of their feeling was taken, when it was unanimously *Resolved*, That W. W. Phelps should be received into fellowship.

"Come on, dear brother, since the war is past,

"For friends at first, are friends again at last."[10]

What a giant of a soul! No wonder Joseph Smith's influence is so enormous throughout the world today.

The following experience shows how the Spirit works with the righteous to accomplish full forgiveness, with attendant increased understanding. On one occasion, impetuous William Smith lost control in a public meeting and orally and physically abused his brother, the Prophet. Serious consequences resulted, including William's threat to renounce the apostleship. Letters were received by Joseph Smith, which Joseph recorded in his diary. Others attempted to intervene, and Joseph also made record of this, as busy as he was, because his family was vital to him. Finally, his father and mother came to enlist the help of Joseph with his brother. The Prophet recorded in his journal, "My father and mother called this evening to see me upon the subject of the difficulty that occurred at their house, on Wednesday evening, between me and my brother William. They were sorely afflicted in mind on account of that occurrence. I conversed with them and convinced them that I was not to blame in taking the course I did, but had acted in righteousness in all things on that occasion. I invited them to come and live with me. They consented to do so as soon as it was practicable."[11]

Then his beloved brother, Hyrum, came after having also received a letter of apology from William. The Prophet recorded, "[Hyrum] tarried most of the forenoon, and conversed freely with me upon the subject of the difficulty existing between me and

Brother William. He said that he was perfectly satisfied with the course I had taken in rebuking William in his wickedness, but he is wounded to the very soul, because of the conduct of William; and although he experiences the tender feelings of a brother towards him, yet he can but look upon his conduct as an abomination in the sight of God."[12]

The tender feelings of Joseph were revealed in an extensive letter that he wrote to William, who had also finally asked Joseph forgiveness but had implied that Joseph had been in error. With much love and respect, Joseph responded. William had asked, "Do not cast me off for what I have done, but strive to save me in the Church as a member."[13] Joseph, in careful counsel to a brother he loved, explained extensively why he had acted as he did and what the error of William's way was, that he might be corrected. One paragraph illustrates his tenderness, yet also shows how specific he was in correcting error:

"You desire to remain in the Church, but forsake your Apostleship. This is the stratagem of the evil one; when he has gained one advantage, he lays a plan for another. But by maintaining your Apostleship, in rising up and making one tremendous effort, you may overcome your passions and please God. And by forsaking your Apostleship, is not to be willing to make that sacrifice that God requires at your hands, and is to incur His displeasure; and without pleasing God, we do not think it will be any better for you. When a man falls one step, he must regain that step again, or fall another; he has still more to gain, or eventually all is lost.

"I desire, Brother William, that you will humble yourself. I freely forgive you."[14]

Later in his diary, he noted this poignant thought. "I have had many solemn feelings this day concerning my brother William, and have prayed in my heart fervently, that the Lord will not cast him off, but that he may return to the God of Jacob, and magnify his

Apostleship and calling. May this be his happy lot, for the Lord of glory's sake."[15] We see the tenderness and the strengthening effect that Joseph had on his own family. Joseph Smith freely forgave his brother William. Yet despite Joseph's sincere efforts, William denounced his apostleship and continued actions that eventually resulted in his excommunication.[16]

If you feel that you have been seriously wronged, or are an innocent victim, don't harbor feelings of anger or hatred at what appears to be unjust. Frankly and genuinely forgive.[17] It may require what feels like a tremendous effort to begin to forgive. But while often difficult, to begin to forgive is the sure path to peace and healing. If your offender requires discipline for a serious transgression against you, leave that to the Church and civil authorities. Don't burden your own life with thoughts of retribution. The mill of justice of the Lord grinds slowly, but it grinds exceedingly well. In His economy, no one will escape the consequences of the violation of His laws. In His time and in His way, a full payment will be required for every evil act others commit for which there has been no adequate repentance.

Remember you are required by the Lord to forgive so that when needed you can be forgiven. Should you discern the need to forgive another as you read this, do it now. Possibly you have felt an impression to help someone forgive another. Help relieve needless suffering by following that guidance now.

We now consider the blessings and benefits of repentance.

CHAPTER 12

THE BENEFIT OF REPENTANCE

WHILE TRAVELING ON AN unfamiliar road, I encountered a large, temporary sign declaring "Rough Road Ahead," and indeed it was. Had I not been warned, that experience would have been disastrous. Life is like that. It's full of rough spots. Some are tests to make us stronger. Others result from our own disobedience. Helpful warnings in our personal life can also save us from disaster.

A damaged road presents the same obstacles to every traveler until others repair it. The highway of life is different. Each of us encounters unique challenges meant for growth. Also, our own bad choices can put more potholes in the path. Yet we have the capacity to smooth out the way, to fill in the depressions, and to beautify our course. The process is called repentance; the destination is forgiveness.

What follows is counsel that may or may not apply to you or a loved one. For simplicity, it has been written as though you were the one that could benefit from the counsel given. Should it not apply, perhaps the principles discussed could help someone you know.

If you have ignored warnings and your life has been damaged or disabled by a rough road, help is available. Through that help you can renew and rebuild your impaired life. You can start over again and change your course from a downward, twisting, disappointing path to a superhighway to peace and happiness. I want to help you find that relief. To do that, it is necessary to give you some background information that will make the remedy more logical and the steps to healing more easily understood.

Every incorrect choice you make, every sin you commit is a violation of eternal law. That violation brings negative results you will generally soon recognize. There also can be other consequences of your acts of which you may not be immediately conscious. They are nonetheless real. They can have a tremendous effect on the quality of your life here and most certainly will powerfully affect it hereafter. A role of justice in our Father's plan of happiness is to require that a payment be made for every law that is violated. Yet unless the demands of justice for broken laws are satisfied, your mortal life will be impaired and eventually you will be ruled out of the presence of God, to suffer endless negative consequences.

Each of us has made and will make mistakes, large or small, which if unresolved will keep us eternally separated from our Holy Father and His Beloved Son. As a consequence, we would be void of enduring peace and happiness. The life, teachings, and most significantly the Atonement of Jesus Christ provide a means to resolve what for us alone would be an impossible challenge.

Through His grueling, indescribably onerous sacrifice of self, Jesus Christ earned the authority and power to save us from the effect of broken law. He has done this through His matchless love and perfect Atonement. This act is the central ingredient of our Holy Father's plan of happiness. That is why the Atonement of Jesus Christ is considered to be the single most significant event that ever has or ever will occur. This selfless act of infinite and eternal consequence, executed by the Savior alone,[1] was essential to the fulfillment of the plan of salvation of our Father in Heaven.[2] Through it Jesus Christ severed the bonds of death, thus assuring our resurrection. By His Atonement He earned the right to be our Final Judge.[3] Because of the Atonement, our obedience to the commandments of Jesus Christ makes it possible to avoid an eternity under the dominion of Lucifer.[4] That supernal act opened the gates to exaltation and eternal life for all who qualify for forgiveness through repentance and obedience.[5]

Through your continuing faith and obedience and the fruits of His Atonement, the Redeemer can satisfy the demands of justice for your violation of God's laws and grant forgiveness through the merciful path of repentance.[6] Full repentance is absolutely required for the Atonement to have its full effect in your life. Without it, no soul can gain the presence of God.[7] Through your study of the Atonement, you will confirm that God is not a jealous being who delights in persecuting those who transgress. He is an absolutely perfect, compassionate, understanding, patient, and forgiving Father. He is willing to entreat, counsel, strengthen, lift, and fortify. He so loves each of us that He was willing to have His perfect, sinless, absolutely obedient, totally righteous Son experience indescribable agony and pain and give Himself in sacrifice for all.[8] Because of the Atonement, you can live in a world where absolute justice reigns in its sphere so that there will be order. The demands of justice are satisfied through mercy, which is attainable through your faith in Jesus Christ and obedience to His teachings.

Do you yearn for peace of conscience and have not yet found it? Have you felt anguish, grief, and turmoil in those quiet moments when you look objectively at your life and recognize the tragic mistakes you have made? You may have endured pain of conscience for a long time, or possibly it results from more recent transgression. Know that only through full repentance, which qualifies you for the forgiveness available through the Atonement of Jesus Christ, can you find peace once more.

Which of us is not in need of the miracle of repentance? Whether your mistakes are small or profoundly serious, the principles of recovery are the same. God has made the length and severity of the treatments conditioned to fit the circumstances of the transgression. Your goal surely must be forgiveness. The only possible path to that goal is repentance, for it is written:

> There is no other way nor means whereby man can be saved, only through the atoning blood of Jesus Christ. . . . He [will] not come to redeem [His people] *in* their sins, but to redeem them *from* their sins. And he hath power given unto him from the Father to redeem them from their sins because of repentance.[9]

Obedience and faith in the Savior give you power to resist temptation. The more temptations you reject, the less need you will have for repentance.

Forgiveness is the sweet fruit of repentance, but you can never taste it until you make a firm decision to repent, with resolute determination to do it completely. The next chapter deals with that decisively important subject and includes a brief summary of the classic elements of repentance. Yes, the fruit of true repentance is forgiveness, which opens the door to receive all of the covenants and ordinances provided on this earth and to enjoy the resulting blessings. When a repentant soul is baptized, all his or her former sins are forgiven. When repentance is full and one has been cleansed, there comes a new vision of life and its glorious possibilities. How marvelous the promise of the Lord: "Behold, he who has repented of his sins, the same is forgiven, and I, the Lord, remember them no more."[10] The Lord is and ever will be faithful to His words.

Because of the Light of Christ, every soul born on Earth, with normal capacities, can discern right from wrong. While many do not follow those promptings, they are nonetheless there. That is why most sincere individuals with sound core values recognize the need to repent of serious errors in life. As noted in the previous chapter, in addition to the usually defined steps to repentance, another step can be taken that will accelerate the progress to obtain the miracle of forgiveness of the Lord Jesus Christ. It is a willingness to truly forgive others who have offended or injured you emotionally or physically, whether or not you feel any responsibility for the offense. While that may be most difficult to accomplish, this is a vital step to warrant the Lord's forgiveness of you. In the Lord's Prayer Jesus pleaded, "Forgive us our debts, as we forgive our debtors."[11] He also taught:

> For, if ye forgive men their trespasses your heavenly
> Father will also forgive you;
> But if ye forgive not men their trespasses neither
> will your Father forgive your trespasses.[12]

In proclaiming another aid to find forgiveness, the Lord indicated that He abhors sin but is compassionate with the transgressor when He said:

> For I the Lord cannot look upon sin with the least
> degree of allowance;
> Nevertheless, he that repents and does the commandments of the Lord shall be forgiven;
> And he that repents not, from him shall be taken
> even the light which he has received; for my Spirit shall
> not always strive with man, saith the Lord of Hosts.[13]

When he was an Apostle, Spencer W. Kimball explained:

"Repentance is a kind and merciful law. It is far-reaching and all-inclusive. Contrary to common thinking it is composed of many elements, each one indispensable to complete repentance. . . .

"There is no royal road to repentance, no privileged path to forgiveness. Every man must follow the same course whether he be rich or poor, educated or untrained, tall or short, prince or pauper, king or commoner."[14]

President Joseph F. Smith counseled:

"True repentance is not only sorrow for sins, and humble penitence and contrition before God, but it involves the necessity of turning away from them, a discontinuance of all evil practices and deeds, a thorough reformation of life, a vital change from evil to good, from vice to virtue, from darkness to light. Not only so, but to make restitution, so far as it is possible, for all the wrongs we have done, to pay our debts, and restore to God and man their rights—that which is due to them from us. This is true repentance, and the exercise of the will and all the powers of body and mind is demanded, to complete this glorious work of repentance."[15]

Valid repentance cannot be forced or hurried. Further, as Alma explained to his son Corianton, all are invited to come to the blessings of repentance.

> Therefore, O my son, whosoever *will* come *may* come and partake of the waters of life freely; and whosoever will not come the same is not compelled to come; but in the last day it shall be restored unto him according to his deeds.[16]

Adultery, fornication, committing homosexual acts, and other deviations approaching these in gravity are not acceptable alternate lifestyles. They are serious sins. Committing physical and sexual abuse are major sins. Such grave sins require deep repentance to be forgiven.

Sometimes the steps of repentance are initially difficult and painful, like the cleansing of a soiled garment. Yet they produce purity, peace of mind, self-respect, hope, and, finally, a new person with a renewed life and abundance of opportunity. This scripture will help you know what to do:

> They did fast and pray oft, and did wax stronger
> and stronger in their humility, and firmer and firmer
> in the faith of Christ, unto the filling their souls with

joy and consolation, . . . because of their yielding their hearts unto God.[17]

Should there be a need, for your peace now and for everlasting happiness, please repent. Open your heart to the Lord and ask Him to help you. You will earn the blessing of forgiveness and peace and the knowledge you have been purified and made whole. Find the courage to ask the Lord for strength to repent now.

To repent is a superb manifestation of trust in the Redeemer and in His limitless power to heal. The next chapter contains doctrine and suggestions that clarify how to repent.

CHAPTER 13

HOW TO REPENT

THE CHAPTERS OF THIS book repeatedly refer to the need for each of us to consistently repent and obey the laws of God to find continuing peace with happiness and joy. You likely do not require repentance for a serious transgression, only for the consequences of lesser broken laws. However, to simplify this chapter, I have written it as if you were in need of profound healing. While it may not fully apply to you, it will probably benefit someone you know and would like to help.

Forgiveness comes through repentance. What is repentance? How is it accomplished? What are its consequences? These may seem to be simple questions, but unfortunately many do not know how to repent.

Stated in concise terms, the path to full repentance and the gift of divine forgiveness consists of the following elements:

Recognition of sin
A fixed determination to repent
An honest, full confession
Abandonment of sin
Restitution to the degree possible
Obedience to all of the commandments
Faith in the Savior's power to heal

Each one of these elements is essential. They are interrelated and must be given sufficient attention and time to yield their full potential of complete repentance and forgiveness. Serious sins such as adultery, fornication, committing homosexual acts, sexual and aggravated physical abuse, addiction to pornography, and the like require the intervention of a judge in Israel such as a bishop or branch president or a stake or district president. You can resolve lesser infractions of the commandments directly with the Lord. If in doubt, ask your bishop or branch president what matters need not be treated with an authorized priesthood leader.

I will now provide a broader explanation of the seven elements of repentance mentioned above.

RECOGNITION OF SIN

Any sexual intimacy outside of the bonds of marriage, that is, any involvement with the private, sacred parts of the body of another, is forbidden by the Lord. Where it has occurred there must be repentance. While the world has other standards, you must keep morally clean. There are many reasons. Chief among them is that it is a commandment of the Lord, the violation of which He considers grievous sin. God regards the power of procreation to be most sacred. He has established protective laws for it, with serious consequences when those laws are violated. To ensure that you keep this sacred commandment, in quiet moments when you feel the influence of the Holy Ghost in your life set specific personal standards. Decide what you will and will not do when temptation comes, for it surely will. When you find yourself in the battlefield, do not deviate from your standards, no matter what the reason or how tempting a proffered exception may appear.

Also, it is wrong to intentionally awaken the physiological and emotional responses within your own body where there is no covenant of marriage. Such arousal should not be done. Those sacred capacities are reserved for appropriate use between a man and woman as husband and wife within the legal commitment of marriage. If it has occurred you must repent and abandon that transgression. Such practices are offensive to the Holy Spirit and can be manipulated by Satan to lead you to pornographic addictions, as well as the grave sins of fornication and adultery.

Satan would use rationalization to destroy you. That is, he would have you twist something you know to be wrong so that under specific circumstances it appears to be acceptable. In this way he attempts to progressively lead you to destruction. Love, as defined by the Lord, elevates, protects, ennobles, enriches, and shows respect for another. It motivates one to make sacrifices for another. Satan promotes counterfeit love. Its true definition is lust. It is driven by a hunger to appease personal appetite. Although it can be camouflaged by pleasing, flattering words, one who practices this deception cares little for the destruction caused another. The motivation for such a pattern is the desire for self-gratification through corrupt thoughts and acts.

You know how to live a clean, righteous life. You are trusted to do it. The Lord will bless you richly and strengthen you in your resolve to be clean and pure. As you live worthily, the precious fruits of obedience will everlastingly be yours. If you have made missteps along the way, recognize those transgressions. Begin now to repent of them so that the Savior can grant forgiveness with the peace and happiness He promises.

With the forgoing brief listing of standards of worthiness in your mind, I invite you with a tenderness and sincerity of heart to thoughtfully consider your life. Have you deviated from the standards that you know will bring happiness? Is there a dark corner that needs to be cleaned out? Are you now doing things that you know are wrong? Do you let your mind fill with unclean thoughts? When it is quiet and you can think clearly, does your conscience tell you to repent?

If you have identified some transgression, study and ponder to determine how serious the Lord defines it to be. Such effort will likely bring remorse and healing sorrow. It will also bring promptings from the Holy Ghost to create a sincere desire for change and a willingness to submit to every requirement for forgiveness. Alma taught, "Justice exerciseth all his demands, and also mercy claimeth all which is her own; and thus, none but the truly penitent are saved."[1]

Sometimes the steps of repentance are initially difficult and painful. Yet when followed to completion they produce peace of mind, purity, self-respect, hope, and finally a new person with a renewed life and an abundance of opportunity. President Howard W. Hunter stated: "To those who have transgressed or been offended, we say, come back. The path of repentance, though hard at times, lifts one ever upward and leads to a perfect forgiveness."[2]

If you have identified transgressions in your life, for your peace now and for everlasting happiness, obtain His forgiveness by repenting, now. Open your heart to your Father in Heaven. Ask Him to help you. You will earn the blessings of forgiveness and peace, and the knowledge that you have been purified and made whole. Find the courage to seek from the Savior strength to repent, now. He loves you personally and will help you. He declared:

> Whoso repenteth and cometh unto me as a little child, him will I receive, for of such is the kingdom of God. Behold, for such I have laid down my life, and have taken it up again; therefore repent, and come unto me ye ends of the earth, and be saved.[3]

His compassion is further revealed in these words:

> Will ye not now return unto me, and repent of

your sins, and be converted, that I may heal you? Yea, verily I say unto you, if ye will come unto me ye shall have eternal life. Behold, mine arm of mercy is extended towards you, and whosoever will come, him will I receive; and blessed are those who come unto me. Behold, I am Jesus Christ the Son of God.[4]

A Fixed Determination to Repent

After you have identified a need for repentance, your next step must be to make an unwavering decision to begin the process with a firm resolution to meet every requirement until forgiveness is granted. A fixed determination to repent, with a resolute commitment not to backslide, invites the support of God through the guidance of the Holy Ghost.

As an Apostle, Spencer W. Kimball taught: "To every forgiveness there is a condition. The plaster must be as wide as the sore. The fasting, the prayers, the humility must be equal to or greater than the sin."[5] "It is unthinkable that God absolves serious sins upon a few requests. He is likely to wait until there has been long-sustained repentance."[6]

The Savior wants to help you resolve past mistakes, but you must take the first steps. Talk to your Father in Heaven about the lesser mistakes. He will hear you and guide you to forgiveness with rejuvenating peace and happiness. Should the offenses be more grievous, decide now to talk to your bishop. Do it immediately. You will never regret your determination to repent. Putting off confession and repentance puts off the blessings that the Savior wants you to receive now.

This statement of President J. Reuben Clark Jr. is most reassuring: "I feel that [the Lord] will give that punishment which is the very least that our transgression will justify. . . . I believe that when it comes to making the rewards for our good conduct, he will give us the maximum that is possible to give." [7] These words of Moroni are also encouraging: "But as oft as they repented and sought forgiveness, with real intent, they were forgiven." [8]

If you have seriously transgressed, you will not find any lasting satisfaction or comfort in what you have done. Excusing transgression with a cover-up may appear to fix the problem, but it does not. The tempter is intent on making public your most embarrassing acts at the most harmful time. Lies weave a pattern that is ever more confining and becomes a trap that Satan will spring to your detriment.

Do not take comfort in the fact that your transgressions are not known by others. That is like an ostrich with his head buried in the sand. He sees only darkness and feels comfortably hidden. In reality he is ridiculously conspicuous. Likewise, our every act is seen by our Father in Heaven and His Beloved Son. They know everything about you and are patiently waiting for you to act so that They can bless you.

It is encouraging to know that repentance, with continuing obedience and faith in the Savior, will give you power to resist temptation. Helaman taught:

> It is upon the rock of our Redeemer, who is Christ, the Son of God, that ye must build your foundation; that when the devil shall send forth his mighty winds, . . . when all his hail and his mighty storm shall beat upon you, it shall have no power over you to drag you down to . . . endless wo, because of the rock upon which ye are built, which is a sure foundation, . . . whereon if men build they cannot fall. [9]

The fruit of true repentance is forgiveness, which opens the door to receive all of the covenants and ordinances provided on this earth and to enjoy the resulting blessings. When repentance is full and one has been cleansed, a new vision of life and its glorious possibilities unfolds. How marvelous the promise of the Lord: "Behold, he who has repented of his sins, the same is forgiven, and I, the Lord, remember them no more."[10] The Lord is and ever will be faithful to His words.

The suggestions in chapter 21 may help you fortify your fixed determination to repent.

AN HONEST, FULL CONFESSION

You always need to confess your sins to the Lord. If they are serious transgressions, of the nature of those described in the beginning of this chapter, they need to be confessed to a bishop (branch president) or stake (district) president. Please understand that confession is not full repentance. It is an essential step but is not of itself adequate. Partial confession by mentioning lesser mistakes will not help you resolve a more serious, undisclosed transgression. Essential to forgiveness is a willingness to fully disclose to the Lord and, where necessary, to His priesthood judge all that you have done. Remember, "He that covereth his sins shall not prosper: but whoso confesseth and forsaketh them shall have mercy."[11]

When he was an Apostle and I was a very young and inexperienced mission president, Elder Spencer W. Kimball taught me much about repentance and forgiveness. As we walked together on one occasion, he asked me to tell him why priesthood leaders ask intimate, personal questions of someone who has transgressed. He noted it was unpleasant for the leader to do so and painful for that individual. I explained that I had been taught to do so as part of the process of helping another repent. He used the example of a rotten apple being placed in a barrel of good ones, noting that soon they all would be ruined. He then inquired what would result if the barrel were emptied and filled with fresh apples. He wanted me to recognize that unless the barrel were carefully cleaned with a stiff brush and powerful soap, those apples would soon be rotten as well. With that powerful visual image, he taught that I must always be sure that I have asked sufficiently detailed questions so as to identify the extent of a transgression.

He shared another powerful insight by describing a doctor who, upon examining a patient, discovered that his appendix was about to rupture. The doctor knew that the patient was poor and that the surgery would be painful and would take significant time to heal. Out of compassion, he gave the patient two aspirin and told him to go home to rest. When asked what I thought of such a doctor, I responded that no doctor worthy of trust would ever do such a thing, for the appendix would rupture and the consequences would be serious. Then Elder Kimball taught a lesson that I have never forgotten: The priesthood bearer who holds the keys of judge in Israel has the obligation to deal with transgression. He must act no matter how sensitive, personal, or difficult the case may be. He can use tenderness and wisdom in his approach, but he must act in a timely manner to resolve the transgression.

Sometime later, while interviewing a young man for a district mission, I asked, "Do you obey the law of chastity?" He said, "Yes." I then had a feeling that either he did not understand the question or did not respond honestly. I again inquired, "Have you ever had sexual relations with another person?" He paused, bowed his head, and said, "Yes, I have." Further questions revealed that he had transgressed with the daughter of a Church leader I knew very well. Then the image of a barrel of rotten apples came into my mind. I thought, what could be worse than what he has just confessed? But following that impression I asked, "Is there anything more you need to tell me?" He shook his head, no. I spoke no more, simply waiting to let the power of the silence work on him. Beads of perspiration began to form, he held his head in his hands, and finally he said, "Yes, there is more. She got pregnant, and I forced her to have an abortion."

Follow-up determined that the abortion was crudely performed. She would likely never have had her own children had there not been corrective surgery. Both he and she were helped through the steps of repentance by an understanding, compassionate branch president. Their lives have subsequently been rich and rewarding.

Serious sin inhibits the direction of the Holy Ghost in one's life. The foregoing example illustrates how Jesus Christ can inspire a judge in Israel to help one caught in the shackles of sin be tenderly led through the steps of repentance for the blessing of forgiveness. If you need such help, seek it now.

How grateful I am for the insight and counsel of kind leaders throughout my life. How I appreciate the promptings of the Spirit that have repeatedly helped me as I have tried to connect some of Father in Heaven's children to Him. Through their repentance and the miracle of forgiveness, He then could untangle and restore peace to their lives.

ABANDONMENT OF SIN

Abandonment of sin is an unyielding, permanent resolve to not repeat the transgression. Keeping this commitment means that the bitter aftertaste of that sin need not be experienced again. It means sealing the door to former sins by resolving never to become entangled with them again. Joseph Smith declared: "Repentance is a thing that cannot be trifled with every day. Daily transgression and daily repentance is not . . . pleasing in the sight of God."[12]

Since God knows your thoughts and intent in addition to your every act, there is no wisdom in publicly appearing to obey but privately transgressing. Yes, He has promised: "Behold, he who has repented of his sins, the same is forgiven, and I, the Lord, remember them no more."[13] But He has also declared: "Unto that soul who sinneth [that is, repeats past sin] shall the former sins return, saith the Lord your God."[14]

If you have lied to ease your conscience and tried to persuade others that you have changed when you have not, realize that your failure to keep commitments causes your words to have no convincing power. Others will not trust you. Consider this Spanish saying: *"Palabras y plumas, el viento las lleva."* The translation: "Words and feathers, the wind carries them away." However, through consistent proper choices, your actions will demonstrate when you have changed for the good. They will help establish a pattern of being truthful that is essential to your peace and happiness. Such a life will garner the respect and support of those who love you.

God has said, "I, the Lord, am bound when ye do what I say; but when ye do not what I say, ye have no promise."[15]

RESTITUTION TO THE DEGREE POSSIBLE

To obtain the forgiveness you seek, you must restore as far as possible all that which you have stolen, damaged, or defiled by transgression. Some things cannot be restored to their original state. These include the loss of another's virtue through the despicable sin of immorality, the damaging of a reputation from slanderous comments, and the disorientation of children through the breakup of a family. But willing restitution of all offenses to the extent possible provides the Lord concrete evidence that you are committed to do all you can to repent. The importance of restitution is evidenced in the Old Testament, where the requirement was not only full restitution for that taken but the addition of an extra fifth as good measure.[16]

Your life will be more rewarding if you remember the need for restitution in even the smaller mistakes of life.

OBEDIENCE TO ALL OF THE COMMANDMENTS

The Lord said, "For I the Lord cannot look upon sin with the least degree of allowance; nevertheless, he that repents and *does the commandments of the Lord* shall be forgiven."[17] Full obedience brings the complete power of the gospel into your life, with strength to focus on the abandonment of specific sins. It includes things you might not initially consider part of repentance, such as attending meetings, paying tithing, giving service, and forgiving others. Full participation to the extent possible will accelerate your recovery and will almost always provide others to help you find your way fully back.

Faith in the Savior's Power to Heal

If your soul is lightly blemished or seriously disfigured from transgression, know that through proper repentance the Savior will restore it. Recognize that He desires to heal you. But He will not force upon you that recovery. You must take the first steps by showing a willingness to repent.

Amulek testified of a principle fundamental to your forgiveness:

> And thus [the Son of God] shall bring salvation to all those who shall believe on his name . . . to bring about the bowels of mercy, which overpowereth justice, and bringeth about means unto men that they may have *faith unto repentance.* And thus mercy can satisfy the demands of justice, and encircles them in the arms of safety, while he that exercises no faith unto repentance is exposed to the whole law of the demands of justice; therefore only unto him that has *faith unto repentance* is brought about the great and eternal plan of redemption.[18]

With faith unto repentance you can determinedly progress through the steps of repentance for full forgiveness. In so doing it is important to understand that forgiveness comes because of the Redeemer and His Atonement. It is essential to know that only on

His terms can you be forgiven. Witness Alma's declaration: "I was . . . in the most bitter pain and anguish of soul; and never, until I did cry out unto the Lord Jesus Christ for mercy, did I receive a remission of my sins. But . . . I did cry unto him and I did find peace to my soul."[19] You will be helped as you exercise faith in the power of Jesus Christ to heal you. That means you trust Him and you trust His teachings. Satan would have you believe that serious transgression cannot be entirely overcome. That of course is a treacherous lie. As a key element of His glorious Atonement, the Savior gave His life so that the effects of all transgression can be put behind us, except the sins of shedding of innocent blood and the denial of the Holy Ghost.

Consider this comforting teaching of President Harold B. Lee: "If the time comes when you have done all that you can to repent of your sins, whoever you are, wherever you are, and have made amends and restitution to the best of your ability; if it be something that will affect your standing in the Church and you have gone to the proper authorities, then you will want that confirming answer as to whether or not the Lord has accepted of you. In your soul-searching, if you seek for and you find that peace of conscience, by that token you may know that the Lord has accepted of your repentance. Satan would have you think otherwise and sometimes persuade you that now having made one mistake, you might go on and on with no turning back. That is one of the great falsehoods. The miracle of forgiveness is available to all of those who turn from their evil doings and return no more, because the Lord has said in a revelation to us in our day: ' . . . go your ways and sin no more; but unto that soul who sinneth [meaning again] shall the former sins return, saith the Lord your God.' (D&C 82:7.) Have that in mind, all of you who may be troubled with a burden of sin."[20]

Our Father in Heaven knew that you and I would make mistakes during our mortal probation on earth. When I contemplate how miserable each of us would be if there were no way to rectify the consequences of our poor choices, my heart overflows with gratitude for the consummate blessing of being able to repent and be forgiven. If there is a need to avail yourself of the boundless mercy and kindness of our Holy Father and His Righteous Son through repentance, please do it now.

PART 4

PEACE, HAPPINESS, AND JOY EVEN WITH THE INEVITABLE TRIALS OF LIFE

CHAPTER 14

TO FIND MORE PEACE
AND JOY IN LIFE

YOU CAN INCREASE YOUR peace and joy each day, regardless of
your personal circumstances. As mentioned in a previous chapter, your life can become one of consistent peace. You can also experience golden moments of pure joy.

The scriptures declare that "men are, that they might have joy."[1]
Why, then, is there so much despair and anguish, so many afflicted
with depression, fear, and suffering? Why are so many lives in turmoil, bereft of peace? Since neither God nor His prophets deceive or
mislead, there must be a way to have peace and joy no matter how
distressing the world becomes. Know that these blessings are available to you as you understand and live the truths upon which a
loving Heavenly Father has founded true peace and enduring happiness. We will review together some of the doctrines that form that
foundation. But first a suggestion about how your days can be filled
with more joy.

One memorable cloudy morning, I stood on the north shore of
a beautiful Pacific island gazing out to sea at daybreak. I was fascinated by the regularity with which the gigantic waves consistently
moved forward to break on the shoreline. It reminded me of the con-
stancy of the plan of happiness of the Lord, with its fixed, eternal

laws that provide the security of enduring justice with the tenderness of mercy. I noticed that each wave would crest at a different point on the horizon to find its unique path to shore. Some cascaded over rocks, leaving rivulets of foaming, white water. Others burst on the shore in delightful, individual patterns. They slid up the moistened sand with playful, frothy edges, then bubbled and swirled in excitement as they receded.

I thought of the unending variety of possibilities the Lord has provided for us. We have so much freedom, so many opportunities to develop our unique personalities and talents, our private memories, our individual contributions. Since commitments precluded further opportunity to observe the majestic sea, I tried to imagine the glorious panorama the brilliant sun would later create. As I watched this magnificent scene in reverence, a window formed in the clouds, and the glistening rays of the rising sun broke through the overcast sky, transforming everything with its luminescence, its color, its life. It was as if the Lord wanted to share an additional blessing, a symbol of the light of His teachings, which light gives brilliance and hope to everyone it touches. Tears of gratitude filled my eyes as I contemplated this wondrous world in which we live and the extraordinary beauty our Heavenly Father so freely shares with all who are willing to see. Truly, life is magnificently beautiful when we look for that beauty.

There is so much joy to be found when with faith in God you look for it. Do you take time to discover each day how rich your life can be? How long has it been since you watched the sun set? The departing rays kiss the clouds, trees, hills, and lowlands good night, sometimes tranquilly, sometimes with exuberant bursts of color and form. What of the wonder of a cloudless night when the Lord unveils the marvels of His heavens—the twinkling stars, the moonlight rays—to ignite our imagination with His greatness and glory? How captivating to watch a seed planted in fertile soil germinate, gather strength, and send forth a tiny, seemingly insignificant sprout. Patiently it begins to grow and develop its own character, following the genetic code the Lord has provided to guide its development. With care it surely will become what it is destined to be: a lily, crowned with grace and beauty; a fragrant spearmint plant; a peach; an avocado; or a beautiful blossom with unique delicacy, hue, and fragrance. When did you last observe a tiny rosebud form? Each day it develops new and impressive character, more promise of beauty, until it becomes a magnificent rose.

Enrich your life with the beauty around you. There is such an abundance of it: the resplendent breaking dawn welcoming a fresh new day, the abundant arms of a blue spruce adorned with golden medallions from adjacent aspen, shimmering ripples in a mountain lake transformed by the brilliant sun, a hushed stillness of a forest glen bathed in moonlight, the exuberance of a child at play, and the love in her mother's eyes. "Rejoice evermore, and in everything give thanks."[2] "And he who receiveth all things with thankfulness shall be made glorious; and the things of this earth shall be added unto him, even an hundred fold, yea, more."[3]

You are of the noblest of God's creations. His intent is that your life be gloriously purposeful and deeply satisfying, regardless of your circumstances. As you are grateful and obedient, you can become all that God intends you to be and can find abundant peace with happiness.

If your life is becoming a bit stale, routine, and uneventful, this suggestion could give it new spark and verve. Attempt to be creative, not in competition with those who are particularly talented, but just for the joy and happiness that it brings. In the later life of Sister Camilla Kimball, when her prophet husband had been called home and she had some lonely hours, she was encouraged to learn to paint with oils. A teacher visited her home to show her how to paint. It was something she had never done before in her life. That effort opened a new series of rewarding experiences in her life. She did not look at a sunset or a cloud or a person's face or a flower or a tree the same way again. She began to see the nuances of color, form, and texture. Not only did she leave a legacy for her children and grandchildren in the works she produced, but she found something extremely interesting that gave her lasting joy.

One way to enjoy your life more fully is to try to express it creatively. Select music or dance or dressmaking or flower arranging or any of a multitude of things that a little imagination can identify. Consider the beauties of music. There is such a rich variety of it that is good. I know individuals who lament not having learned how to play the piano in their youth. It takes longer as an adult, but it can be done. I get a great deal of joy out of a limited ability to improvise on the piano. The left hand provides the chord structure and the right the melody, often from legal "fake" books. (Such books show the traditional melody line with symbols for the corresponding chords.) When no one is near, I can add to a recording of my piano my own clarinet or saxophone lead for well-known standards from the jazz era. The result is not great, but the effort brings satisfaction. Find out for yourself that you don't have to be an expert to enjoy the fruits of your own creativity.

When you attempt to be creative, you not only will have the fascinating benefits that come from your own efforts, but you will also have a capacity to appreciate more the wonderful gifts of those who are truly outstanding in the field you have selected. In my own life, just picking up a watercolor brush and painting for a while is one of the easiest ways to sweep out the cobwebs and let refreshment in. Winston Churchill wrote a small pamphlet about how, during the grueling years of World War II, he found relaxation and renewal in the concentration that came as he would paint with oils.[4]

Attempt to be creative, even if the results are modest. It will help you to find more pleasure and joy in life. Creativity can engender a spirit of gratitude for life and for what the Lord has woven into your being. Think of your extraordinary capacities to reason, to create, to remember, to love, to act, and to rejoice in life. Creativity gives a renewal, a spark of enthusiasm, a zest for life that we all need. If you choose wisely, it doesn't have to absorb a lot of time. Life will become more than just a monotonous routine from one day to another.

A superficial reading of scriptures might lead you to believe that life is intended to be onerous, always challenging, and void of pleasure. That is not the case. As you ponder the deep meaning of the words of the Lord and His prophets, you will find that they are motivated by His perfect love and desire that you in time receive all that He has, with the attendant supernal peace and joy.[5] The Lord inspired Lehi to declare the fundamental truth, previously mentioned, that "men are, that they might have joy."[6] That is a conditional statement: "they *might* have joy." But it is the intent of the Lord that each of us find joy. It will not be conditional for you as you obey the commandments, have faith in the Master, and do the things that are necessary to have joy here on earth.

Some blessings will be delivered here in this life; others will come beyond the veil. The Lord is intent on your personal growth and development. That progress is accelerated when you willingly allow Him to lead you through every growth experience you encounter, whether initially it be to your individual liking or not. Trust in the Lord. Be willing to let your heart and your mind be centered in His will. Ask to be led by the Spirit to do His will. You will then qualify for the greatest happiness along the way and the most fulfilling attainment from this mortal experience. An individual who questions everything he is asked to do, or digs in his heels at every unpleasant challenge, makes it much harder for the Lord to grant blessings. When Lehi asked his son Nephi to accomplish a most challenging task he responded:

> I will go and do the things which the Lord hath
> commanded, for I know that the Lord giveth no

commandments unto the children of men, save he shall prepare a way for them that they may accomplish the thing which he commandeth them.[7]

When severe difficulties arose in his efforts to accomplish his goal, Nephi was valiant:

> As the Lord liveth, and as we live, we will not go down unto our father in the wilderness until we have accomplished the thing which the Lord hath commanded us. . . . I was led by the Spirit, not knowing beforehand the things which I should do. Nevertheless I went forth.[8]

He followed doctrinal truths steadfastly, knowing that his faith and sincere effort would qualify him to receive divine help when needed. He willingly accepted partial answers when they came. He was confident that when he acted on the piece of direction given, more guidance would come as needed. That would be a fruitful practice to follow in your life.

Your moral agency, the right to make choices, is not given so that you can get all you may want. This divine gift is provided so that you will choose what your Father in Heaven wants for you. That path leads to glorious happiness and joy. It will permit Him to lead you to become all that He intends you to be.

Your perspective is vital to your happiness. Some, blind to the bountiful opportunities around them, live lives of sadness and despair with brief moments of joy. Be alive to the abundant potential that surrounds you so that you live a life of peace and happiness with periods of challenging growth. Learn from inspiring individuals who have come to peace with their challenges and therefore live to find joy amid adversity.

My precious wife, Jeanene, although afflicted with an aggressive terminal disease, consistently found joy in life. She understood the plan of happiness, had received the temple ordinances, and was doing her best to qualify for the promised blessings. Her personal journal records: "It is a beautiful fall day. I picked up the mail and sat down on the swing. I was so happy and content in the warm sun, the sweet smell of nature and the trees around me. I just sat and gloried in the fact that I am still alive on this beautiful earth. . . . The Lord is so good to me. How I thank Him that I am still here and feeling so good. I am soooooo happy I just want to shout and dance through this beautiful house as the sun streams into the big windows. I love being alive."

I love my dearest wife, Jeanene. She was always joyously happy, and much of it came from service to others. Even while very ill, in her morning prayer she would ask her Father in Heaven to lead her to someone she could help. That sincere supplication was answered time and again. The burdens of many were eased, and their lives brightened. She was blessed continually for being an instrument directed by the Lord.

A valiant friend of hers, courageously fighting a debilitating illness of her own, spent untold hours laboriously completing a large, challenging needlepoint work of art depicting a soaring eagle. It was a gift to Jeanene to encourage her as she experienced trials. That gift is a priceless treasure, a constant reminder of the precious fruits of resolute effort in the face of adversity. It is an enduring message of hope bound in the bonds of pure love and willing sacrifice.

Children can teach you how to find joy even under the most challenging circumstances. Children haven't yet learned to be depressed by concentrating on the things they don't have. They find joy in what is available to them. I remember a small boy playing along a riverbank in a remote area of Brazil. He had tied a piece of fishing line to the ends of two discarded soft-drink cans. He threw one can over a limb, then filled it with water. He would pull on the other can, then let it go. The weight of the first can would draw the second one up as it fell. He laughed and danced with glee. He found happiness in simple pleasures.

Simple, rejuvenating experiences surround us. They can be safety valves to keep the tension down and the spirit up. Don't concentrate on what you don't have or have lost. The Lord promised to share all that He possesses with the obedient.[9] You may temporarily lack here, but in the next life, if you prove yourself worthy by living valiantly, your blessing will be a fulness.[10]

Find the compensatory blessings in your life when, in the wisdom of the Lord, He deprives you of something you very much want. To the sightless or hearing impaired, He sharpens the other senses. To the ill, He gives patience, understanding, and increased appreciation for others' kindness. With the loss of a dear one, He deepens the bonds of love, enriches memories, and kindles hope in a future reunion. You will discover compensatory blessings when you willingly accept the will of the Lord and exercise faith in Him and His plan of happiness.[11]

To the afflicted people of Alma, the Lord said:

> I will also ease the burdens . . . that even you cannot feel them upon your backs . . . ; and this will I do that ye may stand as witnesses for me hereafter, and that ye may know of a surety that I, the Lord God, do visit my people in their afflictions.
>
> And . . . the burdens . . . were made light; yea, the Lord did strengthen them that they could bear up their burdens with ease, and they did submit cheerfully and with patience to all the will of the Lord.[12]

Willing service to others is a significant key to enduring happiness. President Spencer W. Kimball said: "God does notice us, and he watches over us. But it is usually through another mortal that he meets our needs. Therefore, it is vital that we serve each other."[13]

Reach out to others in need to find the pleasure and enjoyment that come as you act as an instrument motivated by the Lord to bless someone less fortunate or with temporary wants, someone who needs a lift. Do not confine your life to a small circle of Church friends. Build enduring friendships with others. At times there is legitimate criticism that some members of the Church are clannish in that they associate principally with those that they know within the confines of their Church experience. One of the best ways to share the gospel is to lay the foundation stones of understanding by just sharing our personalities, our gifts, our enthusiasm, and our capacity with others who are less gifted in these attributes. Over time, that can build a foundation from which to impart the truths of the gospel that are the source of our happiness.

Another way to enjoy the beauties of this life is to learn how to grow from challenge and affliction so as to consciously not let the disturbing element of a particular challenge completely absorb your life. Some years ago, as I was reading the Doctrine and Covenants, I was impressed to write a note in the margin of my scriptures next to this verse: "Be patient in afflictions, for thou shalt have many; but endure them, for, lo, I am with thee, even unto the end of thy days."[14] The note reads: "This scripture will have increasing importance in your life in the future. You will come to understand how absolutely true it is." I now realize that it is not the affliction part of that scripture that is important. It is the promise, "I am with thee, even unto the end of thy days." His love for you will bring peace and happiness. Challenge, when faced within the framework of the gospel of Jesus Christ and in recognition of the beauties around us, is a path upward to help us grow and earn peace with happiness.

There is a very famous song in Brazil that laments how the poor people earn money for a full year to revel during the few days of the carnival season. The song declares, *"Tristeza não tem fim, felicidade sim."* ("Sadness has no end. Happiness does.") That is a false teaching. I can understand how those without the light of the gospel can be led to believe that error. Truly the reverse is true. Our destiny in life is to have joy.[15] It is to grow to be more like the Savior. As we recognize that, no matter how difficult something is that we or a loved one faces in life, it need not take over our life to be the center of all interest. Don't be as some carnival participants who labor all year for one single event.

This concept is so important to peace and happiness that I will restate it as a principle: *The challenges we face, the growth experiences we encounter, should be like temporary scenes played out on the stage of continuing peace and happiness.* Some people are so absorbed in a matter that they find it difficult to think of much else. They often do not adequately care for themselves and find it difficult to properly care for children or others who depend upon them. It is appropriate to try to resolve the challenges of life, but when one has done what can reasonably be done, the matter should be placed in the hands of the Savior for a while, as he has admonished us to do. Later, when the burden is worked with again, it will appear lighter. The Redeemer illuminates life in ways that confirm that happiness is attainable. Through this approach such individuals are able to find hope, then faith, and finally the abililty to overcome the things that have brought them to such a deplorable state. Much like the mending of the body, the healing of some spiritual and emotional challenges takes time and patience.

Consider two modern parables to help you enjoy the beauties of this life. One is the parable of the stone and the cork. Some people are like stones thrown into a sea of problems. The minute they encounter a challenge, they disappear from sight. Others are like a cork. When they are submerged in a problem, they fight to be liberated. At the first opportunity, they free themselves of the challenge. They bob up smiling to serve again with happiness.

Consider this parable of a well. Once there was a deep well of water. Above it hung a pulley, with a rope over the pulley. At the extreme ends of the rope were two buckets. Water was drawn from the well by pulling the rope down. A full bucket would rise while an empty bucket would go down to be replenished. Those who used the well didn't realize that as the buckets passed they would talk to each other. One bucket was an inveterate pessimist. He was convinced that everything went wrong in his life. Whenever he passed his friend, he would recount what he considered to be deplorable circumstances in his life. His comments would include complaints such as: "I hate being in a cold, dark, wet hole all my life. I work very hard, but no matter how many times I give water to others, they never thank me for it. It's discouraging. The worst part is that I am not succeeding. No matter how many times I come up full I *always* go down empty."

The other bucket was a classic optimist. Every time he would pass, he would try to lift his neighbor with his enthusiasm: "I wish I could share the beauty of my life with you. I am so happy. When I feel myself rising I wonder, 'Will there be sunlight, or will there be glistening stars? Will it be that young boy who takes water for the garden of his mother, or the little girl who helps the mother make bread?' I love to come up because I can always help someone else. They don't know that I can talk, so they thank me with their eyes. My life is so worthwhile. The best part is, no matter how many times I go down empty, I *always* come up full."

Are you a pessimist and feel, "Oh, it isn't going to work. No one will let me do it. I can never do what I want to do." Or will you be an optimist? Optimism can be an expression of faith in Jesus Christ and His promises. Will you realize that you have something incredibly powerful in your life? You have the teachings of Jesus Christ. You have the truth. Continue to read the scriptures and learn more about the Savior, and study how the prophets teach you to communicate with God. Master how to gain a stronger testimony of God. Trust

Him. In these ways you can wipe away any dark cloud of pessimism. You will see that Father in Heaven loves you as His child—His daughter or His son. You can gain confidence that not only will He bless you and your family, but everyone, everywhere to the extent they obey Him. Quietly, but with assurance, you can bring blessings into your own life and the lives of others. You can help build the kingdom of God on earth, with the resultant joy that brings.

When you can see life as a continuum of wonderful experiences, then when a difficult challenge comes it will not color your whole life. It will be confined to its purpose. You can work it through. It is true that some challenges take a long time to resolve, but they need not consume everything you do or think about. They are part of the growth experiences the Lord expects you to overcome here on earth.

Every difficulty we face in life, even those that come from our own negligence or even transgression, can be turned by the Lord into growth experiences, a virtual ladder upward.[16] I certainly do not recommend transgression as a path to growth. It is painful, difficult, and so totally unnecessary, for "wickedness never was happiness."[17] It is far wiser and so much easier to move forward in righteousness. But through proper repentance, faith in the Lord Jesus Christ, and obedience to His commandments, even the disappointment that comes from transgression can be converted into a return to happiness:

> Blessed is every one that feareth the Lord; that walketh in his ways. For thou shalt eat the labour of thine hands: happy shalt thou be and it shall be well with thee.[18]

In summary, no matter how difficult something may be that you or a loved one faces, it should not take over your life and be the all-consuming center of all your interest. Challenges are growth experiences, temporary scenes to be played out on the stage of a pleasant life. Don't become so absorbed in a single event that you can't think of anything else or care for yourself or for those who depend upon you.

Your faith in Jesus Christ gives life enduring meaning. Remember you are on a journey to exaltation. Even when obedient and full of faith, sometimes you will have experiences that yield more happiness than others, but it all has purpose with the Lord.[19]

Thank your Father in Heaven and His Beloved Son for the plan of happiness and the gospel principles upon which it is based. Be grateful for the ordinances and the covenants they have provided. I solemnly testify they have power to crown your life with peace and joy, to give it purpose and meaning. You will confirm that sadness and disappointment are temporary.[20] However, happiness can be everlastingly eternal because of the Atonement of Jesus Christ. He lives. He loves you. He will help you find the gifts of enduring peace, happiness, and joy.

Let's continue our search together, for there is more to learn about how to find that peace, happiness, and joy.

CHAPTER 15

TO LIVE WELL AMID INCREASING EVIL

I HOPE THAT THUS FAR the chapters in this book have helped you find some peace and happiness. Yet there still may be a stumbling block to enduring happiness. You may be excessively concerned about the increasing evil in the world. Let's consider that worsening environment objectively. President Hinckley put world conditions in crystal-clear perspective. Two of his comments illustrate that prophetic vision. First, regarding the challenge we face:

"The traditional family is under heavy attack. I do not know that things were worse in the times of Sodom and Gomorrah. . . . We see similar conditions today. They prevail all across the world. I think our Father must weep as He looks down upon His wayward sons and daughters."[1]

Now concerning our extraordinary opportunities:

"Who in the earlier days could have dreamed of this season of opportunity in which we live? . . . The Church is in wonderful condition. . . . It will grow and strengthen. . . . It is our opportunity and our challenge to continue in this great undertaking, the future of which we can scarcely imagine."[2]

You have a choice. You can wring your hands and be consumed with concern for the future, or you can choose to use the counsel the

Lord has given to live with peace and happiness in a world awash with evil. If you choose to concentrate on the dark side, that is what you will see. Much of the world is being engulfed in a rising river of degenerate filth, with the abandonment of virtue, righteousness, personal integrity, traditional marriage, and family life. Sodom and Gomorrah was the epitome of unholy life in the Old Testament. That condition was fairly isolated then; now it has spread the world over. Satan skillfully manipulates the power of all types of media and communication. His success has greatly increased the extent and availability of degrading and destructive influences worldwide. In the past some effort was required to seek out such evil. Now it saturates significant portions of virtually every corner of the world. We cannot dry up the mounting river of evil influences, for they result from the exercise of moral agency divinely granted by our Father. But we can, with clarity, warn of the consequences of getting close to its enticing, destructive current and counsel to choose to avoid it.

Now look at the brighter side. Despite pockets of evil, the world overall is majestically beautiful, filled with many good and sincere people. God has provided a way to live in this world and not be contaminated by the degrading pressures spread throughout it. You can live a virtuous, productive, righteous life by following the plan of protection created by your Father in Heaven: His plan of happiness. It is contained in the scriptures and in the inspired declarations of His prophets. He clothed your intelligence with spirit and made it possible for you to enjoy the wonder of a physical body. When you use that body in the way He has decreed, you will grow in strength and capacity, will avoid transgression, and will be abundantly blessed.

When God, our Eternal Father, and His Beloved Son appeared to Joseph Smith in that sublime vision in the Sacred Grove, they began to place on earth again that plan of happiness and all required to sustain it. Part of that restoration included additional sacred scriptures to complement the treasured record of the Bible. These precious scriptures are contained in the Book of Mormon, the Doctrine and Covenants, and the Pearl of Great Price. Our Father knew of our day. He prepared the scriptures and provided continuing divine guidance to sustain us. That help will assure that you can live with peace and happiness amid increasing evil.

Consider these verses:

> All things must come to pass in their time. [God knew the challenges we would face, then gave this counsel.] Wherefore, be not weary in well-doing, for ye are laying the foundation of a great work. And out of small things proceedeth that which is great. Behold, the Lord requireth the heart and a willing mind; and the willing and obedient shall eat the good of the land of Zion in these last days.[3]

We should emulate Joshua: "Choose you this day whom ye will serve. . . . As for me and my house, we will serve the Lord."[4]

These are priceless promises. As you continue to center your mind and heart in Him, He will help you have a rich and full life no matter what happens in the world around you.

Paul wisely taught: "Be not overcome of evil, but overcome evil with good."[5]

Knowing of the calamities that would come to the world, Jesus taught:

> Fear not to do good . . . for whatsoever ye sow, that shall ye also reap; therefore, if ye sow good ye shall also reap good for your reward. Therefore, fear not, little flock; do good; let earth and hell combine against you, for if ye are built upon my rock, they cannot prevail.[6]

> He who is faithful shall overcome all things, and shall be lifted up at the last day.[7]

Finally this pattern of success:

> Come unto Christ, and be perfected in him, . . .
> deny yourselves of all ungodliness, and love God with
> all your might, mind and strength, . . . that by his grace
> ye may be perfect in Christ.[8]

An example will illustrate that the plan of happiness can lift and bless you wherever you live. On Christmas Eve 1967, in the light of a full moon, I climbed a small hill in the isolated village of Quiriza, Bolivia. Four young elders and I had spent the day crossing a mountain pass on a treacherous hand-hewn road. Then we struggled up a riverbed to see if the teachings of the Savior would help a destitute people. What we saw that day was discouraging—undernourished children, adults subsisting on meager crops, some with eyes glazed from seeking refuge with alcohol and drugs. I looked at the tiny, barren village below—a cluster of thatched-roof, adobe houses beaten by the harsh environment, with a people imprisoned by false teachings. The only evidence of life was barking dogs searching for food. There was no electricity, telephone, running water, roads, proper sanitation, or doctors there. It seemed so hopeless. Yet a solemn prayer confirmed that we should remain. We found a humble people who embraced the restored gospel with determination to live it. This they did under desperate conditions where severe poverty, alcohol, drugs, witchcraft, and immorality were in plentiful supply.

Under the guidance of exceptional missionaries, the people learned to work hard to cultivate the fields. They produced a harvest of nutritious vegetables and raised rabbits for better protein. But the best lessons came as beloved missionaries labored in the fields with fathers and taught them of a God who loves them, of a Savior who gave His life that they might succeed. Wives and husbands learned how to live in harmony, teach their children truth, pray, and sense guidance from the Spirit.

I watched a six-year-old boy who had attentively observed our first baptismal service act out with his younger sister what he had seen. He carefully arranged her hands, raised his tiny arm to the square, mumbled words, gently lowered her into a depression in the sun-baked earth, then led her to a rock where he confirmed her, and then shook her hand.

The young people learned most quickly. They became obedient to the light of truth taught by the missionaries and in time by their own parents. Through faith and obedience, in one generation youth baptized in that village overcame a seemingly hopeless future. Some have served missions, have graduated from universities, and have been sealed in the temple. Through their diligence and obedience, they found purpose and success in life despite an early harsh physical and evil-saturated environment. If it can be done in an area of extreme poverty, suffocated by such false traditions as were found in Quiriza, Bolivia, it can be done anywhere.

Have you noticed how Satan strives to capture the mind and emotions with flashing images, blaring music, and the stimulation of every physical sense to excess? For those who succumb, there is no opportunity to perceive the quiet promptings of the Spirit. Satan diligently strives to fill life with action, entertainment, and stimulation so that one cannot ponder the consequences of his tempting invitations. Think of it. Some are tempted to violate commandments because of seductive media in movies, on television, and on computer screens, where the violation of the most basic commandments of God is portrayed as acceptable. This transgression is made to seem attractive, even desirable. There seems to be no serious consequence, rather, apparent lasting joy and happiness. But recognize that those performances are controlled by scripts and actors. The outcome of decisions made is manipulated to be whatever the producer wants. Life is not that way. Yes, moral agency allows choices to be made of all the alternatives available to man. You can choose what you will—

but you cannot control the outcome of those choices. Unlike the false creations of man that exploit human weakness, our Father in Heaven determines the consequences of your choices. Obedience will yield happiness, while violation of His commandments will not.

Consider the lives of many of those who create what for some are captivating images of life. They generally turn to the very worst of the destructive influences they depict so appealingly in media. They may be wealthy, but they are miserable and without conscience. Truly the statement of Alma, an inspired prophet and compassionate father, is borne out in their lives: "Wickedness never was happiness."⁹

If, as you read this, you have felt feelings of sadness for having become entangled in transgression from poor choices, and if your conscience is prompting you to do something about it, lay this book down, kneel in prayer, and ask your Heavenly Father to strengthen your resolve to change. Seek out your bishop or a parent, someone who can show you the pattern of repentance that will bring peace and happiness. That pattern will resolve the conflict you feel stirring within you now. This counsel is given as an expression of sincere love and with absolute confidence that, with the Lord's help, you can make those changes needed in your life. Chapters 12 and 13 will help you understand what to do. As you pray to your Father in Heaven, He will give you the strength to do it. Don't let another moment go by. Begin now.

If you have determined to live righteously, don't become discouraged. Life may seem difficult now, but hold on tightly to that iron rod of truth. You are making better progress than you realize. Your struggles are defining character, discipline, and confidence in the promises of your Father in Heaven and the Savior as you consistently obey Their commandments. You are so important. You are so needed. There are so few willing to make the sacrifice you are making to live righteously. If you have not yet been blessed to be sealed to a worthy companion in the temple, exercise your faith that you will be. You can develop the sensitivity, love, and kindness to gain supreme happiness within the covenant of an eternal marriage. It is worth your every effort. It is worth your exercise of pure faith in the promises of the Lord. When you are sealed in the temple (if you have not already done so), you can bless your children with insight the world can never give them. Your example will set the course for their successful life as the world becomes even more difficult. You are needed to strengthen the growing kingdom of the Lord and to be role models for so many who lack the light of truth you have and use.

May I share a motivating insight? As conditions become more difficult in life, those of us who are older and have had our own growing experiences are not as flexible, not as adaptive. We are not able to capture as quickly new conditions and accommodate them to our personal needs. Today as you observe some of the finest examples of youth, you can see that many have developed an internal barrier against evil influences in a difficult world. They can study, learn, and flower in an environment that would have totally distracted me in my youth. Moreover, by righteous living they come away clean and pure. I believe the Lord prepares in premortal life the spirits who will come to earth so that those who are obedient to His counsel, and seek direction of the Holy Spirit, can manage whatever environment they live in. They have been prepared for it.

Maybe you recall how your parents lamented that the world was going to the dogs when you were young. I remember those comments. I felt they were exaggerated, yet now I find myself making similar statements about our current world. When correct principles are understood and applied, the current youth know that they can overcome whatever negative pressures surround them. In time they will grow older and become more fixed in their ways. Then the cycle will be repeated with their children, who will have been prepared for the conditions they will face so they can build their life on truth.

This new, exuberant generation will take their place and accommodate to even more severe challenges.

As previously mentioned, your Eternal Father has a specific plan for your life. He will reveal parts of that plan to you as you look for it with faith and consistent obedience. His Son has made you free—not from the consequences of your acts, but free to make choices. God's eternal purpose is for you to be successful in this mortal life. Don't be overly concerned about how wicked the world becomes—you can still earn that blessing. Deteriorating conditions necessitate the understanding and living of the essential truths found in the scriptures and declarations of the prophets. Seek and be attentive to the personal guidance given you through the Holy Spirit. Continue to be worthy to receive it. Reach out to others who stumble and are perplexed, not certain of what path to follow.

Your security is in God your Father and His Beloved Son, Jesus Christ. I know that He is your hope, your Mediator, your Redeemer. Through your continuing obedience, let Him guide you to peace and happiness amid increasing evil.

The next chapter discusses principles that help overcome worry and loneliness to find peace and happiness.

CHAPTER 16

To Overcome Loneliness
and Worry to Find
Peace and Happiness

Seldom have I struggled as long and as hard to define the feelings of my heart as I have with this topic. But, finally, those sweet, quiet promptings of the Spirit have come to give me confidence to share my thoughts with conviction and assurance. My desire is to help any who are struggling with feelings of inadequacy or being left out or being misunderstood and not appreciated.

Each passing day I am aware that there are many in the Church who understand the teachings of the Savior and apply them faithfully and consistently in their lives. These individuals continue to grow in strength and self-confidence and find their obedience is rewarded with peace, happiness, and self-assurance. If you are such an one, I rejoice.

Living the gospel fully will not eliminate all problems in life, for overcoming them provides growth and increased understanding. Yet significant numbers of members are striving to identify a path that will bring them satisfaction—a sense of belonging and self-worth. Some have an intellectual knowledge of gospel principles but have not incorporated them completely into their own lives. They live the teachings of the Savior partially or superficially and, as a consequence, do not receive the fullness of direction that can come from the Lord, nor the ability to achieve blessings that result from being fully, willingly obedient to His commandments. They have not yet fully discovered the power and inspiration that come from the Lord to aid all of us in the difficult experiences of life. Such individuals strive mightily to face each day's challenges on their own, and they encounter difficulties. They see only a part of the picture and can be stealthily led by Satan down erroneous paths. With deep love and empathy and with all the conviction of my soul, I wish to share with you some personal experiences that a kind and loving Lord has used to help me understand how the power of His gospel can help those in such circumstances.

In my youth I, too, had feelings of deep loneliness and of being left out and not appreciated. All of that has totally changed. What follows shares how that change came about.

I was born into a home where my father was not a member of the Church, and my mother was less active. During my early childhood, I didn't in any way understand the significance of the fact that there was no priesthood-bearing patriarch or consistent teaching of pure gospel principles in our home. No sons could have loved more or been more proud of our father and mother than were the five of us, then and now. My father taught his five boys by noble example the importance of industry, education, manual skills, hard work, integrity, trust, and obedience. We gained self-confidence through the practice of those worthy traits. Because he traveled frequently and left our precious mother alone for significant periods of time to raise five active, exuberant boys, we discovered in her an amazingly marvelous combination of love, patience, firmness, and diligence. She became more a friend and companion than anything else.

I should add that the Lord has since greatly blessed our family. Dad was baptized, became valiant in testimony, and was set apart by

President Spencer W. Kimball to be a sealer in the Washington D. C. Temple. Mother served with him in the temple. Both provided powerful examples of righteous obedience for each of their children, grandchildren and great-grandchildren, as well as those they served so selflessly.

During my youth, through kind, understanding bishops, patient home teachers, and other thoughtful friends, I was encouraged to attend Church and to participate in its activities. I did so, although at times reluctantly for lack of understanding. I remember with sadness the times when we separated for Sunday School classes and I slipped out the back door to walk in the park. Oh, if I could convince others never to do that. I lost so much from that weakness. There were, however, times when I listened to the teachings in class. I'm sure that if anyone had questioned my testimony and understanding of the gospel, I would have fiercely defended it as being strong and vigorous. Only from the perspective of time, along with the marvelous experiences of a mission and more active participation in the Church, do I now realize that I knew very little of the true meaning of the gospel plan. I participated in Church activities but somehow felt I was always at the periphery. I would approach youth activities daydreaming of a glorious evening dancing with the most popular girls in the ward. The reality of each evening was quite different. As I sat on the sidelines and watched others enjoying themselves, I felt left out, not part of the central group. The same occurred in school. Though I felt comfortable in academic and leadership activities, the social and sport endeavors left me feeling alone and unwanted. It wasn't until a lot later in life that I realized these feelings were largely my own fault.

Over time I have learned that one cannot demand love and respect, or require that the bonds of friendship and appreciation be extended, as an inherent right. These blessings must be earned. They come from personal merit. Sincere concern for others, selfless service, and worthy example gain such respect. All my rationalization that others had formed select groups and knowingly ruled out my participation was largely a figment of my imagination. Had I practiced correct principles, I need not have felt alone.

In time I learned how to make friends and feel comfortable socially. I found that if I sought out others who felt shy or lonely and tried to draw them out with a genuine desire to help, I was compensated by gaining personal confidence, great satisfaction, and skill. Some find it difficult to believe that I was ever very shy and found it difficult to initiate friendships. I discovered others felt comfortable in talking about themselves; therefore, it was easy to engage them in conversation when I showed that I was truly interested in them. The result was that their confidence was strengthened. They felt more positive towards me and extended their friendship. The integrated result was that I felt more a part of others' lives and was able to overcome my own self-consciousness. It is true that excessive focus on self is really a form of selfishness.[1]

I learned another important lesson about building friendships from another early experience. As graduation from high school approached, I arranged to have a party at our home for many of the graduating class. One of the activities planned for entertainment that night was the use of a piece of equipment that had just begun to reach the market. It was a Wilcox Gay recorder that cut with a stylus tracks into a blank phonograph disk to record voice and music. That would be no treat for today but then was fascinating to those who had never used such equipment. The plan was to form groups who would go to an isolated place and record their voices, distorting them as much as they could. Later we would listen to the playback and see if we could identify the individuals. In the press of activities, I was organizing the groups and I turned to one young man and said, "Would you be in charge of one of these groups?" Then I realized it was a student that I detested. My pride would not let me retract the

183

invitation. He did not realize I had made a mistake. He thought it was a change of heart and accomplished the assignment very well. I don't even remember now why I disliked him. What I do recall is that we became very close friends from that experience.

Well did President David O. McKay repeatedly observe, "Every . . . person radiates what he or she is. Every person is a recipient of radiation."[2] Where proper gospel principles are observed, that radiation invites friendship and trust—where lacking, there is a negative, unpleasant radiation that closes the doors to righteous companionship.

During my last year at the university, I looked forward to the prospects of a fine professional future and thought I had my life very well outlined. Then a kind and thoughtful Lord placed a bombshell in my little world. Her name was Jeanene Watkins. The election of her father, Arthur Watkins, to the United States Senate had brought her to Washington, D.C., where I lived. The more I knew her, the more fascinated I became. She radiated goodness. She was exuberantly enthusiastic and happy. Each opportunity to be with her deepened the growing love within my heart. One evening as we conversed about the important things of life, she innocently said, "When I marry, I'll marry in the temple, a returned missionary." That comment struck me to the core. It started me on a process of reflection, contemplation, and prayer that resulted in my receiving a call as a missionary to Uruguay. All that I treasure in life began to mature through that missionary experience.

I discovered myself ill prepared to teach the gospel to anyone. I had an intellectual understanding of some of the gospel principles, but I recognized that understanding needed to be converted into a heart-centered, Holy-Ghost-inspired, burning testimony of truth. I struggled to communicate to the Lord feelings of gratitude for the privilege of service, for the blessing of righteous parents, and for the love of one of His most precious daughters. I asked Him to help me become an effective servant in His hands. I strained to forget self. I struggled to help others and, in the process, the skeleton of the teachings I took with me on my mission assumed new life and meaning.

The Lord accelerated my growth with an experience I will not forget. Early in my mission, while I was serving in Montevideo, Uruguay, the daughters of a neighbor invited my companion and me to come to their house the next morning at ten o'clock. They indicated that their mother wanted us to simply tell what the Church believed but to avoid any effort to prove the truthfulness of those beliefs. They indicated another religious leader would be there. The mother planned to choose which of the two churches she would further evaluate with her daughters. When we arrived at the appointment, we found that the head of the Jehovah's Witnesses for South America was the other leader invited. I knew I was in trouble when I suggested that we open with prayer and he responded, "That won't be necessary." I began a simple description of our beliefs. Virtually every time I opened my mouth he cited a scripture from the Bible to undermine that belief and prove me wrong. The contrast was painful. I expressed my thoughts in struggling Spanish. I felt bound by the request not to try to prove our points, but in truth I didn't know enough about the gospel to prove them effectively anyway. In contrast, his presentation was crisp, if combative. He repeated from memory many of the scriptures he used. His Spanish was excellent, and his points were clearly, decisively stated.

When the trial was over, I returned with my companion to our humble lodging. I was embarrassed, crushed, and justifiably rebuked. I suffered in agony throughout the night. I resolved to devote myself to scriptural study and the acquiring of the doctrinal foundation of our beliefs. I was powerfully reprimanded by the Lord for my lack of preparation.

However, the two daughters returned the next morning with an invitation from their mother to teach the family because we had kept our word. In this painful experience I saw the evidence of a kind Father in Heaven, willing to support me yet another time. That kindness further strengthened my commitment to properly prepare and adequately serve.

For some time then and many times later, I poured out my heart to our Father in Heaven and asked for forgiveness for being so ill prepared. I told Him that if He would forgive me, I would humbly seek to learn the doctrines of His gospel and strive diligently to become fluent in Spanish. There were no missionary preparation plans at that time, so for the balance of my mission I did the best I could, arising early to study the scriptures and, from the meager materials we had, to organize some intelligent way of presenting the gospel message. That experience was powerfully motivating. As I recall it as this is written, I am again motivated to serve more effectively, to study more consistently, and to serve with greater devotion and commitment.

Through this and many like experiences I have confirmed that we are not left alone to face the challenges of life, but can receive guidance and strength from a loving, understanding God in heaven. As a missionary I bathed my pillow with tears, pleading for the mercy of the Lord to forgive a wayward soul or to fortify a family in need. I prayed that a heart could be softened or a struggling father could be given a personal witness of truth. As my prayers were answered, I discovered the limitless breadth of the Master's love.

Through prayer and application, I was blessed to have familiar scriptures guide me to new depths of understanding and appreciation. I had read the words before. They now took on new meaning. For example, the powerful commentary on charity made by Mormon[3] while serving under extremely trying circumstances took on a new meaning for me.

What a priceless message for any who would enjoy the comforting circle of true friendship! How I wanted then, as I do now, to share with others those exquisite feelings of love and appreciation—of truly belonging.

I consistently discovered new lessons. Well do I remember the first time when, as I pleaded with the Lord in solemn prayer for the help and guidance and feeling of support I had come to cherish, no answer came. Rather, I felt a barrier, an insurmountable wall. I reviewed my life, my feelings, my acts, and all that could affect such communication and found no problems. It was not until after much more purposeful struggling that the clarification came. What I had felt was not a wall but a giant step, an opportunity to rise to a higher spiritual plane, an opportunity evidencing trust that I would obey correct principles without the necessity of constant reinforcement. After more effort, the peaceful, comforting presence of the Spirit returned.

I sincerely desire that these personal experiences I have shared can help you in your quest for peace and happiness.

I wish I had some magic wand that would allow me to touch your heart as you read this message so it will be truly helpful, but I do not. I can, however, mention five principles that I have come to recognize as the foundation of peace, happiness, and joy—accompanied by the secure feeling of belonging and being strengthened by the companionship of the Lord.

These five principles have brought the deepest feelings of peace with happiness into my own life. The Lord has established them as cornerstones in His eternal plan. Each one is essential. They all work together in harmony and reinforce one another. When they are applied with diligence and consistency, they produce strength of character and an increasing ability to convert the challenges of life into steps to peace and happiness now and forever. They are:

Faith in the Lord Jesus Christ and His teachings and His capacity to bless,

Repentance to rectify the consequences of mistakes of omission or commission,

Obedience to the commandments of the Lord to provide strength and direction in our lives,

Selfless service to enrich our daily existence, and

Gratitude, sincerely expressed.

Satan also knows that these principles, when observed consistently, will render an individual increasingly resistant to his temptations. He has developed a comprehensive plan to undermine or destroy each one of them. For example, to dispose of faith, Satan would plant and cultivate in us the seeds of selfishness. He knows that if left unchecked, these seeds will grow into a monster that can enslave the divine spirit in man. Selfishness is at the root of sin. It leads to unrighteous acts that debauch and deprave the soul. It reinforces destructive habits that produce a dependence on chemical or physical stimulants that destroy the mind and body. Satan's program is based on immediate gratification of selfish desires. He urges us to participate now and pay later. However, the full, terrible consequences of payment are never revealed until it is tragically late. The Spirit of the Lord can overpower the stifling effect of selfishness. That cherished Spirit comes with faith, repentance, obedience, and service.

With evil intent, Satan would destroy repentance with the prompting, "Why confess? No one will ever know. You don't need to have someone else probe into the personal recesses of your life. Besides, you haven't done anything different from what everyone else is doing." He would overcome obedience to the commandments with the subtle whisperings, "Why let others dictate what you do in life? You have your agency. You know what's best for you. You should be able to do what you want to do." He would push aside the benefits of service with the all-too-pervading pattern, "Me first, and I want the biggest." Such an attitude could also rule out the blessings that result from honest expressions of gratitude.

With the other Brethren, I have the privilege of helping sincere youth who have stumbled along the way and yet have painstakingly found their way back. Many are anxious to serve a mission. Their backgrounds vary widely, as does the degree of their transgression. Support from others ranges from strong to nonexistent. Yet there is always a common thread. In every case, each has come to the realization that "wickedness never was happiness."[4] Each has resolved to bring into effect in their lives the saving principles of the gospel. Each has a greater appreciation for the Atonement of the Redeemer and of its fruits in their personal life. The proper use of moral agency produces the miracle of rebuilt useful lives.

I have personally verified that concepts like faith, prayer, love, and humility hold no great significance and produce no miracles until they become a living part of us through our own experience, aided by the sweet prompting of the Holy Spirit. In early life I found that I could learn gospel teachings intellectually and, through the power of reason and analysis, recognize that they were of significant value. But their enormous power and ability to stretch me beyond the limits of my imagination and capacity did not become reality until patient, consistent practice allowed the Holy Spirit to distill and expand their meaning in my heart. I found that while I was sincerely serving others, God forged my personal character. He engendered a growing capacity to recognize the direction of the Spirit. The genius of the gospel plan is that by doing those things the Lord counsels us to do, we are given every understanding and every capacity necessary to provide peace and rich fulfillment in this life. Likewise, we gain the preparation necessary for eternal happiness in the presence of the Lord. Have you exerted the effort to confirm these truths in your own life?

Anyone who paints a picture of life as being easy, without

challenge, is either dishonest or has not yet encountered the growing experiences that the Lord gives each of His children. They prepare us for happiness in this life and the blessing of dwelling in His presence eternally. The purpose of these experiences has been clarified by the Lord:

> And if men come unto me I will show unto them their weakness. I give unto men weakness that they may be humble; and my grace is sufficient for all men that humble themselves before me; for if they humble themselves before me, and have faith in me, then will I make weak things become strong unto them.[5]

To clarify the purpose of growth experiences, Elder Orson F. Whitney wrote: "No pain that we suffer, no trial that we experience is wasted. It ministers to our education, to the development of such qualities as patience, faith, fortitude and humility. All that we suffer and all that we endure, especially when we endure it patiently, builds up our characters, purifies our hearts, expands our souls, and makes us more tender and charitable, more worthy to be called the children of God . . . and it is through sorrow and suffering, toil and tribulation, that we gain the education that we came here to acquire and which will make us more like our Father and Mother in heaven."[6]

We can, however, avoid unnecessary sorrow and distress. President N. Eldon Tanner has wisely counseled: "The first thing to remember is that if we really understand and live the principles of the gospel, we won't find ourselves in some of the predicaments we get into. Much of the loneliness, heartache and despair which is common to so many people have come because either they or someone in their family or their mate did not live the principles of the gospel, or did not apply the principle of repentance."[7]

Remember President Tanner's second point, repentance. If you do get into trouble, or have not kept the commandments and have transgressed, recognize that you have this glorious principle of repentance to help you erase the guilt and consequences and start all over again. The Redeemer has declared:

> Behold, he who has repented of his sins, the same
> is forgiven, and I, the Lord, remember them no more.
> By this ye may know if a man repenteth of his sins—
> behold, he will confess them and forsake them.[8]

Some divert their best efforts from constructive accomplishment by investing them in mental anguish and continual worry. May I share a personal experience related to this matter of not letting excessive worry paralyze you? The Lord taught me a great lesson I will share with you. I had completed a priceless mission, where everything that has subsequently proven to be of eternal value in my life began to mature. I had been granted the marvelous privilege of being sealed in the temple to a wife who for me is one of the choicest spirits of our Father in Heaven—my lovely Jeanene. She had filled her mission while I was serving mine. We began our life together with every expectation of happiness, having committed to live the commandments of God without rationalization. Through the kindness of the Lord, I was blessed, I am convinced, to obtain a job in a pioneer effort to equip submarines and aircraft carriers with nuclear power plants. The work was fascinating, challenging, and absorbing; however, the pressure was intense. When combined with the natural growth experiences inherent in the formation of a new family and a demanding Church assignment, we found each day full to overflowing.

Within eight months, I was in the office of a doctor being examined to see if I had ulcers. Each night for weeks I would return home from work with a severe headache, and only after a quiet period of isolation could I calm my nerves enough to sleep briefly and return to work the next day. I prayerfully considered my plight. It was ridiculous. All I wanted to do was be a worthy husband and father and carry out honorably my Church and professional assignments. However, my best efforts seemed to produce only frustration, worry, and illness.

After much struggling and many profound, sincere prayers (and, I am confident, much private entreaty by my precious wife, Jeanene), I was led to a solution. I was prompted to divide, both mentally and physically, all of the tasks and assignments given to me into two categories. First were those items that I had some ability to control and resolve. These I put into a basket called "Concern." All the rest of the things that were assigned to me by others, which I felt responsibility for but which I could do little to control, I put in a basket called "Worry." I realized that I could not change such things to any significant degree, nor did I have the means to accomplish them, so I strived studiously to completely forget them. The items in the "Concern" basket were given priority. I conscientiously tried to resolve them to the best of my ability. I realized that I could not always fulfill all of them on schedule or to the degree of competence that I desired, but I did my conscientious best.

Occasionally, as I sat in my office, my stomach muscles would tighten and tension would overcome me. I would cease what I was doing and, with earnest prayer for support, concentrate on relaxing to overcome the barrier that worry produced in my life. Over a period of time, these efforts were blessed by the Lord. I came to understand that the Lord is willing to strengthen, fortify, guide, and direct every phase of life. The symptoms of the illness passed, and I learned to face difficult tasks under pressure. I was able to accomplish far more then and throughout the balance of life.

I have described a technique to overcome worry. That which gives it power is the assurance that an understanding Lord is personally aware of our needs and will give us help to the degree we permit it by exercising faith in Him and by being obedient to His commandments. He has assured us: "Let your hearts be comforted . . . ; for all flesh is in mine hands; be still and know that I am God."[9]

Much of life's disappointments come from looking beyond the mark,[10] from seeking success and happiness where they cannot be found. When wealth, position, influence, power, or possessions become measures of success in life, we should not be disappointed when their attainment does not give lasting happiness. They cannot produce satisfaction and blessings comparable to those blessings promised for obedience to the commandments of the Lord. There is much emphasis in the world today on "things." When "things" become an end unto themselves, the prime object of our effort, they no longer are tools to be used to reach greater, nobler goals. Thus they become part of Satan's astute effort to deflect us from the plan of happiness of the Lord. In time, when aggressively pursued, they can lead us carefully down to hell.[11] "Things" do not produce lasting happiness on earth, nor do they provide exaltation. Material things are to be respected for their value as tools. Every artist, surgeon, or writer needs tools. They become instruments for greater good, but they should not at any time be the ultimate goal of life.

The Savior declared as His work and glory "to bring to pass the immortality and eternal life of man."[12] He enthroned love for one another, service to others, and building the kingdom of God for His glory and majesty as noble, worthy goals that produce rewards beyond all power of expression. Mormon gave us precious insight when he declared:

> For behold, the Spirit of Christ is given to every man, that he may know good from evil; wherefore, I show unto you the way to judge; for every thing which inviteth to do good, and to persuade to believe in Christ, is sent forth by the power and gift of Christ;

wherefore ye may know with a perfect knowledge it is of God.

But whatsoever thing persuadeth men to do evil, and believe not in Christ, and deny him, and serve not God, then ye may know with a perfect knowledge it is of the devil; for after this manner doth the devil work, for he persuadeth no man to do good, no, not one; neither do his angels; neither do they who subject themselves unto him.[13]

I have obtained a personal witness that the true value of an individual is measured in worthy accomplishment, not mounds of paper plans or hoards of accumulated possessions. Genuine feelings of self-worth distill from worthy acts in righteousness. The eternal progress you attain in your own life and help others to accomplish is measure enough for the worthwhileness of your efforts here on earth. No matter who you are, what lofty position you hold, or what powerful influence you wield, such things in and of themselves are of no lasting moment. The measure of success lies in how well you serve as instruments in the hands of the Lord to accomplish His divine will in home and family and elsewhere. Success is governed by how devotedly you obey His commandments and worthily you receive His ordinances. In the final analysis, all success can be measured by how effectively you can know and accomplish the will of our Father in Heaven in your own life, the lives of your own family and loved ones, and the lives of His other children you are blessed to serve.

I hope the content of this chapter has been helpful. Perhaps it can help someone you know who may be lonely or misunderstood or captured by excessive worry. Loneliness is a terrible burden to carry needlessly. As I have described, once in my life I had feelings of being left out. I now share the companionship of incomparable brotherhood and sisterhood, a feeling of belonging, of being useful. I recognize that it has come only from sincere striving to live the commandments of the Lord. There are those around you who would justify taking a path contrary to the Lord's plan because they feel rejected. Oh, how essential it is for you to touch such hearts and help such people feel the expanding influence of the Holy Ghost. Show them how most problems of life can be corrected when the gospel is allowed to flow freely into one's life. Such a pattern will also help them to endure well problems that can't be altered.

The next chapter has been prepared to help you or some you love meet and overcome additional difficult challenges.

CHAPTER 17

"I Can't Do It."
"Yes, You Can."

S O MANY DETOUR FROM the path of purpose and genuine happiness because they lament their portion in life—too thin, too fat, too short, too tall, twenty-nine and not married, too poor, can't make friends, no one really cares, misunderstood, sometimes left out. This condition may not apply to you, but it could apply to someone you love.

Some seem to give up without really trying. "I can't memorize. I'm not a good student and never will be." Perhaps the following experience will motivate a change and open the door to accomplishment, for it embodies true principles for success.

One afternoon, in a country far away, I had one of those experiences that leaves its impress for a lifetime because pure truth was conveyed to my mind and heart. I will try to relate the circumstances of the experience and then draw some principles from it. I was attending a stake conference in a place where, because of the difficult political circumstances, it had been a long time since a General Authority of the Church could visit. Unemployment was very high. Those who wanted to go to the university often found their schooling interrupted for long periods because of the political instability. There was gas and food rationing. It was a challenging life from every perspective.

When the conference ended, I knew it would be difficult for the stake president to drive me in his little truck to the airport. I did not want him to use his meager rationed gas on me. I found a way for him to complete ordination of new elders and the setting apart of a new high councilor while I tried to slip quietly out the front door to find a taxicab. Most of the people had gone home. As I walked out the door, a young man took my briefcase and bag and asked, "How can I help you?" I told him I was looking for a taxi. He responded, "Don't worry, we'll take care of that."

Within a moment, there stood at my side a beautiful young lady in a lovely red dress with a radiant smile, sparkling eyes, and carefully combed hair. She inquired, "Can I take you where you would like to go?" And I thought, "How privileged she is to have a car at a time like this." We walked out to the curb, and I saw the vehicle. It was a very small car. I'm not sure what color it was. It was an ingenious combination of parts from different cars that seemed to be barely hanging together. I wondered if we could make it to the airport.

As we drove along, I was interested in her perspective of life. It was so different from many of the people I had been with in that country. She seemed happy; in fact, she *was* happy. She was radiantly happy. I found that the young man who had taken my bags was married to another charming young lady. They were in the back seat with my things piled on top of them. As I looked out at the wobbling front fender, I wondered how our driver was able to get this car. Then the young man said, "She's a doctor, almost. She's in her last year," and I thought, "How fortunate that her parents could support her in medical school under these difficult times."

As we continued our journey, I found more things about that remarkable young lady. She was the fourth of five children. The others were not members of the Church. Her father was out of work, and somehow she was making her own way in life. Her older sisters were bitter, complaining, and constantly telling her that her honeymoon experience with the Church would soon be over and she would find out the painful realities of life. I thought about some of the challenges she must face, a beautiful young woman in the medical profession, in that particular country. She said, "I always talk about the Church to those around me. Sometimes they ridicule me, but I don't mind. There are those who understand the truth. Also I establish the principles that I live for, and that avoids an awful lot of problems." And I understood, without her having to tell me, what she meant. She was not apologetic for her car as maybe some of us would be. She just wanted to share it. Then I found it wasn't even hers alone. She shared it with eight other students, who somehow had put this device together and made it operate. As we drove along, I wondered how I could help her pay for the gas. I began to discreetly mention the subject, and she replied, "Oh, Marybelle," her car's name, "is a special vehicle. We don't put much gas in it, just a whiff of vapor now and then."

Earlier in the day, I had heard criticism of some of the local neighborhood organizations that were doing things that were opposed to Church principles. Many had counseled that the local people should not participate in them. This young woman had a wonderfully different perspective. She said, "I go, and when they talk about things they shouldn't do, I tell them why it's wrong, and when they ask me to do things on the Sabbath I say that I can't. I tell them that I have principles I live by. You know, Elder Scott, when we don't do that, we're criticized, we're not understood, and our message doesn't help the people like it should."

As we drove on that beautiful sunny day, I looked out the windows and saw burned-out factory buildings and armed soldiers. I saw the poor and the needy and those who were downcast. There were a lot of negative things in that country, but I remembered Moroni's counsel:

> If ye will lay hold upon every good thing, and condemn it not, ye certainly will be a child of Christ. And now, my brethren, how is it possible that ye can lay hold upon every good thing? . . . By faith, they did lay hold upon every good thing.[1]

As we continued to drive, I was able to observe more carefully this young woman, who initially seemed so beautiful. I realized she had some physical flaws. I noticed that her dress was carefully handmade. I began to realize that it was the person that was so beautiful. Truly,

> Whatsoever thing ye shall ask the Father in my name, which is good, in faith believing that ye shall receive, behold, it shall be done unto you. . . . And Christ hath said: If ye will have faith in me ye shall have power to do whatsoever thing is expedient in me.[2]

I continued to ponder how I might share some of the expense of that long trip. I realized that it would offend them. I knew I couldn't do it. They wanted to share even the little that they had. Their generosity was a freely given gift and would be recompensed by the Lord.

Somehow, as we parted, my heart sang. I rejoiced and expressed my thanks to the Lord for the gospel and for those who live it regardless of their circumstances. The years have passed. In a later visit to that country, I again met that woman, and I was lifted again by her radiant spirit. She had become a doctor. Now she was a devoted wife and mother imbuing her children with confidence. She was laying in their lives the foundation of faith and doctrine that has served her so very well. She had earned her peace and happiness.

Here are some suggestions crafted to help, should you or someone you know despair at overcoming what seem to be overwhelming barriers to enduring peace and happiness.

First, be full of faith. Life is what we choose to see in it—cruel, demoralizing, ugly, difficult, challenging, lonely, unfair, or full of opportunity, fulfilling, rich, rewarding, happy, satisfying.

Second, be aware that no life is without challenge. It is how we face those challenges that results in happiness or sadness in our life, not the absence of them. Faith in Jesus Christ and consistent application of His truths will always yield peace and happiness.

Third, find security in the only place it truly can be found, in the gospel of Jesus Christ. There are hardships the world over. There are places where others find it most difficult to achieve true security. President Spencer W. Kimball has wisely said, "Security is not born of inexhaustible wealth but of unquenchable faith."[3] Spiritual security comes from obedience. That will allow the Spirit to give promptings pertaining to physical security when needed.

Fourth, apply correct principles. Some time ago, I was in an airport. It was dawn. The sun was beginning to shine. All was silent about me, and then I became aware of two women who were nearby, each with a child in arms. One was eagerly describing the joy she found in life. She explained how it wasn't easy, how she had had to find a job to help her husband while he was finishing his education. She even mentioned what their meager salary was. I couldn't help but hear the response of the other girl, who said, "You're crazy. I don't work. I'm on welfare, and I get more than you are earning." I wanted to hear the end of the conversation because I didn't know what the first young lady would say. She hesitated for a while and, finally straightening up, she answered, "Well, maybe we see things differently. I'm grateful to share a part of the responsibility to bring to our home what we need from our own efforts." Follow correct principles for happiness.

Fifth, be yourself. I testify that the Lord has given each of us that portion which, if well used, will bring happiness and purpose in life. It sometimes takes a lot of digging and a lot of discovering to find the ingredients, but they are there. Sometimes the characteristics we are dissatisfied with just need to become polished a little to become our best talents and traits. I remember when I was growing up, my mother told me of an experience which taught her a great lesson. She said for many days she tried to change her hairstyle to match that of another girl she greatly admired, but couldn't. Then she discovered that girl was trying to copy her hairstyle. Be yourself. In the Doctrine and Covenants we read:

> And if your eye be single to my glory, your whole bodies shall be filled with light, and there shall be no darkness in you; and that body which is filled with light comprehendeth all things.
>
> Therefore, sanctify yourselves that your minds become single to God, and the days will come that you shall see him; for he will unveil his face unto you, and it shall be in his own time, and in his own way, and according to his own will.[4]

Sixth, be grateful. When President Gordon B. Hinckley prays in our meetings, more than two-thirds of the content is a sincere expression of gratitude for specific blessings the Lord has granted. Expressing gratitude for as many blessings as one can identify— whether for the Lord or others' thoughtful kindnesses—has multiple compensations.

Seventh, don't let worry paralyze your progress. In Mosiah, we find counsel particularly useful to those who face daily challenges of how best to use time and what should be done first. The pressure can be unrelenting. The Lord declared,

> And see that all these things are done in wisdom
> and order; for it is not requisite that a man should run
> faster than he has strength. And again, it is expedient
> that he should be diligent, that thereby he might win
> the prize; therefore, all things must be done in order.[5]

Eighth, make the most of what resources you have. This comment of President Kimball helps: "I found down on the reservation a young woman who was on a full-time mission who was sent out among the Indians and who has charge of Primary work, and she did not have anything to help her. She just was resourceful and went forward with a great heart to inspire children. She went to the store and got a common roll of ordinary wrapping paper and a bunch of crayons and she went to work. And she drew as she taught these children the story of the Book of Mormon. She drew the waves of the sea as the little barks went on their way across the ocean to the promised land. She drew a ship as best she could. She drew for these children the bow and arrow which the Lord had inspired Nephi to find and make so that he could provide food for the group. She drew the mountain from which the ore was taken, from which the plates were made. In a crude way she drew these pictures that taught the children the story of the Book of Mormon. . . . And so she put over her lessons.

"Now, I would be very grateful if you had all the tools for which you might wish in your work among them, but if you do not . . . you can improvise them."[6]

Ninth, act righteously. A knowledge of truth is not sufficient. We have so many good examples of noble, righteous acts of individuals committed to live the teachings of the Master. I briefly mention some of the righteous acts observed in the Presidents of the Church I have known. My earliest recollection of meeting a prophet of the Lord was in a chapel in Washington, D.C. President George Albert Smith patiently stood as members passed through to shake his hand.

I vividly remember feeling the purity, the righteousness, the peace of his soul as he looked into my eyes and took my small hand in his. His righteousness radiated from him.

My earliest memory of Harold B. Lee was from a priesthood session I heard by telephone connection to that same chapel. He introduced a plan to correlate the diverse activities and organizations of the Church. It was a comprehensive plan, and I was touched by his commitment, vigor, and determination to carry out the assignment he had been given to accomplish that unity.

The immense love of President Spencer W. Kimball for anyone and everyone, whatever their condition, led him to act in righteousness, even if it meant entering into a place where he personally felt uncomfortable to rescue one wavering with temptation. When an Apostle, he was introduced by Franklin D. Richards to mission presidents with three words, "Work, work, work." Elder Kimball humbly stood and replied, "I have to work long hours. The Brethren I serve with are so gifted and so capable they complete their work quickly. But I am such a dull blade, it takes me longer." His constant, consistent righteous acts defied that comment.

I observed then-member of the Twelve Elder Ezra Taft Benson when he served as Secretary of Agriculture for our nation: with television cameras rolling, others made accusations for political purposes that he and they knew were false. He never showed anger but acted with strength and resolve, yet ever in the character of a righteous Apostle. In all eternity, I can never forget his tenderness, love, and spirituality when, as President of the Church, he extended a call for me to be an Apostle of the Lord Jesus Christ.

Kind, considerate, devoted President Howard W. Hunter, in ways unknown to others, repeatedly acted righteously to bless my wife with encouragement and strength when both he and she were seriously ill.

One example of President Gordon B. Hinckley: I was present

when one steeped in sin attacked President Hinckley ferociously. He listened with a calmness devoid of anger, then acted righteously, politely but firmly responding to the need.

Let each of us emulate such examples by doing righteous acts in our own lives.

Tenth, be pure. Purity brings peace. Purity also brings inspiration that we may know what to do, and have the power of God to do it. The Lord has promised, "Ye are to be taught from on high. Sanctify yourselves and ye shall be endowed with power, that ye may give even as I have spoken."[7]

If as you read this you know anyone who is on the wrong side of purity, please help them back. Never get on the wrong side of that line yourself. Willingly live the gospel principles. The Lord requires, "Ye shall bind yourselves to act in all holiness before me."[8]

Eleventh, be considerate of others' needs. Try to satisfy some of them. One of the best-kept secrets of happiness is to serve others while honestly forgetting self. I will share four brief experiences I had with President Spencer W. Kimball when he was an Apostle, and later as President of the Church, to show how he lived this principle so eloquently.

Because Elder Spencer W. Kimball liked to pack his day completely with meaningful activity, as he toured missions in Argentina he managed to visit a few members of the Church in Santiago del Estero during the few minutes the plane was on the ground there. As we landed, from the window I could see about three or four hundred young, radiant-faced children in their white school attire, ready to greet the dignitary of another church who was also on our plane. A young girl had a bouquet of flowers in eager anticipation. At her side was the teacher who had clearly worked long and hard on songs they would sing and the reception they would give. As the plane came to a halt, the church leader, who apparently had much to do, stepped off the plane and walked right by the children to a waiting limousine without even looking in their direction. As he drove off, my heart sank at the disappointed faces of the children.

Then I watched a servant of the Lord. He walked over to a small group of members he had never met who were worried about greeting one of the Lord's anointed. One by one, he gave them a hug. He looked into the eyes of each one and talked to them. Then Elder Kimball said, "Let's sing," and for a few minutes they sang hymns together, and he spoke briefly. There was rejoicing. When every available second had been given to the small group, he hurried back onto the plane. Be considerate and sensitive to the needs of others.

I relate another act of kindness. It may seem a small thing to you, but to me it reveals the inner man. It was in a mission presidents' seminar, and Elder Kimball was expressing a very important doctrinal principle when his throat became dry. He needed water. He was handed a glass. He drank from it. Then although very interested in continuing his message, he looked around for a place to set the glass. He reached in his pocket and took out a handkerchief and placed it under the glass, so that the moisture on its exterior wouldn't damage the furniture. He was a man who was aware of everything around him and completely dedicated to selfless service.

I was at the Washington D.C. Temple when ambassadors, key representatives of other governments, and other significant officials had been invited to a very special open house. Somehow in the midst of all of this, two tourists had wandered in, dressed in shorts and T-shirts. They soon realized that everyone around them was more formally attired. They became embarrassed. I could see they almost wished they could become invisible. Just at that moment, President Spencer W. Kimball walked out of the temple with Mrs. Ford, wife of the President of the United States, on his arm. You could see that she was completely at ease, enjoying the experience. Then he noted the tourists' feeling of uneasiness. He stopped and made them welcome, while the first lady of the nation also felt supported. Be considerate and aware of the needs of others. Help others, not because it's easy, but because it's right.

I'll mention one final experience, which occurred when Elder Kimball was an Apostle. He was at a stake conference and had made very active use of the time. He found there was someone in the hospital who had a need but was told that there was not enough time to make a visit. Yet he said, "Let's go." They then ran hurriedly to the patient's door. Just before entering, he stopped, then quietly entered the room. While there he spoke slowly, as though he had all the time in the world, gave a blessing, walked quietly out again, and then broke into a dead run to meet another commitment.

You may not become wealthy, powerful, influential, or renowned. You may never have great political influence, but these are false means of measuring success. Live the principles that will qualify you to have enduring, even eternal, peace and happiness.

CHAPTER 18

TO COPE WITH
WHAT IS UNFAIR

A N IMPORTANT PRINCIPLE of finding peace is to recognize that
sometimes life is intended to be a challenge to foster character
development. This chapter deals with lesser things that *seem to be*
unfair. The next chapter will address major challenges that *are truly*
unfair.

There are some principles in a letter of a father to his missionary
daughter that might help you understand how to manage growth
experiences encountered in service given to others, particularly in circumstances where a supervisor or leader is growing in his or her
responsibility and perhaps not handling it the best way. The sensitive
daughter had encountered some rules that a new mission president
had required that were sincere but not ideal. These were complicat-
ing the daughter's own growth experiences. This insightful, hand-
written letter is used by permission of both father and daughter.

"For some time I have pondered, meditated and prayed about
the following and made several notes as the Spirit seemed to direct. I
sincerely pray that it will be of some value to you in your wonderful
mission.

"First I want you to know how your mother and I thrill with the
evidence of the strong, righteous character you are developing. We

rejoice at your determination to do what is correct and are deeply moved as we see your urgent prayers answered by a loving Father in Heaven. You are so precious; there is nothing we would not do for you, but experience has taught me that some lessons are best learned and forever mastered through wrenching, silent struggles within our own hearts. You have proven your faith and sincerity and He is rewarding you. Perhaps the following observations can help you see a little more clearly what is happening.

"You have also observed that mission presidents grow in experience as they serve, just as you are doing. He may change some of the policies he is now using as he becomes more familiar with the mission personally and is less dependent upon his very well-meaning staff. Through his prayers he will learn many things as he feels comfortable in his calling and is more consistently directed by the Lord. Some current practices are natural human reactions to a tremendous responsibility. He will be led. He has been called by the Lord. Also, his priesthood line officer will visit with him and give him counsel. You and other missionaries can help as prompted by the Spirit. For example, in a private interview you might say, 'President, what do you think of the idea of . . . ? I have considered this deeply, and it seems to me that . . .'

"Now the Lord has given you a great blessing. He has revealed to your mind and heart—so easily that were you less perceptive you might have mistaken it for your own idea—that in the mission field as in few other circumstances in life we are bound only by ourselves. Yes, there are things that can annoy you. Some things you are asked to do may even appear to waste your time, but they must not control you. Consider the following quote:

"'Sydney Harris wrote . . . : I walked with my friend, a Quaker, to the newsstand the other night, and he bought a paper, thanking the newsie politely. The newsie didn't even acknowledge it. "A sullen fellow, isn't he?" I commented. "Oh, he's that way every night," shrugged my friend. "Then why do you continue to be so polite to him?" I asked. "Why not?" inquired my friend. "Why should I let him decide how I'm going to act?"[1]

"You have learned this precious lesson: there is great freedom in a positive attitude when it coincides with the will of the Lord. No matter how difficult the day, you can have the realization, 'I am here by choice. I will conform my attitude and obedience to this call. I accepted it by the exercise of my agency. I have thus qualified, as I am obedient, for the inspiration of the Holy Ghost and the magnifying power of God. This aid I will receive as I do my part. There may be some things I am asked to do that are really unnecessary, but my obedience to them without allowing them to become a stumbling block develops my character.'

"My dear, not everything in life is 'fair' on an immediate daily balance sheet. In aggregate over a period of time, we are much blessed for accepting seeming 'injustices.' I have come to know by sacred experience that sometimes when we are asked to do unreasonable things, it is a test of our willingness to live by every word that proceedeth from the mouth of the Lord or His servants. There will always come compensatory blessings.

"As one qualifies to be directed by the Spirit, many blessings follow. You may feel that care of your body at certain times of the month or other needs prompt you to want to adjust one of the rules temporarily. Discuss your feelings with your mission president and follow his advice. Some policies are never to be broken without exception. They are easy to identify. They are the ones some would break by *rationalization* not *inspiration*.

"Now comes the challenging subject of happiness and joy in the work. I have much to tell you. If it seems disjointed forgive me, for I want to convey so much to you.

"Do you remember sometimes playing with the children and then commenting to them 'Aren't we having a wonderful time?' 'Isn't this fun?'—and then seeing them react with broader smiles and more genuine happiness? They were doing the same thing but somehow their attitude changed through understanding. They were not tricked, nor did they convince themselves of something that was not real. They just opened their eyes and hearts to reality. This same thing happens in our adult lives too when we avoid the tragedy of thinking only of tomorrow.

"Can you understand that a person can be happy and sad at nearly the same time? Your mother and I are supremely happy. Perhaps you children don't often see that. You have seen our momentary sadness when one has not understood the need to be self-motivated in obedience or to exercise self-control when challenges are met. I have observed in others that deep sadness from an interview for transgression can turn to radiant joy as understanding and a decision to abandon sin occurs. Yet the satisfying feeling of peace and calmness would not have come had not the challenge been squarely met. You are meeting valiantly the growth experiences you face and will surely overcome them for greater peace. My dear, it has been years since I have known real fear of any kind. What is a blessing like that worth?

"I have wept tears when I have not fully met goals established under the influence of the Spirit for self-improvement—or not controlled my feelings as I should have. But I have never had to face the bitterness of great wickedness. Consequently, life becomes more beautiful, our love deepens, and pure happiness increases. To the degree our service is motivated by 'want to' or 'get to' desires rather than 'have to' compulsion we are happy. 'Have to' is an understandable result of our unconscious desire to excel, to do one's best. With some effort and enlightenment it can be converted into a 'want to' desire that yields much different personal feelings.

"I will share in confidence an experience with a capable General Authority to illustrate. During the process to select a stake president in Baltimore, in the midst of important interviews with the leadership of the stake waiting to be interviewed, he turned to me and said, 'Come. Let's go for a walk.' He spoke of the trees, the sounds of the insects, how temperature could be related to their native call, etc., while the pressing need to select a stake president seemed to wait. Without comment, he began to teach me precious lessons. He was ridding himself of all that would impede his mind and heart from being the instrument through which the Lord could reveal His will. I observed, then he confirmed, that each question he asked was intended only to provide a basis to know the will of the Lord, not to work out a logical conclusion. He was working hard, but in the way he has learned to work. Energy-draining, spiritual communion, not as the world works. Experience with this exceptional leader has taught that he works diligently because of his drive to serve, not for what others will think, but to please the Lord. Further, he has learned to care for his body and is consequently a more useful servant.

"You are taking care of your physical body. We're pleased with that decision; it's right. Perhaps now you need to address in like manner your feelings. Your statements about not enjoying the mission because it does not bring sustained periods of happiness indicate a need to further understand how the Spirit can direct you. You won't always be happy, but there must be periods of sustained inner peace. An important but most difficult change to make in life is to exchange what we have come to feel as 'right' or 'proper' for what the Lord would really have us do when His desire is different from what we want to do. When should one feel that it is not necessary to push continually to attain the requisite hours or some other artificial goal? When it begins to interfere with the direction of the Spirit and therefore legitimately affects our inner peace. An illustration:

"A member of the Presiding Bishopric years ago lost a son preparing for a mission from a train accident. Both he and his wife anguished over the loss for some time while he continued his service.

One night the son appeared to the mother consoling her. He explained that his death was an accident, that he was happy and productively occupied. Then the significant statement: 'I have been trying for some time to communicate with father but he is too busy.'[2]

"When we are being directed by the Spirit and feel inner peace we can work with tremendous energy and power. President Gordon B. Hinckley has mastered that ability as few others have. Further, he *has* to work tirelessly to accomplish all he has to do. So the Lord sustains him in activity that would cause others great difficulty. As you grow in the ability to detect promptings to avoid 'busy-ness' and to discern the needs and feelings of others as your own, you will understand this principle more clearly. It will not come without much effort and some struggling. Like all of the Lord's teachings, it comes line upon line. On occasion you have indicated 'I can't do . . . ' You can change anything the Lord would have you change—anything. It requires singular effort, but is part of your eternal progression.

"You have before you a full life of service. What you do in convert baptisms is important, but not the most important result of your mission. Even more vital is the development of an understanding of, and consistent application of, eternal principles. An adjunct to such effort is the gift of recognizing divine direction and the ability to seek and receive it in your life. You will be a queen in Father's kingdom and with your eternal companion will ever use these principles.

"You have asked, 'How do I develop an ability to be led by the Spirit?' Talking with the Lord is the way I most easily learn. Not praying as you have heard others do, but talking and listening with *mind* and *heart*. Remember He is your Father. Tell Him honestly how you feel, what challenges you face, what changes you would make, what motivation you would have, what strengths you would acquire for service to Him. Tell Him you want to know His Son better, to feel Him closer. Listen then, while praying and always.

Have paper and pencil nearby at night, during meetings, testimony time, and record the answers He will pour out to you in His due time. Be careful. Don't think you will remember without writing the important ones down. And most critical, if you would be further enlightened, follow the direction given with exactness. You may make mistakes, fall short at times, but your exercise of moral agency to obey His will without reservation qualifies you for His sustaining power, even when unintentional error occurs. When your mistakes are not premeditated, nor is there conscious decision to go your own way, you will be aided and strengthened.

"Determine the most important long-term objectives and follow them. Decide what motivations He would have you follow and adhere to them. Take time to recognize the happy moments in each day like saying 'Isn't this fun!' and it truly will be.

"Learn to be truly happy as you: counsel contacts and recognize the promptings of the Spirit; relax in deep scriptural study; have a companion inventory session; walk with the sunlight in your lovely face; talk to and listen to your Father in Heaven.

"There is so much more I would tell you—and will again. I am afraid I have sounded like an eager father speaking to a child. Yet I realize you are a mature woman finding your way. Know that we love you, totally trust you, respect your judgment, and know of your complete devotion to your call. I am not urging you to work harder—just more spiritually directed so that you will find still greater success and happiness.

"Our prayers are with you as a family—as individuals. We love you, dearest daughter. You are precious.

"Your Dad"

Ponder what you have just read. What are the principles the father shared with his daughter that, when used, can bring you greater peace and happiness? In the next chapter we will consider major challenges that are truly unfair. The circumstances likely will not apply to you, but they may to a loved one or friend who can use the principles discussed to cope with and overcome the consequences of the unrighteous, unwarranted acts of others.

CHAPTER 19

TO COPE WITH MAJOR CHALLENGES THAT ARE COMPLETELY UNFAIR

Perhaps you, someone you love, or another you have befriended have experienced the shattering effects of events that are completely unjust and unwarranted. I speak of devastating experiences that at times come through no personal fault. Contrary to what is often taught, I know that the consequences of such events can be healed. That healing comes as a result of understanding how the Atonement of Jesus Christ can resolve the effects of all that is unfair, unjust, and undeserved.

By using the example of the heinous sin of sexual abuse, I will share principles that form the foundation of coping with and finally resolving the devastating consequences of others' unrighteous acts. I will also give an explanation of how understanding and applying the fruits of the Atonement of Jesus Christ can heal that which is profoundly unjust. This chapter likely does not apply to you, but perhaps you know of another whose suffering can be alleviated by the principles it contains and the understanding it can provide. This chapter is written as though I am addressing one who has been abused.

I speak from the depths of my heart to you who have been scarred by the ugly sin of abuse, whether you are a member or non-member of the Church. I would prefer a private setting to discuss this sensitive subject and ask that the Holy Spirit will help us both, that you may receive the relief of the Lord from the cruelty that has scarred your life.

Unless you are healed by the Lord, mental, physical, or sexual abuse can cause you serious, enduring consequences. As a victim, you have experienced some of them. They include fear, depression, guilt, self-hatred, destruction of self-esteem, and alienation from normal human relationships. When aggravated by continued abuse, powerful emotions of rebellion, anger, and hatred are generated. These feelings often are focused against oneself, others, life itself, and even Heavenly Father. Frustrated efforts to fight back can degenerate into drug abuse, immorality, abandonment of home, and, tragically, in extreme cases, suicide. Unless corrected, these feelings lead to despondent lives, discordant marriages, and even the possibility of the transition from victim to abuser. One awful result is a deepening lack of trust in others, which becomes a barrier to healing.

To be helped, you must understand some things about eternal law. Your abuse results from another's unrighteous attack on your moral agency. Since all of Father in Heaven's children enjoy agency, there can be some who choose willfully to violate the commandments and harm you. Such acts temporarily restrict your freedom. In justice, and to compensate, the Lord has provided a way for you to overcome the destructive results of others' acts against your will. That relief comes by applying eternal truths with priesthood assistance.

Know that the wicked choices of others cannot completely destroy your agency unless you permit it. Their acts may cause pain, anguish, even physical harm, but they cannot destroy your eternal possibilities for happiness. You must understand that you are free to determine to overcome the harmful results of abuse. Your attitude and efforts can control the change for good in your life. It allows you to have the help the Lord intends you to receive. No one can take away your ultimate opportunities when you understand and live eternal law. Because of the laws of your Heavenly Father and the Atonement of the Lord, you need not be robbed of the opportunities that come to the children of God.

You may feel threatened by one who is in a position of power or control over you. You may feel trapped and see no escape. Please believe that your Heavenly Father does not want you to be held captive by unrighteous influence, by threats of reprisal, or by fear of repercussion to the family member or another who abuses you. Trust that the Lord will lead you to a solution. Ask in faith, nothing doubting.[1]

I solemnly testify that when another's acts of violence, perversion, or incest occur, against your will, you are not responsible and you must not feel guilty. You may be left scarred by abuse, but those scars need not be permanent. In the eternal plan, in the Lord's timetable, those injuries can be made right as you do your part. Here is what you can do now.

If you are now or have in the past been abused, seek help now. Perhaps you distrust others and feel that there is no reliable help anywhere. Begin with your Eternal Father and His Beloved Son, your Savior. Strive to comprehend Their commandments and follow them. They will lead you to others who will strengthen and encourage you. There is available to you a priesthood leader, normally a bishop, at times a member of the stake presidency. They can build a bridge to greater understanding and healing. Joseph Smith taught: "A man can do nothing for himself unless God direct him in the right way; and the Priesthood is for that purpose."[2]

Talk to your bishop in confidence. His calling allows him to act as an instrument of the Lord in your behalf. He can provide a doctrinal foundation to guide you to recovery. An understanding and application of eternal law will provide the healing you require. He has the right to be inspired of the Lord in your behalf. He can use the priesthood to bless you.

Your bishop can help you identify trustworthy friends to support you. He will help you regain self-confidence and self-esteem to begin the process of renewal. When abuse is extreme, he can help you identify appropriate protection and professional treatment consistent with the teachings of the Savior.

These are some of the principles of healing you will come to understand more fully:

Recognize that you are a beloved child of your Heavenly Father. He loves you perfectly and can help you as no earthly parent, spouse, or devoted friend can. His Son gave His life so that by faith in Him and obedience to His teachings you can be made whole. He is the consummate healer.

Gain trust in the love and compassion of your elder brother, Jesus Christ, by pondering the scriptures. As with the Nephites, He tells you, "I have compassion upon you; my bowels are filled with mercy. . . . I see that your faith is sufficient that I should heal you."[3]

Healing best begins with your sincere prayer asking your Father in Heaven for help. That use of your agency allows divine intervention. When you permit it, the love of the Savior will soften your heart and break the cycle of abuse that could transform a victim into an aggressor. Adversity, even when caused willfully by others' unrestrained appetite, can be a source of growth when viewed from the perspective of eternal principle.[4]

The victim must do all in his or her power to stop the abuse. Most often, the victim is completely innocent because of being disabled by fear or the power or authority of the offender. Yet no matter what the circumstance is, the healing power of the Atonement of Jesus Christ can provide a complete cure.[5] Forgiveness can be obtained for all involved in abuse when the corresponding laws of

God are obeyed.[6] Then comes a restoration of self-respect, self-worth, and a renewal of life.

As a victim, do not waste effort in revenge or retribution against your aggressor. Focus on your responsibility to do what is in your power to correct. Leave the handling of the offender to civil and appropriate priesthood leaders. Whatever they do, eventually the guilty will face the Perfect Judge. Ultimately the unrepentant abuser will be punished by a just God. The purveyors of filth and harmful substances who knowingly incite others to acts of violence and depravation and those who promote a climate of permissiveness and corruption will assuredly be sentenced by God if not adequately by man. Predators who victimize the innocent and justify their own corrupted life by enticing others to adopt their depraved ways will be held accountable. Of such the Master warned:

> But whoso shall offend one of these little ones which believe in me, it were better for him that a millstone were hanged about his neck, and that he were drowned in the depth of the sea.[7]

Understand that healing can take considerable time. Recovery generally comes in steps. It is accelerated when gratitude is expressed to the Lord for every degree of improvement you feel.

During prolonged recovery from massive surgery, a patient anticipates complete healing with patience, trusting in others' care. He does not always understand the importance of the treatment prescribed, but his obedience speeds recovery. So it is with your struggling to heal the scars of abuse. Forgiveness, for example, can be hard to understand and even more difficult to give. Begin by withholding judgment. You don't know what abusers may have suffered as victims themselves when innocent. The way to repentance must be kept open for them. Leave the handling of aggressors to your bishop or stake president. They will engage civil authorities when warranted.

As you experience an easing of your own pain, full forgiveness will come more easily.

You cannot erase what has been done, but you can forgive, and healing will surely come when sought properly.[8] Forgiveness heals terrible, tragic wounds, for it allows the love of God to purge your heart and mind of the poison of hate. It cleanses your consciousness of the desire for revenge. It makes place for the purifying, healing, restoring love of the Lord.

The Master counseled, "Love your enemies, bless them that curse you, do good to them that hate you, and pray for them who despitefully use you and persecute you."[9]

Bitterness and hatred are harmful. They produce much that is destructive. They postpone the relief and healing you yearn for. Through rationalization and self-pity, they can transform a victim into an abuser. Let God be the judge—you cannot do it as well as He can.

To be counseled to just forget abuse is not helpful. You need to understand the principles that will bring healing. I repeat, most often that comes through an understanding priesthood leader who has inspiration and the power of the priesthood to bless you.

I caution you not to participate in two improper therapeutic practices that may cause you more harm than good. They are:

• Excessive probing into every minute detail of your past experiences, particularly when this involves explicit, penetrating dialogue in group discussion.

• Blaming the abuser for every difficulty in your life.

Recognize that some discovery is vital to the healing process. However, the almost morbid probing into details of past acts, long buried and mercifully forgotten, can be shattering. There is no need to pick at healing wounds to open them and cause them to fester.

The Lord and His teachings can help you without destroying self-respect.

Stated more simply, if someone extensively soiled your carpet, would you invite the neighbors to determine each ingredient that contributed to the ugly stain? Of course not. With the help of an expert, you would privately restore its cleanliness.

Likewise, the repair of damage inflicted by abuse should be done privately, confidentially, with a trusted priesthood leader and, where needed, the qualified professional he recommends. There must be sufficient discussion of the general nature of abuse to allow you to be given appropriate counsel and to prevent the aggressor from committing more violence. Then, with the help of the Lord, bury the past.

There is another danger. Detailed leading questions that probe your past may unwittingly trigger thoughts that are more imagination or fantasy than reality. They could lead to condemnation of another for acts that were not committed. While likely few in number, I know of cases where such therapy has caused great injustice to the innocent from unwittingly stimulated accusations that were later proven false. Memory, particularly adult memory of childhood experiences, is fallible. Remember, false accusation is also a sin.

I humbly testify that what I have told you is true. It is based upon eternal principles I have seen the Lord use to give a fulness of life to those scarred by wicked abuse.

If you feel there is only a thin thread of hope, believe me, it is not a thread. It can be the unbreakable connecting link to the Lord that puts a life preserver around you. He will heal you as you cease to fear and place your trust in Him by striving to live His teachings.

Please, don't suffer more. Ask now for the Lord to help you.[10] Decide now to talk to your bishop. Don't view all that you experience in life through lenses darkened by the scars of abuse. There is so much in life that is beautiful. Open the windows of your heart and let the love of the Savior in. And should ugly thoughts of past abuse come back, push them out by remembering His love and His healing power. Your depression will be converted to peace and assurance. You will close an ugly chapter and open volumes of happiness.

May the following true experience give you the courage to try and the means to have success. It demonstrates how healing can be complete.

Some time ago I met an exceptional young woman as an outstanding missionary in a distant land. Later, when we met again, she had married a most impressive returned missionary. They were deeply in love, yet challenged. The memory of extensive child abuse by her own father had returned and severely complicated the sacred, private relationship of husband and wife. She and her husband responded to an invitation to discuss the matter. We reviewed pertinent scriptures and principles and clarified that an evil spirit has no power over a righteous person. Yet that spirit can enter into the mind and heart of another human. Through temptation that individual can, through force, commit acts that are contrary to the will of another. Those experiences temporarily overpower one of our Father in Heaven's greatest gifts to His children—moral agency. That means there must be a way to heal completely the consequences of totally unjust and unwarranted acts such as sexual abuse.

Together we reviewed how one of the precious fruits of the Savior's infinite Atonement was to rectify the consequences of those things that are unmerited and unjust. They accepted assignments to read more of the Master's Atonement from suggested resources. I offered that when she was confident that through her faith and understanding the Lord could heal the consequences of her early tragedy, she should return and I would give her a blessing. They completed these requests and the day came when they returned for the blessing. As I saw her devoted, loving, righteous husband by her side I felt, "This isn't right. He should pronounce the words of the blessing, not me." I said, "I'll keep my word for a blessing; but who do you want to be the voice, your husband or me?" With evidence of profound love she turned to her husband and nodded to him. He pronounced a marvelous, extensive blessing, and as they left I felt that the residue of heavy burdens she had carried so long for the unrighteous acts of her father were left behind. She was free of the consequences.

Some time later she called for another appointment. I thought, "How can it be? I know she has been healed. Why does she need to come again?" Nevertheless, an appointment was made. She came with an older couple. As we sat around the table, I could sense she loved the two very deeply. With a lovely smile, she said, "Elder Scott, this is my father. I love him. He's concerned about some things that happened in my early childhood. Could you help him like you helped me?" That is confirming evidence of the Savior's capacity to completely heal the consequences of unjust acts where there is sufficient faith, understanding of the Savior's Atonement, and the required obedience.

PART 5

Peace, Happiness, and Joy through Developing Righteous Character

CHAPTER 20

THE SUSTAINING POWER OF FAITH AND CHARACTER

D O YOU FEEL A need of assurance in the turbulent times in which we live? Do you feel a need for a stabilizing influence in your life? As we have reviewed, a fundamental purpose of earth life is personal growth and attainment. Consequently there must be times of trial and quandary to provide opportunity for that development. What child could ever grow to be self-supporting in maturity if all the critical decisions were made by parents? So it is with us as we seek to grow to spiritual maturity. Our Heavenly Father's plan of happiness is conceived so that we will have challenges, even difficulties, where decisions of great importance must be made so that we can grow, develop, and succeed in this mortal probation.[1] Gratefully, in His perfect love He has provided a way for you to resolve those challenges while growing in strength and capacity. I speak of the sustaining power of faith and character in times of uncertainty and testing.

God has given us the capacity to exercise faith that we may find peace, joy, and purpose in life. Strong character enhances your capacity to exercise faith. Yet to employ its power, faith must be founded on something secure. There is no more solid foundation than faith in the love Heavenly Father has for you, faith in His plan of happiness, and faith in the capacity and willingness of Jesus Christ to help you succeed in this life and to return triumphant to live in the celestial kingdom.

For many, faith is not adequately understood and consequently is not used to full advantage. Some feel that religion and the guidance one can receive through robust faith have no rational basis. However, faith is not illusion or magic, but a power rooted in eternal principles. Are you one that has tried to exercise faith and have felt little benefit? If so, you likely have not understood and followed the principles upon which faith is founded. An example will illustrate what I mean.

Years ago I participated in the measurement of the nuclear characteristics of different materials. The process used an experimental nuclear reactor designed so that high energy particles streamed from a hole that penetrated to the center of the nuclear reactor. These particles were directed into experimental chambers where measurements were made. The high energy particles could not be seen, but they had to be carefully controlled to avoid harm to others. One day a janitor entered while we were experimenting. In a spirit of disgust he said, "You are all liars, pretending that you are doing something important, but you can't fool me. I know that if you can't see, hear, taste, smell, or touch it, it doesn't exist."

That attitude ruled out the possibility of his learning that there is much of worth that can't be identified by the five senses. Had that man been willing to open his mind to understand how the presence of nuclear particles is detected, he would have confirmed their existence. In like manner, never doubt the reality of faith. Exercise faith and you will confirm its power. You will gather the fruits of faith as you follow the principles God has established for its use.

Some of those principles are:

Trust in God and in His willingness to provide help when needed, no matter how challenging the circumstance.

Obey His commandments and live to demonstrate that He can trust you.

Be sensitive to the quiet prompting of the Spirit. Act courageously on that prompting.

Be patient and understanding when God lets you struggle to grow and when answers come a piece at a time over an extended period.

Motivating faith is centered in trust in the Lord and in His willingness to answer your needs. For "the Lord . . . doth bless and prosper those who put their trust in him."[2] The consistent, willing exercise of faith increases your confidence and ability to employ the power of faith.

You can learn to use faith more effectively by applying this principle taught by Moroni: "Faith is things which are hoped for and not seen; wherefore, dispute not because ye see not, for *ye receive no witness until after the trial of your faith*."[3] Thus, every time you "*try your faith*," that is, act in worthiness on an impression born of the Spirit, you will receive the confirming witness that is of the Lord. Those feelings will fortify your faith. As you repeat that pattern your faith will become stronger. The Lord knows your needs. When you ask with honesty and real intent, He will prompt you to do that which will increase your ability to act in faith. With consistent practice faith will become a vibrant, powerful, uplifting, inspiring force in your life. As you walk from the boundary of your understanding into the twilight of uncertainty, exercising faith, you will be led to find solutions you would not obtain otherwise. I have repeatedly confirmed that to be a true principle.

Even when you exercise your strongest faith, God will not always reward you immediately according to your desires. Rather He will respond with what in His eternal plan is best for you. Indeed, were you to know His entire plan, you would not ask for that which is contrary to that plan even though your feelings might tempt you to do so. Sincere faith gives understanding and strength to accept the will of your Heavenly Father when it differs from your own. You can accept His will with peace and assurance, confident that His infinite wisdom surpasses your own ability to comprehend fully His plan as it unfolds a piece at a time.

Exercising faith is not like just pushing a button and getting an answer. The Lord declared: "As many as I love, I rebuke and chasten: be zealous therefore, and repent."[4] Brigham Young observed, "God never bestows upon His people, or upon an individual, superior blessings without a severe trial to prove them."[5] Personally, for some vital decisions I have experienced the grueling, anguishing struggle that precedes a confirming answer. Yet those trying experiences have been edifying. It is comforting to know that God will never try you more than you can manage with His help.[6]

God uses your faith to mold your character. Character is the manifestation of what you are becoming. Strong moral character results from consistent correct choices in the trials and testing of life. Your faith can guide you to those correct choices. Clearly, it is what you do and what you think about that determines what you are and what you will become. Therefore, the choices you make need to be inspired by the Lord. Others can encourage you to make the right decisions, but those choices must not be prescribed by them. You need to ponder, pray, and exercise faith and willingly make choices consistent with the teachings of the Master. Such choices are made with trust in things that you believe. They will be confirmed when acted upon.[7] Only enough guidance is given to lead you aright and not to weaken your growing character. That guidance will solidify your trust in Heavenly Father and the Savior.

The worthy character of the prophets of God is like a fabric woven from countless threads of correct choices, some small, some great, some difficult to make, others less challenging. You can grow your worthy character in the same way. Your exercise of faith in the defining moments of life is the substance of great character. Your faith will forge a strength of character that will be available to you in times of urgent need. Such character is not developed in moments of great challenge or temptation. That is when it is used. Character is cultivated patiently from attention to principle and doctrine, and by obedience to truth. In James we read: "The trying of your faith worketh patience. But let patience have her perfect work, that ye may be perfect and entire, wanting nothing."[8]

The bedrock of character is integrity. Worthy character will strengthen your capacity to obediently respond to the direction of the Spirit. Righteous character is what you are becoming. It is more important than what you own, what you have learned, or what goals you have accomplished. It allows you to be trusted. Righteous character provides the foundation of spiritual strength. It enables you in times of trial and testing to make difficult, extremely important decisions correctly even when they seem overpowering. I testify that neither Satan nor any other power can weaken or destroy your growing character. Only you can do that through disobedience.

Understand and apply this vital principle to your life: *Your exercise of faith builds character. Fortified character expands your capacity to exercise greater faith. Thus, your confidence in conquering the trials of life is enhanced. And the strengthening cycle continues. The more your character is fortified, the more enabled you are to exercise the power of faith for yet stronger character.*

The example of Nephi, the son of Helaman, shows how righteous character provides a conduit for blessings. While returning home from a harrowing experience in which he displayed true character, a voice came to him. It signaled the important characteristics of his life that you can emulate: serving consistently, unwearyingly declaring the word, not fearing, seeking the will of the Lord, and obeying the commandments.[9] Because he had proved himself so consistently, God knew the goodness of his character and trusted him.

Therefore He gave him extraordinary power, confident that he would use it only as guided by the Spirit.

> Because thou hast done this with such unwearyingness, behold, I will bless thee forever; and I will make thee mighty in word and in deed, in faith and in works; yea, even that all things shall be done unto thee according to thy word, for thou shalt not ask that which is contrary to my will.[10]

The declaration "thou shalt not ask that which is contrary to my will" was not a commandment, rather a witness of Nephi's exceptional character.

No matter what occurs, no matter how topsy-turvy the world becomes, you can always have the sustaining power of faith. That will never change. The perfect love of your Father in Heaven will never change. He tabernacled your eternal intelligence with a spirit body and gave you the opportunity of coming to earth to grow through trials and testing and the opportunity to choose for yourself whether to follow His plan or not. His gospel plan gives life meaning and can assure your peace and happiness. His plan is not only for you to prove yourself here on the earth but also that you may receive the growth that comes from correct decisions prompted by faith, enabled by your obedience.

Why worry about future calamities or uncertainties over which you have no control? Your righteous life magnifies the probability that you will never have to suffer them. When challenges and testing do come, your faith will lead you to solutions. Your peace of mind, your assurance of answers to vexing problems, your ultimate joy depend upon your trust in Heavenly Father and His Son, Jesus Christ. Right will ultimately prevail. It will yield blessings now as you in faith obey the commandments of God. Remember that an unfailing, continual, ever-present source of peace and comfort is available to you. It is the certainty that your Father in Heaven loves you no matter what your circumstance, no matter what winds of trial, turmoil, and tribulation whirl about you. That certainty will never change. Your ability to access that support depends on the strength of your faith in Him and your conviction of His certain willingness to bless you.

Exercise strong faith that God will sustain and guide you through the Holy Spirit in an increasingly challenging world. I testify that application of the principles you have reviewed in this chapter will strengthen your character and will help you avail yourself of the sustaining power of faith in times of uncertainty and testing.

Among your friends and loved ones there are likely those who are confused and are seeking solutions to life's perplexing problems. Will you share your testimony of truth and of the power of faith with them? Will you help them understand how faith in God and His teachings, restored in their fulness in The Church of Jesus Christ of Latter-day Saints, can bless their lives now, in these turbulent times? Do it. The Lord will help you. Your faith will guide you and sustain you.

CHAPTER 21

FORTIFY YOUR RESOLVE
TO DO BETTER

HAVE YOU DISCOVERED that the most difficult part about changing is making an unwavering decision to do it? Be assured that once that beginning is securely made, you will find the rest of the path becomes easier than you imagined. Some days are more difficult than others, but the movement toward permanent change for good becomes easier. Through your use of agency, you qualify for the Lord's help, and He will magnify your efforts.[1] This chapter gives suggestions about how to accomplish significant changes in life. If you do not need this counsel, perhaps it could help another you know who is in substantial difficulty.

Once you've decided to make changes in your life, is it difficult to get the required motivation to accomplish your goals? Proper motivation can facilitate the accomplishment of seemingly impossible goals, as this experience illustrates. One dark, moonless night a young boy realized he was very late in returning home. He knew he would soon be in trouble with his parents, so he decided to take a shortcut through the cemetery, even though he was deathly afraid of that place. As he ran homeward, he unwittingly fell into a large hole that had been dug for a burial the next day. The opening was so deep and the vertical sides so carefully dug that there was no place for a foothold. His determined struggling to free himself was fruitless. Reluctantly, he decided he would have to spend the night there until he could call for help the next morning. He was unaware that a second boy with a similar problem had also begun to run through the cemetery. As luck would have it, he fell into the same hole. The first boy sat quietly, unseen in a corner, watching the second struggle without success. Finally the first lad said in a soft voice, "You'll never get out of here." But powerfully motivated, he did. Witness the power of the right motivation!

To reach a goal you have never before attained, you must do things you have never before done. Don't confront your problem armed only with your own experience, understanding, and strength. Count on strength from the infinite power of the Lord by being consistently obedient to His teachings.[2] He will help you find the courage to obtain help from others when needed.

Previously, in chapters 12 and 13 we discussed the specific steps that will bring you refreshing relief. They define the process of repentance and the vital roles of the Redeemer, our Savior, and of a compassionate judge in Israel.

As you pray for help and decide to find it, the Lord will often place in your path priesthood leaders who will counsel and friends who will give support if you'll let them. But remember, they can help only by your following the rules that the Savior has set out for the journey. Any lasting improvement must come from your own determination to change.

Permanent, worthwhile change is attainable, but often not without great effort and the honest application of truth. Worthy accomplishment is founded in integrity. Righteousness is fundamental to happiness and desirable attainment. Righteousness is anchored in a pure heart and mind. Indeed, it protects one from the contamination of the filth of the world. Righteous love is a superb motivation for constructive change. The examples of our Father in Heaven and the Savior, together with Their teachings, are the perfect sources of motivation and direction for life.

May this counsel of the Master benefit you as much as it has me:

> Look unto me in every thought; doubt not, fear not. Behold the wounds which pierced my side, and also the prints of the nails in my hands and feet; be faithful, keep my commandments, and ye shall inherit the kingdom of heaven.[3]

> For behold, it is not meet that I should command in all things; for he that is compelled in all things, the same is a slothful and not a wise servant; wherefore he receiveth no reward. Verily I say, men should be anxiously engaged in a good cause, and do many things of their own free will, and bring to pass much righteousness; for the power is in them, wherein they are agents unto themselves. And inasmuch as men do good they shall in nowise lose their reward.[4]

I know He fulfills that promise.

This admonition of Alma to his son Helaman will provide you much help.

> Counsel with the Lord in all thy doings, and he will direct thee for good; yea, when thou liest down at night lie down unto the Lord, that he may watch over you in your sleep; and when thou risest in the morning let thy heart be full of thanks unto God; and if ye do these things, ye shall be lifted up at the last day.[5]

As you discipline yourself through careful obedience to the commandments of the Lord, you will qualify to receive inspiration and direction in your life. You will grow in capacity, devotion, understanding, compassion, and meaningful service. Your worthy life will allow you to interpret and apply the inspiration that will come through the Holy Ghost. Your love of Heavenly Father and His Son will increase. It will be a love of reverence, awe, and gratitude of a child to the Two Greatest of all. It will become a love of total submission to Their will. It will result from a pure desire and resolute determination to obey Them always.

This world is in trouble. The nation in which I live is in difficulty. If you live elsewhere, your nation is likely struggling also. There is a continual crumbling of obedience to principle, the bedrock of civilization and an absolutely essential ingredient to happiness. Oh, there can be transitory pleasure from power, influence, or material wealth. But true, lasting happiness, the kind that can be felt in the early hours of the morning when you are honest with yourself, can be obtained only by obedience to the teachings of God as you are now doing. Honesty, integrity, chastity, virtue, maturity (that is, willingness to forego for the moment something seemingly desirable, for a greater future good) are essential to true success in life. Develop the capacity, when circumstance demands, to lay everything on the altar to defend a principle. There are so few with the strength to do that. The world needs more like you who are willing to place principle above personal gain, businessmen who are honest and morally clean, attorneys who defend justice, government officials who strive to preserve honor and integrity because it is right. You can be that shining light, that righteous influence, the leaven in the loaf to increase the moral fiber of your nation. Your prayers and humble study of the teachings of the Master, with the twenty-four hour application of those teachings every day of the week, will provide required strength in your life. They will contribute to the stability the world needs.

There is great satisfaction in life that comes as you defend that part of the line the Lord has given you to preserve. Show those in the world around you a better way. Some things are wrong because God decreed that they are wrong. Truth is not determined by what men think, no matter how influential they may be. It was determined by Almighty God before the creation of this earth and will exist forever. We serve. We make our contribution. We pass on. Let it never be said of you what was heard at the passing of an individual with great potential and resources: "He left no legacy."

Will you prayerfully consider what we have discussed together? If there is a need to repent of some improper action, do it. Likewise if there is need to repent from failure to act, correct that. There are many who can be persuaded to follow your righteous example. Because you have been enlightened, you owe to those who follow the best example you are capable of giving. Not only will they be blessed, but your life will be enriched as well. I have come to know of the great influence for good that flows from individual acts born of conscience and principle founded in truth. Resolve that each moment of your life will reflect your determination to be a humble example of righteousness, integrity, and conviction. Keep the Sabbath day holy. Honor and live temple covenants as you receive them. Drink deeply from the fountain of the revealed word of God. Hold fast to His word. You are succeeding in the purpose for which you came to earth.

Establish specific objectives and move steadily toward them. A rudder can't control a drifting vessel; the vessel must be underway. Similarly, you need to be moving forward to keep control of your life. Recognize that you must truly decide to change for the right reasons. If you have transgressed, you must feel sorrow for sin, not just be sorry you were discovered. Your resolve must be genuine, not just a simulated desire to improve. Don't let anything discourage you. Your initial efforts will be the most difficult. In most cases loved ones, Church leaders, and members will readily respond to your needs. Should a loved one seem to ignore you, it is likely because they don't know what to do. Their past attempts to help may have been rejected; you likely have acted as though you did not welcome assistance. Seek them out with trust. Ask them for support in your sincere efforts to improve. Give them reason to know that this time is different because you are determined to change and want to do it the Lord's way.

After you have decided to change, should you then discover that there is a way to cheat on your promise without anyone knowing, don't do it. That will destroy your self-confidence and will weaken others' trust in you, for in time they will know. It will discourage them from helping you. There is simply nothing good about cheating yourself by being disobedient to trust. Absent would be the positive elements of reinforcement that come from obedience. Moreover, you would lose what you most need, the strength and inspiration of God.

Few things will undermine your commitment to change more than lying to yourself. Demosthenes proclaimed: "Nothing is easier than self-deceit. For what each man wishes, that he also believes to be true."[6]

Satan would have you rationalize. He will attempt to have you believe that something you know to be wrong can be forced into a pattern that appears to be a valid exception to the rules. He will tempt you to undermine your resolve to change with the thought, "Just one more time," or "You need relief from the strain. Just once again—no one will know." Or perhaps he will prompt you to think, "Others will get upset when I reveal the mistake I have made. They will give me another lecture. But if I just suffer through all that, they will feel sorry for me and get me out of the problem again."

Perhaps you have said to one sincerely trying to help you overcome an ingrained habit, "You just don't understand. You don't know how hard it is to stop. I don't think I can do it." Anyone who trusts his Creator and obeys His commandments can, in time, overcome temptation.

Rationalization (that is, twisting something wrong so that it appears acceptable) will lead you into fruitless blind alleys. It will drain spiritual power. It will barricade your path to happiness because it has the power to distort your understanding of truth. Overcome rationalization with positive decisions based upon your prayers and pondering, your study of the scriptures, and the inspired feelings that will come to you. In time, such decisions will form character, resistant to the eroding influences you are striving to overcome. The counsel of trusted friends can be a great source of encouragement.

President David O. McKay taught how to be strengthened by resisting temptation: "Your weakest point will be the point at which Satan tries to tempt you, and will try to win you, and if you have made it weak yourself before you have undertaken to serve the Lord, he will add to that weakness. Resist him and you will gain in strength. He will tempt you in another point. Resist him and he becomes weaker and you become stronger, until you can say, no matter what your surroundings may be, 'Get thee behind me, Satan: for it is written, Thou shalt worship the Lord thy God, and him only shalt thou serve.' (Luke 4:8.)"[7]

Don't judge your capacities, your opportunities, your power to accomplish by what you see, hear, feel, and experience while you are in trouble. Your compliance with correct principles and sound counsel will give you unexpected strength, insight, and ability to accomplish your goals. At first you will likely not recognize that you possess such capacities. As you continue in faith, those capacities will increase. The implementation of your resolve to be better will lift your life to a higher level, your performance will improve, and your ability to sustain progress will be powerfully enhanced. A key to your success in renewing your life is resolute willpower. You must direct your life so that proper fundamentals based on eternal principles are followed in preference to appetite, convenience, and the path of least resistance. Be diligent in fulfilling decisions you have been prompted to make, and you will be strengthened and empowered to accomplish the necessary changes in your life. Counsel with the Lord in prayer and follow the feelings you receive, as well as the proper guidance of those who love you. You will confirm that the needed capacity lies within you. I know it does.

Your efforts to distill truth from reading and pondering the scriptures, from analyzing and striving to understand the inspired messages of the prophets, will provide you with a source of power in your life. As you apply truth, it will protect you from evil influences and lay a foundation for peace, happiness, security, and purpose in your life. Truth will help you stay on the right path. Initially the power of such truth must be accepted on faith. The confirming witness of the value of truth comes as you apply it in your life and as you express gratitude for the growth, maturity, and blessings its use provides. That confirmation will strengthen your capacity to discipline your life to avoid those things you know to be unproductive and harmful. Such a witness provides encouragement and the confidence to center your life in the truth of the teachings of the Savior and the plan of happiness of the Father.

How could the Lord state it more clearly than this: "I, the Lord, am bound when ye do what I say; but when ye do not what I say, ye have no promise."[8]

Your individual experience in life colors your understanding of truth. This fact is confirmed in Proverbs: "For as [a man] thinketh in his heart, so is he."[9] The more obedient you are to eternal laws and principles, the more clear will be the path to happiness. The less obedient you are, the more distorted it becomes. Tragically, continued serious violation of commandments creates an environment that becomes real to the transgressor, even to the point where he or she can conclude that lasting satisfaction in life can never be attained. Our enemy, Satan, strives to reinforce that conclusion. The truth is that even the most severe cases of addiction, violations of the law of chastity, abuse, or other serious impediments in life can be healed by the Savior through His Atonement and the plan of happiness of our Father in Heaven.

The first steps can begin in a variety of ways—with caring parents or an understanding companion, a spiritually guided bishop or stake president, or a professional counselor. However, the full healing will occur through the Master. That healing is made possible through His Atonement. You may not fully understand this concept now, but trust it. It is intended to give hope and to motivate you to never vary from your decision to make worthy change permanent. Please remember that the only secure way to true peace and happiness is the way of the Lord. Those blessings will result from consistent obedience to His counsel.

An analogy will help you understand what is happening to you. It came as I watched an impressive composer conduct an orchestra of gifted musicians. That experience has helped me understand more clearly our Father's plan of happiness. The conductor had created the musical score being played. He understood better than anyone else what he desired to be accomplished through the music. He had crafted a role for each individual instrument. He was anxious to communicate to the musicians that vision so that by working in harmony together, they could make reality what he had defined in a complex musical score.

Each instrumentalist or percussionist had a part to play. They were experienced musicians and had polished innate talents through long, tedious hours of practice. They had studied their specific parts privately and attempted to master them. But it was not until they began to perform together, under the direction of an inspired leader, that the full beauty and grandeur of their combined efforts could be realized.

The result was overwhelmingly moving and edifying. Each individual carefully followed the conductor, striving to the utmost of his or her capability to play the part accurately, with feeling, emotion, and precision. They were not forced to perform. It was done willingly. While individual performances were outstanding, it was the combined effort of all that created the sublime result. Can you imagine how one discordant note could mar or destroy the power of their combined efforts? How one individual intentionally modifying the musical score could wreak havoc and destroy the beauty of the others' performances?

I understood with greater clarity how our Father in Heaven and His Beloved Son have schooled us in the premortal life, preparing us for this mortal experience so we might make the most of it. As we now seek it, we can receive individual guidance from the Lord, through the Spirit, to perfect our own talents and abilities. As we learn to work together and yield our will to the divine conductor, we become fitted for the unique contribution that we are expected to make in fulfilling His personal plan for us.

Certainly those who work diligently to learn truth and to live it willingly will make the greatest progress here. Just as it would be a demoralizing experience for an untrained individual to attempt to play in an orchestra of skilled musicians, so it would be painful punishment to attempt to live in a celestial realm for which you are not prepared. Your personal understanding of truth, your willing obedience to it, and the resulting growth, development, and perfection attained in mortal life will determine your happiness here and lay the foundation for what your contribution will be in eternity.

A musician can perfect his or her skill with practice and determined effort to succeed—privately, correcting mistakes as they come. That effort is enhanced by the influence of a caring teacher who is anxious to share counsel for improvement and to identify specific areas where performance can be bettered. In a like manner the Lord, through the Holy Spirit, can perform those functions in your life so that this mortal experience may yield the development, perfection, and understanding that you should gain in your personal plan of happiness. By qualifying here you can live and serve in the celestial kingdom.

As you make progress in your efforts to improve, you will experience feelings that you haven't had for a long time—feelings of concern for others, feelings of unselfish love, feelings of a desire to be near loved ones, and feelings of self-respect and confidence. These stirrings are evidence of progress, like increasing light at the end of a tunnel.

If you are ever tempted to experiment with the alluring offerings of Lucifer, first calmly analyze the inevitable consequences of such choices. Pray for help that you can overcome the temptation. Resist it and your life will not be shattered. You cannot ever sample those things that are forbidden of God as destructive of happiness and corrosive to spiritual guidance without tragic results.

I wish I could replace any doubt you may have with my certainty. But I can't just give it to you. I *can* provide the invitation to make unwavering your decision to repent and change your life. I promise you that the Master will help you. As you exercise faith, He will be there in every time of need. You will feel that support through the Holy Ghost. The Savior gave His life so you can overcome the mistakes you may have made and be able to renew your life. I promise you that in time you will feel His love, strength, and support. Trust Him completely. He is not going to make any mistakes. He knows what He is doing. Please do not allow your determination to change to be weakened through temptation. Be obedient to His teachings and He will bless you. I know that as you seek His help and live for it, He will strengthen you.

The next chapter gives further suggestions to keep your resolve to make positive changes in your life.

CHAPTER 22

THE POWER TO OVERCOME

THIS CHAPTER IS ADDRESSED to you who want to do right—who have had those stirrings in your heart to live worthily no matter what others may say—and to you who want to have such feelings. I have a strong desire to share truths which, if understood and lived, can fundamentally change your life if needed. I ask you to help me. As you read, will you prayerfully consider these things in your mind and your heart, so that my prayer that you will be helped can be answered?

For a piece of wood to catch fire, it must first be heated to a temperature at which it ignites; then it can burn by itself. The initial heating requires energy from outside. When the wood is ignited and the conditions are right, it becomes self-sustaining and gives beneficial light and heat. In the same way, the early years of life are often spent in absorbing help from parents and others as one prepares to be more self-sufficient. I want to help you catch fire spiritually, that you may enjoy the marvelous experience of radiating strength to others while you continue to grow and develop yourself.

There is a more intense fire than that of burning wood. It is produced from a mixture of aluminum powder and metal oxide. By itself, this mixture is cold and lifeless, but when it is heated to the ignition temperature, it becomes a self-sustaining source of brilliant light and intense heat. Once it ignites it cannot be put out by ordinary means. It will burn under water or in other environments that extinguish an ordinary flame. When it burns, it does not depend on its surroundings for support. It is self-sustaining. The spiritual flame in some is easily quenched by the world around them. Yet others live so as to be strengthened and nurtured by the Lord. They not only overcome the temptations of the world, but their unquenchable spirit enriches the lives of others around them. They burn brightly in all circumstances. You can be that way if you are not already.

Two missionaries who were aflame spiritually had spent an active day establishing a branch of the Church in the remote village of Chacopampa, Bolivia. The tiny village had no electricity, no running water, no streets, and not even rustic sanitary facilities. The reputation of trusted, devoted missionaries in the adjacent village of Quiriza had preceded them. They had been in this humble place but a few days.

At 5:30 that morning, they had taught a family before the husband left for the fields. Later they had struggled to plaster their adobe walls to keep out blood-sucking insects. During the week they had laid a small cement floor and had hung a five-gallon can with a shower head to keep clean. They had begun a sanitation facility and put new gravel and sand in their water filter. For part of the day they had worked beside men in the fields to later teach them. They were exhausted and ready for welcome rest.

Then they heard an anxious knock at their crude wooden door. A small girl was crying. She had been running and was gasping for air. They struggled to piece together her message, delivered amid sobs in a torrent of words. Her father had suffered a severe head injury while riding his donkey in the darkness. She knew he would die unless the elders saved his life. Men of the village were at that moment carrying him to the missionaries. She pleaded for her father's life, then ran to help him.

The seriousness of their desperate situation began to engulf these missionaries. They were in a village with no doctors or medical facilities. There were no telephones. The only means of communication was over a rough road up a riverbed, and they had no vehicle. The people of the valley trusted them. The missionaries were not trained in medicine but they were two elders with the priesthood of God. They did not know how to care for a serious head wound, but they knew Someone who did. They knelt in prayer and explained their problem to an understanding Father in Heaven. They pleaded for guidance, realizing that they could not save a life without His help. They felt impressed that the wound should be cleansed, closed with needle and thread, and the man given a blessing. One companion asked, "How will he stand the pain? How can we cleanse the wound and bless him while he is in so much suffering?" They knelt again and explained to their Father, "We have no medicine. We have no anesthetic. Please help us to know what to do. Please bless him, Father."

As they arose, friends arrived with the injured man. Even in the subdued candlelight, they could see he had been severely hurt. He was suffering greatly. As they began to cleanse the wound, an unusual thing occurred. He fell asleep. Carefully, anxiously, they finished the cleansing, closed the wound, and provided a makeshift bandage. When they laid their hands on his head to bless him, he awoke peacefully. Their prayer had been answered and the danger to his life resolved. He recovered completely. The trust of the people increased, and a branch of the Church was strengthened.

The missionaries were able to help in an emergency because they trusted in the power of the Lord. They knew how to pray with faith for help with a problem they could not resolve themselves. Because they were obedient to the Lord, He trusted them and answered their prayer. They had learned how to recognize the answer when it came as a quiet prompting of the Spirit. You have that same help available to you as you continue to live for it. For the Savior has taught, "Whatsoever ye shall ask the Father in my name, which is right, believing that ye shall receive, behold it shall be given unto you."[1]

Two young missionaries were walking down a dusty road. In their hands they carried the scriptures, and in each heart burned a desire to share truth. They saw on the ridge of a hill a group of horsemen laughing and pointing toward them. They sensed they were in severe danger. Each prayed for help as a huge man on a powerful horse galloped down the hill toward them. His menacing whip slashed the air and cracked threateningly. He thundered closer. The sneer on his face communicated his cruel intent to harm them. Suddenly, he reined in his horse, paused, whirled, and disappeared down the valley. These elders had prayed urgently in their minds and hearts for help. They were living worthily. The Lord therefore could protect them against the danger they were helpless to avoid. Your determination to live righteously will make it possible for you to be protected from the dangers that surround you. It will also provide great peace.

God can protect whom He wills to protect. If someone is hurt or killed, that does not necessarily mean that the person is living unworthily. What I have shared in the above examples is to illustrate that your obedience and your faith give you the greatest assurance of protection in times of need.

You may be facing overwhelming challenges. Sometimes they are so concentrated, so unrelenting, that you may feel they are beyond your capacity to control. Don't face the world alone. "Trust in the Lord with all thine heart; and lean not unto thine own understanding."[2] Trust is one of the principal foundation stones to a life of peace with happiness and joy.

In many ways, the world is like a jungle, with dangers that can harm or mutilate your body, enslave or destroy your mind, or decimate your morality. It was intended that life be a challenge, not so that you would fail, but that you might succeed through over-coming. Throughout life you face difficult but vitally important decisions. There surrounds you a potent array of temptations, destructive influences, and camouflaged dangers. I am persuaded that today, no one, no matter how gifted, strong, or intelligent, will avoid serious problems without seeking the help of the Lord. I repeat: Don't face the world alone. Trust in the Lord.

I repeat an admonition expressed in other chapters: if you or one you love has seriously sinned, it is essential to repent—now. It is not good to violate the commandments of the Lord. It is tragic to do nothing about it. Sin is like cancer in the body. It will never heal itself. It will become progressively worse unless cured through the medicine of repentance. Where there is a need you can be made completely whole, new, purified, and clean every whit through the miracle of repentance. Trust in the Lord. He knows what He is doing. He already knows of your problems. And He is waiting for you to ask for help.

Have you ever had the feeling you are walking alone down a dark tunnel that gets ever more depressing? That no one seems to care? That life gets more and more complicated and discouraging? You may have been following a path many others have trod. It often begins with self-pity, then develops into self-indulgence, and, if not checked, leads to gross selfishness. Unless overcome by serving others, selfishness leads to serious sin, with its depressing feelings and binding chains. It is the crowbar Satan uses to open a heart to temptation in order to destroy agency. He would bind mind and body through crippling habits and separate us from our Father in Heaven and His Son by cultivating selfishness.

If you have had such feelings of depression, turn around—literally, turn your life around. The other end of the tunnel is filled with light. No matter where you have been or what you have done, that light is always available to you. Satan will try to convince you that you have gone too far to be saved. That is a lie. Or he will try to persuade you that there is a shortcut to relief. There is none. It must be done the way God has decreed.

You will need some help to get started. The scriptures are a good place to begin. A father, mother, brother, sister, bishop, or friend will help. As you move nearer to the light through repentance, you will feel better about yourself and more confident in your future. You will rediscover how wonderful life really is. The Savior gave His life so you and I can correct mistakes, even the most serious ones. Our Father's plan is perfect. It always works for each one who follows the rules.

Getting through the hazards of life requires understanding, skill, experience, and self-assurance like that required of a basketball player to sink a difficult basket under pressure. In the game of life, that is called righteous character. When strengthened by obedience and worthy acts, correct decisions forge strong character that will bring victory in time of great need.

Righteous character is a foundation of spiritual strength that enables you to make difficult, extremely important decisions correctly when they seem overpowering. Righteous character is what you *are.* It allows you to be trusted. Be honest. Righteous character is based on integrity. Never lie to yourself. A lie can give temporary advantage, but it brings with it long-term difficulties. Make no premeditated plans to do wrong, no lies to gain advantage, no falsehood to cover mistakes. When you are completely honest with yourself and measure your acts against what you know is right, you will not be dishonest with anyone. Moreover, you will make sure the Lord can bless you when you need it. When you are tempted to break a commandment and hide it from others, don't do it. It will always hurt you. Satan will see to that. He'll make it known at the worst possible time because he wants to destroy you.

You may have observed how some of your friends try to live a double standard of life. They want to appear to their family and Church leaders as though they are doing the right things, but secretly they do otherwise. They may have moments of excitement they consider pleasure, but they can never be at peace or truly happy. They fight against themselves internally and run the risk of destroying mind and body. When you are alone with your friends, talk about doing good and being good. The feelings you will have, the promptings that will come to you, will powerfully motivate you for good. Those who do wrong and scheme to get away with it will never know such feelings. If you don't feel comfortable with the thought of discussing good with your friends, they are not your friends. Find better friends.

Each of us has a natural, powerful desire to be accepted, to be liked, to be somebody. Years ago, I learned something of the price we must pay for trust and worthy recognition. During a summer break, I found a job on an oyster boat in Long Island Sound. Eight of us lived together in an area not much larger than twice the size of the cab of a big semitrailer tractor. At first, I was considered a spy for the owner, then a kid who didn't have courage to live like a man. They were very hard on me. Finally, when they understood I would not abandon my principles, we became friends. Then privately, one on one, some asked for help.

You know what is right and wrong. Be the leader in doing right. At first, you may not be understood. You may not have the friends you want right away, but in time they will respect you, then admire you. Many will come privately to receive light from your spiritual flame. You can do it. I am confident that you can do it. When your life complies with the will of the Lord and is in harmony with His teachings, the Holy Ghost will be your companion in need. You will be able to be inspired by the Lord to know what to do. When needed, your efforts will be fortified with divine power. Like the missionaries we have discussed, you can be protected and strengthened to do what alone would be impossible.

The Lord needs you for His purposes. Live His commandments. Learn to follow the promptings of the Spirit. Keep your spiritual flame burning brightly. Live to have trust in the Lord. Live to be trusted and helped by Him.

As you have read this message, you may have been prompted by the Spirit regarding private things the Lord wants you to do something about. You may have been impressed to know what to do. Those feelings are the very most important thing you can gain from this chapter. They are a personal message from the Lord to you. Remember that message. Write it down. Follow it precisely, now, for your enduring happiness.

PART 6

ADDITIONAL POWERFUL SOURCES OF PEACE, HAPPINESS, AND JOY

CHAPTER 23

TO FIND PEACE AND
DIRECTION FROM THE
SCRIPTURES AND PROPHETS

IF YOU WERE TO undertake a difficult, demanding journey to a vitally important destination, you would undoubtedly carefully prepare. You would likely talk to individuals who had experience with the journey, overcome the challenges, and proven themselves capable of reaching the desired destination. You might search to find maps, to better understand the route and its unique conditions. You would try to become familiar with the blessings and opportunities that would result from successful completion of the journey.

In reality you *are* on a vitally important journey, fraught with challenges, yet replete with rich opportunities and wonderful blessings along the way. There are unexpected twists and turns in this journey of mortal life. Success in this endeavor is assured when you understand and follow the counsel of those who have been successful in this portion of our testing and growth.

The counsel of the Lord Jesus Christ is paramount to ponder and apply. No one is better prepared to give you advice, support, and inspiration as you proceed. Also the words, counsel, warnings, and explanations of His prophets will be essential to your success. Much of this counsel is contained in the scriptures recorded in the four standard works of the Church. The inspired direction of His prophets for the unique conditions of our day is also available to you in the current messages of the First Presidency and Quorum of the Twelve.[1]

THE ADMONITION AND COUNSEL OF JESUS CHRIST

A few representative examples of indispensably important guidance and admonition given by Jesus Christ for our benefit follow:

The Savior admonished:

> I now give unto you a commandment . . . to give diligent heed to the words of eternal life. For you shall live by every word that proceedeth forth from the mouth of God. For the word of the Lord is truth, and whatsoever is truth is light, and whatsoever is light is Spirit, even the Spirit of Jesus Christ. And the Spirit giveth light to every man that cometh into the world; and the Spirit enlighteneth every man through the world, that hearkeneth to the voice of the Spirit. And every one that hearkeneth to the voice of the Spirit cometh unto God, even the Father.[2]

> Therefore, whoso repenteth and cometh unto me as a little child, him will I receive, for of such is the kingdom of God. Behold, for such I have laid down my life, and have taken it up again; therefore repent, and come unto me ye ends of the earth, and be saved.[3]

Jesus Christ promised:

> I will pray the Father and he shall give you another Comforter, that he may abide with you for ever; even the Spirit of truth; whom the world cannot receive,

because it seeth him not, neither knoweth him: but ye know him; for he dwelleth with you, and shall be in you. I will not leave you comfortless: I will come to you. . . . These things have I spoken unto you, being yet present with you. But the Comforter, which is the Holy Ghost, whom the Father will send in my name, he shall teach you all things, and bring all things to your remembrance, whatsoever I have said unto you.[4]

And whatsoever thing persuadeth men to do good is of me; for good cometh of none save it be of me. I am the same that leadeth men to all good.[5]

The Savior consoled, knowing that each of us would face disturbing difficulties in life:

Peace I leave with you, my peace I give unto you: not as the world giveth, give I unto you. Let not your heart be troubled, neither let it be afraid.[6]

Draw near unto me and I will draw near unto you; seek me diligently and ye shall find me; ask and ye shall receive; knock, and it shall be opened unto you. Whatsoever ye ask the Father in my name it shall be given unto you, that is expedient for you.[7]

The Master gave assurance, to strengthen us when we become discouraged:

And if men come unto me I will show unto them their weakness. I give unto men weakness that they may be humble; and my grace is sufficient for all men that humble themselves before me; for if they humble themselves before me, and have faith in me, then will I make weak things become strong unto them.[8]

And if your eye be single to my glory, your whole bodies shall be filled with light, and there shall be no darkness in you; and that body which is filled with light comprehendeth all things. Therefore, sanctify yourselves that your minds become single to God, and the days will come that you shall see him; for he will unveil his face unto you, and it shall be in his own time, and in his own way, and according to his own will.[9]

The Redeemer taught us how to live in an ever more difficult world:

Ye are commanded in all things to ask of God, who giveth liberally; and that which the Spirit testifies unto you even so I would that ye should do in all holiness of heart, walking uprightly before me, considering the end of your salvation, doing all things with prayer and thanksgiving, that ye may not be seduced by evil spirits, or doctrines of devils, or the commandments of men.[10]

And now, verily, verily, I say unto thee, put your trust in that Spirit which leadeth to do good—yea, to do justly, to walk humbly, to judge righteously; and this is my Spirit. Verily, verily, I say unto you, I will impart unto you of my Spirit, which shall enlighten your mind, which shall fill your soul with joy; . . . by this shall you know, all things whatsoever you desire of me, which are pertaining unto things of righteousness, in faith believing in me that you shall receive.[11]

The Prince of Peace explained:

All things must come to pass in their time. Wherefore, be not weary in well-doing, for ye are laying the foundation of a great work. And out of small things proceedeth that which is great. Behold, the Lord requireth the heart and a willing mind; and the willing and obedient shall eat the good of the land of Zion in these last days.[12]

The Admonition and Counsel of His Prophets

Throughout mortal history the prophets of Jesus Christ have given precious, sensitive, inspired counsel to the inhabitants of the earth. A few examples follow:

Thy word is a lamp unto my feet, and a light unto my path.[13]

My son, despise not the chastening of the LORD; neither be weary of his correction: for whom the LORD loveth he correcteth; even as a father the son in whom he delighteth.[14]

Trust in the LORD with all thine heart; and lean not unto thine own understanding. In all thy ways acknowledge him, and he shall direct thy paths. Be not wise in thine own eyes: fear the LORD, and depart from evil.[5]

Paul wisely taught:

Be not overcome of evil, but overcome evil with good.[16]

All scripture is given by inspiration of God, and is profitable for doctrine, for reproof, for correction, for instruction in righteousness.[17]

Nephi showed love and concern for his people by citing scriptures.

And I did read many things unto them which were

written in the books of Moses; but that I might more fully persuade them to believe in the Lord their Redeemer I did read unto them that which was written by the prophet Isaiah; for I did liken all scriptures unto us, that it might be for our profit and learning.[18]

The prophets of Jesus Christ in our time continue to admonish us to be blessed through study and application of the word of God.

Joseph Smith explained how to gain a testimony of truth: "Search the Scriptures—search the revelations which we publish, and ask your Heavenly Father, in the name of His Son Jesus Christ, to manifest the truth unto you, and if you do it with an eye single to His glory, nothing doubting, He will answer you by the power of His Holy Spirit. You will then know for yourselves and not for another. You will not then be dependent on man for the knowledge of God; nor will there be any room for speculation."[19]

President Joseph Fielding Smith admonished: "Today we are troubled by evil-designing persons who [endeavor] to destroy the testimonies of members of the Church, and many . . . are in danger because of lack of understanding and because they have not sought the guidance of the Spirit. . . . It is a commandment from the Lord that members . . . be diligent . . . and study . . . the fundamental truths of the gospel. . . . Every baptized person [can] have an abiding testimony . . . , but [it] will grow dim and eventually disappear [without] study, obedience, and diligent seeking to know and understand the truth."[20]

President Benson counseled: "We should make daily study of the scriptures a lifetime pursuit. . . . I . . . say to you that one of the most important things you can do . . . is to immerse yourselves in the scriptures. Search them diligently. Feast upon the words of Christ. Learn the doctrine. Master the principles that are found therein. . . . Few other efforts . . . will bring greater dividends to [you]. . . . Few other ways [will result in] greater inspiration. . . . You must . . . see that studying and searching the scriptures is not a burden laid upon [us] by the Lord, but a marvelous blessing and opportunity."[21]

President Marion G. Romney declared with characteristic candor: "I don't know much about the gospel other than what I've learned from the standard works. When I drink from a spring I like to get the water where it comes out of the ground, not down stream after the cattle have waded in it. . . . I appreciate other people's interpretation, but when it comes to the gospel we ought to be acquainted with what the Lord says. . . . You ought to read the Book of Mormon and the Doctrine and Covenants; and . . . all the scriptures with the idea of finding out what's in them and what the meaning is and not to prove some idea of your own. Just read them and plead with the Lord to let you understand what he had in mind when he wrote them."[22]

As evidence that President Romney obeyed that counsel personally, on one occasion he said, "I was reading in the Book of Mormon last night—I have read the Book of Mormon through many, many times—and I read a scripture that impressed me more than it ever has before."[23] He then shared valuable insights that his pondering of the scriptures had afforded him.

President Gordon B. Hinckley encouraged reading the Book of Mormon: "Without reservation I promise you that if you will prayerfully read the Book of Mormon, regardless of how many times you previously have read it, there will come into your hearts an added measure of the Spirit of the Lord. There will come a strengthened resolution to walk in obedience to his commandments, and there will come a stronger testimony of the living reality of the Son of God."[24]

"I love Moroni. My heart reaches out to Moroni, that great, lonely figure who wandered for years and years, with all of his people gone. He saw them go down by the thousands, walking in their evil ways and forsaking the Lord and going to destruction. He and his father were left alone, and then his father died, and Moroni walked alone. These great final words of his always touch me: 'Despair cometh because of iniquity' (Moroni 10:22). Moroni was a man of hope, of optimism, forward-looking. Despair cometh of iniquity. 'And now I speak unto all the ends of the earth—that if the day cometh that the power and gifts of God shall be done away among you, it shall be because of unbelief' (Moroni 10:24). That's as applicable to us today as it was in his day. 'I exhort you to remember these things; for the time speedily cometh that ye shall know that I lie not, for ye shall see me at the bar of God; and the Lord God will say unto you: Did I not declare my words unto you, which were written by this man, like as one crying from the dead, yea, even as one speaking out of the dust? . . . And God shall show unto you, that that which I have written is true' (Moroni 10:27, 29). Marvelous. Read those things, and ponder them in your hearts."[25]

SPENCER W. KIMBALL AND THE
IMPORTANCE OF THE SCRIPTURES

While there are many who have helped me appreciate the importance of the scriptures, there is one who has had a greater impact than the others. He taught me indelibly the imperative need to consistently ponder the scriptures and to use the lessons learned to bless family, self, and others. His own life was an impressive example of living what he proclaimed. That individual is Spencer Woolley Kimball. He taught as an Apostle, as President of the Quorum of the Twelve, and as President of the Church. Since he may not be as well known to you today, I will relate a few of the many eternally significant lessons I learned from that giant among men.

Once after a very moving missionary zone conference when acting as our supervisor, then an Apostle, Elder Spencer W. Kimball found an opportunity to teach me a great lesson regarding scripture study. He taught with love and patience but with an eternal impact. He said, "President Scott, you used a scripture from the Book of

Mormon that I had never thought of using that way." Now that was the preparation for an important lesson. Then he commented, "And to think I've read the Book of Mormon many, many times." What was he gently telling me? He wanted me to know that I needed to continuously study the scriptures all my life to be able to gain knowledge of their content and benefit from personal application of their truths. You will be blessed by applying that principle in your own life.

On another occasion, Elder Spencer W. Kimball taught me a lesson that has become a fundamental part of my life and essential to my service to the Lord. He was kind enough to invite my wife, Jeanene, and me to participate with him in the creation of the first stake in Argentina. We went down from our mission field in the northern part of Argentina to spend a glorious two days observing how this marvelous giant among men used the Spirit to communicate truth and to touch lives. I had the privilege of being a translator in private interviews where Elder Kimball seemed to take a life apart, clean it, and put it back together to run better than before. At the end of the day, I realized that since I was out of my mission area, I didn't have any further responsibilities. I thought of how I could use the evening hours. I garnered enough courage to ask Elder Kimball if he would let me borrow his scriptures. I told him that I wanted to mark mine like he had marked his. I was particularly interested in the passages related to the Lamanites that he loved so much, for they have played a prominent part in my own life.

He gave me the scriptures he had copiously marked. Suddenly I had no desire for food, drink, or rest. I went to a small, isolated room in the mission home, opened my Book of Mormon, and began to mark in it as rapidly as I could the things that he had underlined in his book, paying special attention to the marginal notes. It seemed like the hands of the clock spun around. About 2:00 o'clock in the morning, I realized that what I had attempted to do was a monumental task. I knew that I had to accelerate my progress, so I used a small recorder to note the passages he had marked. That worked well until about 3:30 A.M., when the batteries went dead. I started again to laboriously mark the scriptures. I was so engrossed in the fascinating task that I shut out the outside world. At about 4:30 A.M. I was startled when I felt a heavy hand on my shoulder and heard that singular voice that so touched the hearts of those who love its owner. "Richard, what are you doing here this time of the morning?" I'll confess that the thought came to my mind to ask him the same question, but I didn't. I explained to him that I had been marking my scriptures. He said, "How far did you get?" Somewhat embarrassed for the lack of progress, I responded, "To the Words of Mormon." With expressions of gratitude, I returned his triple combination to him. He was preparing for a 10:00 A.M. stake conference session at 4:30 in the morning. He wanted to be sure it was done right. He asked me if I could translate some of his comments so he could speak to the people in their own native language. I became so involved in that activity, and felt so grateful to be at the side of such a marvelous leader, that my mind moved on from the experience with his scriptures. He did not forget however.

A few weeks passed. One day I opened a letter. In it were three typewritten sheets wherein were noted all of the remaining scriptures marked in his copies of the Book of Mormon, Doctrine and Covenants, and Pearl of Great Price. That extraordinary kindness, provided for my use alone, so moved me that I resolved to spend the rest of my life studying them.

We can never search the scriptures too much. These are words of valuable counsel from Spencer W. Kimball: "We overestimate our scriptural knowledge. I ask us all to honestly evaluate our performance in scripture study. It is a common thing to have a few passages of scripture at our disposal, floating in our minds, as it were, and thus to have the illusion that we know a great deal about the gospel.

In this sense, having a little knowledge can be a problem indeed. I am convinced that each of us, at some time in our lives, must discover the scriptures for ourselves—and not just discover them once, but rediscover them again and again."[26]

Further, President Kimball has said, "The years have taught me that if we will energetically pursue this worthy personal goal in a determined and conscientious manner, we shall indeed find answers to our problems and peace in our hearts. We shall experience the Holy Ghost broadening our understanding, find new insights, witness an unfolding pattern of all scripture; and the doctrines of the Lord shall come to have more meaning to us than we ever thought possible. As a consequence, we shall have greater wisdom with which to guide ourselves and our families."[27]

The following experience of young Spencer W. Kimball motivated me to read the Old Testament; perhaps it will help you do the same, if you have not already done so.

"When I heard a Church leader from Salt Lake City [Sister Susa Young Gates] tell us at conference that we should read the scriptures, and I recognized that I had never read the Bible, that very night at the conclusion of that very sermon I walked to my home a block away and climbed up in my little attic room [and] lighted a little coal-oil lamp . . . , and I read the first chapters of Genesis. A year later I closed the Bible, having read every chapter in that big and glorious book. . . .

"I found that there were certain parts that were hard for a 14-year-old boy to understand. There were some pages that were not especially interesting to me, but when I had read the 66 books and 1,189 chapters and 1,519 pages, I had a glowing satisfaction that I had made a goal and that I had achieved it."[28]

HOW TO STUDY THE SCRIPTURES

Let us now consider together various ways to study and ponder the scriptures. The suggestions apply to all of the standard works of the Church: the Old and New Testaments of the Bible, Book of Mormon, Doctrine and Covenants, and Pearl of Great Price. The exceptional teaching aids that are conveniently bound in many versions of the scriptures are a good place to begin. One must never take for granted the extraordinary footnotes that were laboriously prepared by hundreds of knowledgeable individuals, enhanced by the remarkable organizational power of the computer. The precious insights provided by the Topical Guide and the Bible Dictionary have proven to be most valuable resources to all who avail themselves of them. That help is further enlarged by the carefully researched maps and photographs, which provide greater understanding of historic events and places. The citations from the Joseph Smith Translation of the Bible contain additional valuable wisdom to be pondered. There is a lifetime of resource material available to each of us in the standard works alone.

No other church provides the wealth of resources to assist the sincere truth seeker to understand the counsel and commandments of our Eternal Father and His Beloved Son. It is impressive that references from all four standard works used in the footnotes, the content of the Topical Guide, and Bible Dictionary cover a time line that spans the history of man on earth. Yet there is no conflict of doctrine or principle in any of the relationships identified. Truly, together the standard works and the abundant teaching aids provide a solemn testimony of the truthfulness of the message of the Restoration and of the validity of The Church of Jesus Christ of Latter-day Saints as the kingdom of the Lord on earth today.

Consider these three ways to acquire light, truth, and inspiration from the scriptures:

Read, ponder, and pray about the meaning of specific verses.

This is probably the most common way to use the scriptures. The meaning of each word is carefully analyzed. Key concepts and phrases can be underlined. Thought is given to who made the declaration, under what circumstances it was given, how the truth revealed relates to me, and whether there is something I need to do or change.

Be instructed through inspiration as you ponder the scriptures. You have likely had this experience: As you have thought about a specific verse, the words seem to disappear from the page and you begin to be prompted by the Spirit. You cannot control when this blessing of having a conduit open to inspiration of the Holy Ghost will come, but you will benefit from this source of guidance and understanding as you consistently search the word of God in His holy scriptures. Often the impressions that come have nothing to do with the verses you have been reading. This is one way the Lord can teach you truths He knows that you need.

Analyze and unite the core content of related scriptures, then prepare a statement of principle that incorporates the truths distributed throughout several passages. This approach requires much more effort than studying individual verses, but the significant rewards obtained warrant the additional effort required. It is like assembling the individual components of a car. The whole is far more useful than any individual component. The result is an understanding of truth that isn't contained in any one scripture but is embodied in the resulting combination.

Any gospel topic can be analyzed in this way, such as the blessings of the Atonement, the power of the priesthood, the fruits of faith, and so forth. To illustrate, here is an example of scriptures that can show you how to increase your capacity to be inspired by the Holy Ghost. I identified these scriptures by searching for occasions when individuals were guided by the Spirit. I studied each pertinent scripture to identify the key truths that allowed the individual to qualify for the guidance of the Spirit. These truths were organized under a heading that provided unity to the effort. I will show the beginning results of such an effort. There are of course many more scriptural references that can be used to identify more ways to be guided by the Spirit.

In order to qualify to be led more powerfully by the Spirit I must:

Respond immediately to an impression of the Spirit.[29]
Exercise faith in Jesus Christ.[30]
Be diligent in keeping the commandments of the Lord.[31]
Seek the will of the Lord and obey it.[32]
Serve the Lord and His children.[33]
Unwearyingly declare the word of the Lord.[34]
Not fear.[35]
Forget myself.[36]

Sometime you can look for other scriptures to extend the foregoing list. There are many. You would also benefit from applying this study pattern to many other topics. For example, try to identify the key content of scriptures from the Topical Guide and your own marked scriptures to list under this heading: "For the Atonement to have greater influence in my life I must . . . "

Another fact worth noting is that many of the doctrines in the scriptures are clearly applicable to each of the children of Father in Heaven. It is also true that some scriptures are addressed to specific individuals, but they also embrace true principles. And when those principles apply to your life, you can, with confidence, consider that such scriptures have been directed to you individually. For example, the Lord gave specific instructions to Emma, the wife of Joseph Smith: "Continue in the spirit of meekness, and beware of pride. . . . Keep my commandments continually, and a crown of righteousness thou shalt receive."[37] That specific counsel to an individual was followed by the Lord's statement: "Verily, verily, I say unto you, that this is my voice unto all. Amen."[38]

LISTEN TO SCRIPTURES

Another way to study the scriptures is by listening to recordings. This approach yields the best results when there is a calm environment so that the truth can sink deeply into the mind and heart. That is a good way to memorize specific verses. But I would offer a caution about your use of the scriptures on a computer or handheld device: It is an effective way of identifying specific verses for a talk or for teaching, since it enables you to quickly identify needed references. But you should not replace the tried and true use of your own volumes of the standard works. There is something that brings a special spirit when you heft your own carefully annotated volume in your own hands in a quiet place where you can ponder and be moved by the Spirit for greater understanding and inspiration.

MEMORIZE SCRIPTURES

Your effort to memorize treasured verses of the word of God can enrich your life and bring you peace and comfort in times of need. An example will help confirm this truth. Once I was in a foreign country assigned to fulfill a difficult task that, if done properly, would bring significant good to members of the Church. I awoke in the middle of the night restless with concern and worry about the outcome. I knew that I needed rest to be prepared for the challenge of the next day, but I could not go to sleep. Then I began to repeat time and again from memory the following scripture:

> The LORD is my shepherd; I shall not want.
> He maketh me to lie down in green pastures: he leadeth me beside the still waters.

He restoreth my soul: he leadeth me in the paths of righteousness for his name's sake.

Yea, though I walk through the valley of the shadow of death, I will fear no evil: for thou art with me; thy rod and thy staff they comfort me.

Thou preparest a table before me in the presence of mine enemies: thou anointest my head with oil; my cup runneth over.

Surely goodness and mercy shall follow me all the days of my life: and I will dwell in the house of the LORD for ever.[39]

Somewhere in the process I fell into a peaceful sleep that lasted until morning. Refreshed and blessed by the Lord, I was able to successfully complete the assignment.

There is a related phenomenon that I don't completely understand but have come to know is true. Somehow reading, listening to, and repeating aloud passages of scripture accelerates learning another language. Moreover, sometimes as I have read a passage of scripture in another language, new insight seems to jump out from the page. I am not sure why. The translated meaning is the same. Perhaps it is the different structure or arrangement of words that causes that to occur.

THE POWER OF SCRIPTURES

When scriptures are used as the Lord has caused them to be recorded, they have intrinsic power that is not communicated when paraphrased. There is great solace, direction, and power that flow from the scriptures, especially in the unaltered words of the Lord and His prophets, as this example illustrates:

> Therefore, let your hearts be comforted . . . ; all
> flesh is in mine hands; be still and know that I am
> God.[40]

I hope you have discovered the mighty, enduring, motivating force that comes from pure doctrine. Doctrine, when understood and applied, becomes a sustaining power in your determination to live righteously. You build that secure foundation for life through your prayerful study, analysis, and pondering of the priceless scriptures available to you. That foundation is enhanced and tailored to meet the needs of today as you drink deeply from the counsel and admonition of the living prophets.

Another aspect of the power of the word of God as He has inspired it to be written is manifest in an experience I had some years ago. I received an assignment to go to another part of the world to investigate allegations that a Church leader had fathered a child out of wedlock. Knowing that the assignment would be difficult, I arranged for the help of a very spiritual mission president. The accused was a friend. We interviewed him, as well as those who made the accusations, and those who supported him. After two days of concentrated effort, I could not honestly say I had a clear impression of innocence or guilt. Each time there appeared to be damaging evidence, other evidence appeared to confuse or refute it. Late into the night I continued to wrestle with the matter in prayer and meditation. I searched the scriptures and was led to some I felt would be helpful.

We met with him again the next morning. This time I was impressed to take a different approach. I began. "Whoever is responsible for the act has this scripture to face. Would you read it and then explain in your own words its meaning?" He read it perfectly, but as he began to explain, he hesitated and stumbled. I continued, "This next verse speaks of the authority of those sent by the servants of the Lord. Would you read it and explain its meaning?" Other scriptures followed. By then, his whole attitude had changed, and he was perspiring and nervously shifting. There came a knock at the door, and he said, "I see you have another interview. I'll just wait outside." About forty-five minutes later, the phone rang. It was that man. He asked, "Can I see you privately?" As he entered the room, he sat down and pulled from his pocket a piece of paper, which he pushed across the table. It was a signed, full confession. How grateful I am for the scriptures that penetrated his heart and initiated full repentance, which, in time, brought a complete restoration of his blessings.

The Peace and Direction the Scriptures Afford

As you may have done, I have spent years studying the scriptures and the declarations of inspired servants of the Lord relating to spiritual communication. I have pondered those truths and faithfully endeavored to try to apply them so as to distill their essence into my heart and soul. Sacred personal experiences have resulted for my own guidance and direction. I have come to know that the Lord has given us no magic wand to provide immediate answers to life's challenges. I know there is no mystic source of solutions, rather, that God communicates with us on the basis of simple, understandable, verifiable principles that can be found in the scriptures. I testify that all righteous, obedient children of God can understand and apply these principles.

I love the scriptures. They are a source of continuing inspiration. They often open the channel of spiritual communication. I am sure that you have had the same experience I have enjoyed. As you have read the scriptures and have prayed for an understanding of their meaning, some times suddenly, other times quietly over a period of time, you have received a distillation of truth and an ability to see its application in your life. In this way you can develop a capability to understand through the Spirit how the scriptures can strengthen your own capacity, or resolve some difficulty in your life, or fortify you as an instrument to help another.

The scriptures attest that earth life is not the confusing, conflictive, painful, disjointed experience Satan portrays it to be, where he paints the objective as "me first" and "my wants must be satisfied"; where success is measured in personal wealth, notoriety, power, human recognition; where the most important being is oneself; where deceit, deception, and betrayal are considered simply tools to secure personal advantage and one's personal objectives have precedence over the rights of others; where hate is justified if another gets in the way and love is a sign of weakness.

How can we ever adequately express to our Father in Heaven our gratitude for His plan of salvation, which is so clearly defined in the scriptures? We can know the purpose of mortal life and how it should be lived for happiness now and forever. How can we ever show sufficient gratitude for His Beloved Son, our Savior and Redeemer, for His incomparable Atonement and for all the opportunities and blessings that flow from it? Certainly a lifetime devoted to the study and application of the inspired counsel of the Father, His Son, and the prophets that have been and will be called is a small price to pay for what They have done for each of us. And it is not a sacrifice, for by so doing we are abundantly blessed with inspired direction and solutions to the perplexing challenges of life.

When your life is lived by the rules of our Eternal Father, which are central to His Plan of Happiness, He will make of your life a rich, productive, often magnificently purposeful experience. It will be one of peace and immense satisfaction. Let us ever be grateful for the scriptural light and inspiration our Father in Heaven has provided through His Son and the holy prophets for our continuing peace and happiness.

CHAPTER 24

THE PEACE AND HAPPINESS TEMPLE ORDINANCES CAN PROVIDE

ONE OF THE MOST beautiful, comforting doctrines of the Lord, one that brings immense peace, happiness, and unbounded joy, is the principle of eternal marriage. This doctrine means that a man and woman who love each other deeply, who have grown together through the trials, joys, sorrows, and happiness of a shared lifetime, can live beyond the veil together forever with their family members who also earn that blessing. That is not just an immensely satisfying dream—*it can be a reality*. What husband and wife who have shared the joys of marriage here on earth would not want that blessing hereafter? However, only those who meet the requirements established by the Lord will earn that supernal gift.

If you have not already received the ordinances of the temple, decide now that at the appropriate time you will obtain them all. Don't let anything overcome that resolve. I bear witness that all those things that have and will bring my wife, our family, and me the greatest happiness have roots in the temple ordinances we have received and the covenants we have kept.

The essential, indispensable importance of temple ordinances and covenants is stressed by God in numerous scriptures. For example:

> For all who will have a blessing at my hands shall abide the law which was appointed for that blessing, and the conditions thereof, as were instituted from before the foundation of the world.[1]

> Therefore, if a man marry him a wife in the world, and he marry her not by me nor by my word, . . . their covenant and marriage are not of force when they are dead. . . . Therefore, when they are out of the world they neither marry nor are given in marriage; but are appointed angels in heaven . . . to minister for those who are worthy of . . . an exceeding, and an eternal weight of glory. For these angels did not abide my law . . . but remain separately and singly, without exaltation, . . . and from henceforth are not gods, but are angels of God forever and ever.[2]

> If a man marry a wife by my word, which is my law, and by the new and everlasting covenant, and it is sealed unto them by the Holy Spirit of promise, by him who is anointed, . . . it shall be done unto them in all things whatsoever my servant hath put upon them, in time, and through all eternity; and shall be of full force when they are out of the world; and they shall pass by the angels, and the gods, which are set there, to their exaltation and glory in all things, as hath been sealed upon their heads, which glory shall be a fulness and a continuation of the seeds forever and ever . . . because they have all power, and the angels are subject unto them. Verily, verily, I say unto you, except ye abide my law ye cannot attain to this glory.[3]

In the celestial glory there are three heavens or degrees; and in order to obtain the highest, a man must enter into this order of the priesthood [meaning the new and everlasting covenant of marriage]; and if he does not, he cannot obtain it. He may enter into the other, but that is the end of his kingdom; he cannot have an increase.[4]

Joseph Smith was inspired to declare:

It may seem to some to be a very bold doctrine that we talk of—a power which records or binds on earth and binds in heaven. Nevertheless, in all ages of the world, whenever the Lord has given a dispensation of the priesthood to any man by actual revelation, or any set of men, this power has always been given. Hence, whatsoever those men did in authority, in the name of the Lord, and did it truly and faithfully, and kept a proper and faithful record of the same, it became a law on earth and in heaven, and could not be annulled, according to the decrees of the great Jehovah.[5]

Brethren, shall we not go on in so great a cause? . . . Courage, brethren; and on, on to the victory! Let your hearts rejoice, and be exceedingly glad. Let the earth break forth into singing. Let the dead speak forth anthems of eternal praise to the King Immanuel, who hath ordained, before the world was, that which would enable us to redeem them out of their prison; for the prisoners shall go free. . . . How glorious is the voice we hear from heaven, proclaiming in our ears, glory, and salvation, and honor, and immortality, and eternal life; kingdoms, principalities, and powers![6]

The temple ordinances are the culminating, transcendent gifts our eternal Heavenly Father has prepared for your peace and happiness on earth and for eternity. We now review how they can be obtained.

If you are now ready to receive the ordinances of the temple, prepare carefully for that crowning event. Before entering the temple you will be interviewed by your bishop and stake president for your temple recommend. Be honest and candid with them. That interview is not a test to be passed but an important step to confirm that you have the maturity and spirituality to receive the supernal ordinances and to make and keep the edifying covenants offered in the house of the Lord. Personal worthiness is an essential requirement to enjoy the blessings of the temple. Anyone foolish enough to enter the temple unworthily will receive the deserved condemnation of the Lord.

Since many aspects of the temple experience are significantly different than regular worship services, get the counsel of your bishop to help prepare you before you enter the temple. Parents who have been endowed in the temple can also assist you. Your bishop can arrange for a specially trained individual to discuss important aspects of the temple to help you understand and appreciate more fully that sacred experience. The endowment and sealing ordinances of the temple are so gloriously rich in meaning that you will want to allow significant time to receive those ordinances and to ponder their meaning. I suggest that you divide your endowment and sealing into separate visits. On your first visit, if possible, take an endowed member of your family or close friend of your own gender to escort you. Because of the sacred nature of the temple experience, you would want to limit those who accompany you for your sealing (marriage) to a few family or close friends. Do not let receptions, wedding breakfasts, farewells, or other activities overshadow the sacred temple experience. Above all, do not be overly concerned about doing correctly all that will be asked of you in the temple. Understand that you will be helped in every step by caring temple workers thoroughly familiar with the temple ordinances. They will be intent on making your visit the glorious experience you anticipate.

Outside of the temple, we do not speak of the specific, sacred matters shared there. However, while within the temple, authorized individuals can help answer your questions. On your first visit you will receive carefully prepared, specific instructions regarding those matters that are not discussed outside of the temple walls. May your first experience in the temple be as moving and inspiring as was mine. I know that it will be, as you carefully prepare.

When you are sealed forever in the house of the Lord, a new family unit is created. Parents, who have had direct responsibility for you since your birth, now move into an advisory role. Their counsel will be precious after you are sealed, but you and your eternal companion will prayerfully make the important decisions together.

How grateful I am that President Hinckley has been inspired by the Lord to construct new temples at an unprecedented rate so that the ordinances are more accessible to members throughout the world.

If you have received temple ordinances but do not now visit the temple, even when there is one nearby, with all the tenderness of my heart I invite you to come back to the temple. There are many reasons. It is a place of peace, solitude, and inspiration. Regular attendance will enrich your life with greater purpose. It will permit you to provide deceased ancestors the exalting ordinances you have received, without which they cannot receive a fulness of blessings.

Seek out your unendowed ancestors and provide those ordinances essential to their eternal happiness. Go as regularly as you are able to the temple. You know it is the right thing to do. If you have been lax in temple attendance and can go without great sacrifice, do it now. If the temple is still far away, always have a current temple recommend. You could unexpectedly have the opportunity to participate. In any event, a determination to hold a current recommend will help you stay centered in obedience so that God can bless you more fully.

For some, the closer they live to the temple the less consistently they attend. When there is a great sacrifice required to participate, once plans are made nothing is permitted to conflict with attendance. But when a temple is nearby, unless there is the same resolve to plan a specific appointment time, little things can distract and interfere with temple worship. Be consistent and determined, wherever you live.

The temple ordinances are so imbued with symbolic meaning that they provide a lifetime of productive contemplation and learning. Ponder each word and activity in the temple. Study how they interrelate. As you think about the significance of each matter presented, think of them in light of your relationship to the Savior and His to our Father in Heaven. Contemplate how the understanding you receive enhances your earth life by giving proper emphasis to things that are critically important. Arrange to participate for deceased ancestors in the sealing and all of the other ordinances, as well as the endowment. Participation in baptism and confirmation ordinances for the deceased is most rewarding. A worthy elder can officiate in these ordinances by making prior arrangements with the temple.

I find it helpful when receiving ordinances for another to try to relate specifically to that individual. I think of him and pray that he will accept the ordinance and benefit from it. Do these things with a prayer in your heart that the Holy Spirit will enhance your understanding and enrich your life. Those worthy prayers will be answered.

It has been said that near the end of his ministry, in a meeting with the First Presidency and Twelve in the Salt Lake Temple, President David O. McKay began to recite from memory the endowment ceremony. That was completely appropriate in that set-ting. After repeating a significant portion of the ceremony from memory, he paused, meditating for some time, and then said, "I believe I'm finally beginning to understand." What a powerful con-firmation that consistent temple worship throughout life can be most refreshing and rewarding.[7]

President Ezra Taft Benson counseled: "I promise you that, with increased attendance in the temples of our God, you shall receive increased personal revelation to bless your life."[8]

Clear from your mind all other concerns so your full attention is given to the temple experience. Occasionally, when possible, devote an entire day to temple worship. The benefits multiply greatly with unhurried temple participation. I always remove my watch in the temple to avoid being distracted and so that those souls beyond the veil know that they are very important to me.

You can come to appreciate more the depth and breadth of the blessings that flow from temple worship by observing how it has enabled the Lord to touch other's lives to lift them. Recognize that through similar obedience you can grow and find joy. The following experience illustrates what I mean. In the highlands of Guatemala, members barely subsist. Going to the temple requires great sacrifice. A visit takes a year of preparation. There is hard work, sacrifice to save money and food, the spinning, dyeing, and weaving of new clothing. There is the long, barefoot walk out of the mountains, the crossing of Lake Isabel, the bus rides with little food. Tired and worn, they arrive at the temple. They scrub until they shine, dress in their new clothing, and enter the house of the Lord.

Reclothed in white, they are taught by the Spirit, receive ordi-nances, and make covenants. One highland woman was greatly touched by the spirit and meaning of the endowment. As she entered the celestial room she was overcome with the light she saw and felt. She observed that others were seated, with heads reverently bowed.

Innocently, she knelt at the entrance to the room, oblivious to others. She bowed her head, sobbed, and for twenty minutes poured out her heart to her Father in Heaven. Finally, with her dress soaked with tears, she raised her head. The sensitive temple matron asked, "May I help?" She responded, "Oh, would you? This is my problem: I've tried to tell Father in Heaven of my gratitude for all my blessings but I don't feel that I've thanked Him enough. Will you help me tell Him how grateful I am?" Perhaps her example will lead you to be more aware of the blessings of the Lord in your life. It has done that for me.

Are you by any chance preparing for that sweet period of discovery known as courtship leading to eternal marriage? It can be a wondrously beautiful time of growth and sharing. It is a time when you should focus your thoughts, actions, and plans on two individuals: the parents of your future children. Prepare to be a successful parent by being completely worthy in every thought and act during courtship. Be sensitive to the needs, desires, and worthy aspirations of your eternal companion-to-be.

Be worthy. To commit in courtship intimate acts, intended to unfold only within the bonds of marriage, is transgression. Such activity offends the Holy Ghost, and lays the foundation for heartache and disappointment. It could mask traits and characteristics that could prove conflictive or incompatible within the covenant of marriage. Seeds of distrust that mature in divorce and loss of temple blessings are often sown through violation of the laws of personal purity prior to marriage. Don't make that mistake. Protect each other from anything that would be inappropriate.

There is more to a foundation of eternal marriage than a pretty face and attractive figure or a strong, manly body and record of an outstanding sports career. There is more to consider than popularity or charisma. As you seek an eternal companion, look for someone who is developing the essential attributes that bring happiness: a deep love of the Lord and of His commandments and a determination to live them. Seek one who is kind, understanding, forgiving of others, and willing to give of self, with the desire to have a family crowned with beautiful children. Pray for a companion with a commitment to teach children the principles of truth in the home.

If you are a man, as a husband and worthy priesthood bearer you will want to emulate the example of the Savior, whose priesthood you hold. You will make giving of self to wife and children a primary focus of your life. Your wife and children must have higher priority than your personal interests. As you live that principle, you will confirm the truth that it is more rewarding to give of self than to be served. Occasionally a father attempts to control the destiny of each family member. He seeks to make all the decisions. His wife is subjected to his personal whims. Whether that is the custom or not is immaterial. It is not the way of the Lord. It is not the way a Latter-day Saint husband treats his wife and family. It is certainly not the way a priesthood holder should serve his wife and children.

An honorably completed full-time mission provides a foundation for your life as husband, father, and worthy priesthood bearer in the home.

If you are a woman, your noble ambition should be that of a wife and mother. You should be developing the sacred qualities that God has given you as one of His daughters to excel as a wife and mother: patience, kindliness, a love of children, and a desire to care for them rather than placing first priority on professional pursuits. You should acquire a good education to prepare for the demands of motherhood. Should future circumstances require it, that education could facilitate your financial support.

While not required of you, where feasible, a full-time mission would provide invaluable preparation. You should seek a husband who honors his priesthood and uses it in service to others. His having completed an honorable mission would be strong evidence of such a commitment. Look for a man who accepts his role as provider of the necessities of life and has the capacity to do it. He should be making concerted efforts to prepare himself to fulfill those responsibilities. Hopefully, he will be able to provide well enough that you can be in the home with your children during the years of their critical development.

I suggest that you not ignore many possible candidates who are still developing these attributes by seeking only the one who is perfected in them. You will likely not find that perfect person, and if you did he or she might not develop interest in you. These attributes are best polished together as husband and wife facing the challenges of life together as one.

Some feel anguish when eternal marriage is mentioned because they believe their spouse will not prepare for that sacred experience by reason of deeply rooted characteristics or habits. I share a personal experience to help you. Throughout my youth and mission I did what I could so that my nonmember father and less-active mother would qualify to be sealed in the temple. After our marriage, my wife joined me in the effort. About five years into our marriage, we had a growing experience. Our precious two-year-old son, Richard, died while undergoing surgery to correct a congenital heart defect. Within six weeks, our daughter, Andrea, passed away at birth. Father loved little Richard very much. He said to Mother, "I cannot understand how Richard and Jeanene seem to be able to accept the loss of these children. I don't think it's fair." Mother, responding to a prompting, said, "Kenneth, they have been sealed in the temple. They know that their children will be with them for eternity if they continue to live righteously. But you and I will not have our five sons because we have not made those covenants."

My father pondered those words. Privately he began to meet with missionaries and was soon baptized. In time, that decision resulted in Mother, Dad, and their five children being sealed into an eternal family in the Idaho Falls Temple. Years later, President

Spencer W. Kimball put his hands on my father's head, promised him the vigor and strength of a younger man, and conferred the sealing power. Our father worked as a temple sealer for eleven years in the Washington D.C. Temple, with Mother serving there also. You do your part. Ask the Lord to help you. Don't abandon hope for a temple marriage.

If you are single and haven't identified a solid prospect for celestial marriage, live for it. Pray for it. Expect it in the timetable of the Lord. Do not compromise your standards in any way that would rule out that blessing on this or the other side of the veil. Never find yourself complaining because others often speak of family and eternal marriage. The Lord knows the intent of your heart. His prophets have stated that you will have that blessing as you consistently live to qualify for it. We do not know whether it will be in this life or the next, but God will keep His promise. As you qualify, that supernal blessing will be yours in the timetable of the Lord.

Temple ordinances will bless your life now, during your mortal probation, as well as giving you great reason to rejoice hereafter. An example will clarify what I mean. Some time ago I was assigned to work with leaders and members in a country that was being severely threatened by rebel activity. In the height of the turmoil, dangerous threats, and overall uncertainty, a newly called stake president abandoned his flock. He disappeared to resurface in the United States, where he felt that the opportunities of life would be more abundant. Some time later as I walked through the halls of a Salt Lake hospital, he emerged from a doorway pushing a garbage can, evidence of menial labor. When his eyes met mine he turned and ran, ashamed for what he had done, unable to speak to me. That man had not received the temple ordinances nor gained the strength and understanding that would have enabled him to face the challenges of his native country.

At about the same time, I learned that another stake president in the same country was on a list to be assassinated by the rebels. His father and a brother had been killed because of their opposition to the group trying to overtake the country. I quietly arranged for him and his family to be moved to another nation to avoid his also becoming a victim. After all the plans were in place, I met with him and explained what I had done. He responded, "Elder Scott, I'm the stake president. I can't leave my people under these circumstances. I've made covenants in the temple, and I'm going to keep them. I know if the Lord wants to He can protect me. And if He doesn't, that is not a great concern. I will not leave my people." That courage, engendered by temple ordinances, was honored by the Lord. He lived through those dangerous circumstances safely, despite the threats of the rebel group.

Have you noticed how, as the end of a prophet's service on earth approaches, he seems to be preoccupied with the temple and its ordinances? There is evidence of this concern in the life of each prophet from Joseph Smith to our current president. Their sermons mention the blessings of the temple, and they personally attend. Such an interest motivated Sister Camilla Kimball to continue weekly temple worship long after her husband, President Spencer W. Kimball, was called home. When they were not traveling, President and Sister Benson participated in temple ordinances nearly every Friday morning during his ministry as President of the Church. That consistent example taught the vital importance of the temple and its ordinances more than a host of sermons would have.[9]

Each of us should share a knowledge of this magnificent work, personally or through missionaries, with our friends and neighbors that they may join the kingdom of God on earth. Then they themselves can receive the consummate, eternal blessings provided through temple ordinances and covenants.

I testify that, with unimaginable suffering and agony and at an incalculable price, the Savior earned His right to be our Intermediary, our Redeemer, our Final Judge. Through faith in Him and receipt of the requisite ordinances and covenants, you will earn your right to the blessings of eternal marriage made possible through His infinite Atonement. You will qualify through continuing obedience for the glorious privilege of eternal life in the celestial kingdom with your qualified loved ones.

The Savior has declared:

> Therefore, verily I say unto you, that your anointings, and your washings, and your baptisms for the dead, and your solemn assemblies, and your memorials for your sacrifices by the sons of Levi, and for your oracles in your most holy places wherein you receive conversations, and your statutes and judgments, for the beginning of the revelations and foundation of Zion, and for the glory, honor, and endowment of all her municipals, are ordained by the ordinance of my holy house, which my people are always commanded to build unto my holy name.[10]

I am confident that Jesus Christ, our Savior, is the true source of inspiration for the increasing capacity of Church members to receive ordinances and to make covenants of eternal consequence in the beautiful, peaceful, sacred sanctuaries of holy temples. Our Redeemer is prompting the development of powerfully improved tools and information to help us identify our ancestors, that we may go to the temples to receive ordinances for and in behalf of them. This is done that they may enjoy the promised blessings of the Lord as they qualify to receive the temple ordinances. They thus can make personally the covenants that will allow them to enjoy the fulness of blessings in eternal realms. This is His work. He guides it. He has given His life that, even in our weakness, we may overcome our mistakes through repentance and obedience to His gospel. Oh, what a favored people we are to have this light, this knowledge, these opportunities for happiness on earth and throughout the eternities.

For almost twelve years (as of this writing) since my dear wife was called home, I have kept a personal commitment to participate some way in temple ordinances every week. I will continue to do so. When travel on assignment has precluded temple attendance, upon return I have attended more frequently to maintain my commitment. I do not have the capacity to express meaningfully the enduring peace and serenity and the inexpressible joy that have come from that temple worship. I also am grateful for the vicarious ordinances others beyond the veil have received by reason of that commitment.

I know the exquisite joy that comes from an eternal marriage sealed at a temple altar through the holy sealing power. When there is righteousness, a commitment to give of self, obedience to the commandments of God, and the resolve to seek His will in all things, that joy increases. I do not have words to express the fulfillment and peace that flow from such a supernal experience, even when there is a temporary interruption of the glory of life as husband and wife together on earth. I am sustained daily by the conviction that as I remain faithful, I will be able to live eternally with my precious Jeanene. It is that joy and happiness I want so much for you, if you do not yet have it. More important, that is what your Father in Heaven wants to give you as you qualify for it.

As you contemplate the grandeur and magnificence of the temple and its ordinances, commit to receive any ordinances that may be lacking in your own life. Resolve that as you are able, you will identify ancestors and act in their behalf, that they may obtain the sacred ordinances of eternal salvation.

Come to the temple, now. It will greatly bless your life and provide essential ordinances for those beyond the veil that they cannot obtain by themselves.

We now consider the consummate power of love.

CHAPTER 25

THE ROLE OF LOVE

U NQUESTIONABLY THE greatest manifestation of love that has ever occurred is described in these classic verses:

> And as Moses lifted up the serpent in the wilderness, even so must the Son of man be lifted up: that whosoever believeth in him should not perish, but have eternal life.
>
> For God so loved the world, that he gave his only begotten Son, that whosoever believeth in him should not perish, but have everlasting life. For God sent not his Son into the world to condemn the world; but that the world through him might be saved.[1]

There is no love as deep and enduring, as pure and selfless, as motivating and inspiring as that of our Heavenly Father and His matchless Son. It is timeless, limitless, and the same for each and every one of the children of our Father in Heaven. When understood and appreciated it becomes the immovable, indestructible foundation of peace, happiness, and joy in your life.

The highest priority of life should be love of Father in Heaven and His Holy Son, Jesus Christ, manifest by obedience to Their teachings. Love of spouse, children, and parents should be the next priority.

Our Father in Heaven personally or through His Holy Son and prophets has explained how love can benefit your life in multiple ways.

FOR PERSONAL IMPROVEMENT

My son, despise not the chastening of the LORD; neither be weary of his correction: for whom the LORD loveth he correcteth; even as a father the son in whom he delighteth.[2]

Ye have heard that it hath been said, Thou shalt love thy neighbour, and hate thine enemy. But I say unto you, Love your enemies, bless them that curse you, do good to them that hate you, and pray for them which despitefully use you, and persecute you; that ye may be the children of your Father which is in heaven: for he maketh his sun to rise on the evil and on the good, and sendeth rain on the just and on the unjust. For if ye love them which love you, what reward have ye? do not even the publicans the same? . . . Be ye therefore perfect, even as your Father which is in heaven is perfect.[3]

FOR PEACE

And it came to pass that there was no contention in the land, because of the love of God which did dwell in the hearts of the people. And there were no envy-ings, nor strifes, nor tumults, nor whoredoms, nor lyings, nor murders, nor any manner of lasciviousness;

and surely there could not be a happier people among all the people who had been created by the hand of God. There were no robbers, nor murderers, . . . but they were in one, the children of Christ, and heirs to the kingdom of God. And how blessed were they! For the Lord did bless them in all their doings, . . . and there was no contention in all the land.[4]

FOR PROTECTION

Ye that love the LORD, hate evil: he preserveth the souls of his saints; he delivereth them out of the hand of the wicked.[5]

FOR BLESSINGS

And it shall come to pass, if ye shall hearken diligently unto my commandments which I command you this day, to love the LORD your God, and to serve him with all your heart and with all your soul, that I will give you the rain of your land in his due season, the first rain and the latter rain, that thou mayest gather in thy corn, and thy wine, and thine oil. And I will send grass in thy fields for thy cattle, that thou mayest eat and be full.[6]

Wherefore, ye must press forward with a steadfastness in Christ, having a perfect brightness of hope, and a love of God and of all men. Wherefore, if ye shall press forward, feasting upon the word of Christ, and endure to the end, behold, thus saith the Father: Ye shall have eternal life.[7]

As the Father hath loved me, so have I loved you: continue ye in my love. If ye keep my commandments, ye shall abide in my love; even as I have kept my Father's commandments, and abide in his love. These things have I spoken unto you, that my joy might remain in you, and that your joy might be full. This is my commandment, That ye love one another, as I have loved you. Greater love hath no man than this, that a man lay down his life for his friends. Ye are my friends, if ye do whatsoever I command you.[8]

FOR SERVICE TO GOD AND OTHERS

And thou shalt love the LORD thy God with all thine heart, and with all thy soul, and with all thy might.[9]

Master, which is the great commandment in the law? Jesus said unto him, Thou shalt love the Lord thy God with all thy heart, and with all thy soul, and with all thy mind. This is the first and great commandment. And the second is like unto it, Thou shalt love thy neighbour as thyself.[10]

A new commandment I give unto you, That ye love one another; as I have loved you, that ye also love one another. By this shall all men know that ye are my disciples, if ye have love one to another.[11]

See that ye love one another; cease to be covetous; learn to impart one to another as the gospel requires.[12]

If thou lovest me thou shalt serve me and keep all my commandments.[13]

Jesus saith to Simon Peter, Simon, son of Jonas, lovest thou me more than these? He saith unto him, Yea, Lord; thou knowest that I love thee. He saith unto him, Feed my lambs. He saith to him again the second time, Simon, son of Jonas, lovest thou me? He saith unto him, Yea, Lord; thou knowest that I love thee. He saith unto him, Feed my sheep. He saith unto him the third time, Simon, son of Jonas, lovest thou me? Peter was grieved because he said unto him the third time, Lovest thou me? And he said unto him, Lord, thou knowest all things; thou knowest that I love thee. Jesus saith unto him, Feed my sheep.[14]

An example of the edifying power of love comes from Parley P. Pratt: "It was Joseph Smith who taught me how to prize the endearing relationships of father and mother, husband and wife; of brother and sister, son and daughter. It was from him that I learned that the wife of my bosom might be secured to me for time and all eternity. . . . It was from him that I learned the true dignity and destiny of a son of God, clothed with an eternal priesthood, as the patriarch and sovereign of his countless offspring. It was from him that I learned that the highest dignity of womanhood was, to stand as a queen and priestess to her husband, and to reign for ever and ever as the queen . . . of her numerous and still increasing offspring."[15]

Pure love is the incomparable power for good. Pure love bridges deep cultural differences, heals heartache, increases compassion, and solidifies the bonds of friendship. It is the strongest, most effective influence to settle anger, soften hate, and resolve serious misunderstanding.

As a lubricant in life, it must be administered in the proper dose. A precious stone is created as a skilled artisan polishes the rough gem against a grinding wheel. He uses a water-based solution as the lubricant. If he applies too much lubricant no polishing occurs; if he uses too little the gem overheats and shatters. So it is in life. Misplaced love that takes away appropriate growth opportunities in another's life can stunt the growth of character; insufficient love can strain and destroy a relationship.

Righteous love is the secure foundation of a successful marriage. It is the primary cause of contented, well-developed children.

Who can justly measure the extent of the righteous influence of a mother's love? What enduring fruits will result from seeds of truth a mother carefully plants and lovingly cultivates in the fertile soil of her child's trusting mind and heart? When a mother is consistently in the home, at least during the hours the children are predominantly there, she can detect the individual needs of each child and provide ways to satisfy them. Her divinely given instincts help sense a child's special talents and unique capacities so as to nurture and strengthen them. Consider these examples of how compassionate love and sensitivity of parents, particularly mothers, bless children's lives.

A mother overheard her son, four, tell his brother, six, "I don't believe in Jesus." The older brother responded, "You have really hurt my feelings." Sensing a need, the mother reinforced the younger boy's understanding of the Savior. She placed a picture of the Redeemer in his room and continued to teach all of her children more about the Master. Sometime later the younger son commented, "Mom, you're my best friend, next to Jesus."

Another lovely mother has consistently read scriptures to her children to teach them truth. While overseas with no satisfactory schools, she spent much time and energy painstakingly tutoring them, with amazing results. Once her husband went to help their five-year-old daughter with evening prayer. He found her kneeling, sharing her tender feelings with her Heavenly Father. Sensing his presence, she looked up. He said, "Do you know how wonderful it makes Father in Heaven feel when you talk to Him?" She responded, "Oh, Daddy, I will always talk to my Father in Heaven." Such is the pure heart of a five-year-old who has been carefully, spiritually nurtured.

Another mother read gospel stories to her children from a young, formative age. Once, as she read of the crucifixion of the Savior, her two-and-a-half-year-old son sobbed. She realized he was a spiritually sensitive child. Through the years, that child has become a righteous, disciplined young man who loves the Lord and keeps His commandments. Profanity, so prevalent today, is particularly offensive to him. As he shuns it and other evils, he is criticized for being too "churchy." While it is difficult now, as he continues his resolve to be righteous, he will become a powerfully strong husband, father, and leader.

When two-year-old Clayton overheard the family sharing feelings about his grandmother serving a mission in Swaziland, Africa, his little heart was touched. Often he would fold his arms, bow his head, and say, "Gam-ma on mission. Jesus. Amen." When she returned, he did not recognize her until she said, "This is your missionary grandma." Instantly, he broke into a smile, ran, and threw his arms around her. Other grandchildren now want to be missionaries.

If you are a mother carefully nurturing your children, how grateful you must feel as you see some of the fruits of your sacrifice. You have a vision of the power of obediently, patiently, lovingly teaching truth, because you look beyond the peanut butter sandwiches, soiled clothing, tedious hours of routine, struggles with homework, and long hours by a sickbed.

The incomparable, all encompassing love of our Father in Heaven is superbly manifest in His plan of happiness. Through a singular dream that has left its indelible impress in my soul I understood more of that plan and saw more clearly the profound depth of His love. This is what occurred:

I had a very difficult and challenging dream. When I awoke from it, my heart was pounding, my muscles ached, and the bedclothes were saturated with perspiration. I had experienced those feelings that come when you have faced a great challenge. Initially I felt that it had been a nightmare. Then I noticed that the transition from sleep to wakefulness was not discernable, a sign I have come to recognize as evidence of a dream with an important message. I began to analyze the dream to discover its purpose. I had been searching for my precious deceased wife, Jeanene. As I searched everywhere for her, individuals around me commented that I was wasting my time for it would be impossible to find her. Because I love her very much I would not be dissuaded.

Others around me were also searching for individuals. As they listened to those who prompted them to give up, they were convinced of the futility of their search. Soon they became absorbed with despair and finally hopelessness. Then they were overcome with rage and began to condemn the Lord.

The more I searched, the more intense were the suggestions that I would never be able to find her. As others saw that I would not abandon my quest, they changed their approach. They said that they were just trying to protect me from heartache, for if I found her I would discover that she had changed. They said she didn't love me anymore. While there was not a shred of support that I could find her, I thought: "That can't be. That is not the way it is. I will find her. I don't know how and I don't care how long it takes. I will find her. She has not changed. We have been sealed in the temple and have kept the covenants. We have been promised eternal life together." That thought filled me with determination. I made the decision that I would find her no matter what.

At that point I seemed to be lifted out of that environment. I could see that I had been in an evil, controlled atmosphere where there was an attempt to force me. Others were trying to manipulate me. Their intent was to discourage me so that I would abandon

Father's plan of happiness. They themselves were miserable and wanted me to be likewise.

As I realized what I had been taught in the dream, I was filled with the most extraordinary feeling of gratitude and love for our Father in Heaven and His plan of happiness. It is perfect. His laws are completely just and His mercy unending. I knelt beside the bed and poured out my heart in thanksgiving for justice. I have long appreciated mercy, I was beginning to realize how precious is justice.

No evil power can ever take away what through love we have worthily earned on earth: the profound love of an eternal companion, of children, parents, and treasured friends. Where we honor our covenants, the eternal bonds of temple ordinances are ours forever. No devilish power can wrench them from us. All understanding and knowledge gained through study and pondering will be available through the quickening power of the Holy Ghost. Oh, it can be lost from our own disobedience, but that is in our power to control.

The contrived environment that Satan was trying to create is not real life nor the real world in which we live. I felt the deepest expression of gratitude that worthy character cannot be destroyed. Our unique identity is forever our own. True, what we gain from our experience on earth depends on how obedient we are to the teachings of the Lord; but no one can take away our individuality. That is absolutely guaranteed because of Father in Heaven's plan. The precious fruits of pure love are ever ours unless threatened by our own unworthiness.

If it were not for the Savior and His Atonement, you would literally be living in that corrupt environment for all eternity. There Satan would manipulate you and, as horrible as the thought is, in time you and I would have become like him.[16] There could be no love, no progress, no companionship, and no happiness. By His transcendent sacrifice and its infinite consequence, the Redeemer brought into your life the influence of mercy. He has made it possible for you to be forgiven of your mistakes.

Charity is a form of love that is particularly potent for good, as eloquently evidenced in these words of Mormon:

> Charity suffereth long, and is kind, and envieth not, and is not puffed up, seeketh not her own, is not easily provoked, thinketh no evil, and rejoiceth not in iniquity but rejoiceth in the truth, beareth all things, believeth all things, hopeth all things, endureth all things. Wherefore, my beloved brethren, if ye have not charity, ye are nothing, for charity never faileth. Wherefore, cleave unto charity, which is the greatest of all, for all things must fail—but charity is the pure love of Christ, and it endureth forever; and whoso is found possessed of it at the last day, it shall be well with him.[17]

A thought to ponder: I believe that the phrase "charity is the pure love of Christ" is intended to refer not only to His perfect love of each one of us but also to the deep love we should have for Him. Do you agree?

Never let anyone or anything cause you to question God's ever-present, continuing, all-pervading love for you. Our Father in Heaven may not appreciate everything you do and will ever seek for you to overcome error. But He will never cease to love you and to strive for you to live to enjoy eternal peace and happiness. Should you have any thoughts or feelings to the contrary, when you are living worthily, they are not motivated by the Lord. They must be cast aside by sincere prayer, even when there is no desire to pray.

Should you ever feel distanced from the Lord, it will be for one of two causes: either you have done something wrong, or the Lord has given you a growth experience. Prayerfully try to determine the cause of feelings of isolation. If the separation is caused by your breaking of a commandment, plead for the strength and courage that you can repent and be forgiven. If it results from a challenge the Lord wants you to overcome for your growth and development, patiently work to overcome it. While doing so, seek sustaining power from God. In either of these challenges, as you continue to plead for help He will guide you to accomplish what you must do to restore your confidence that He is near. He is always near. When any barriers to communication are removed, that reality will be confirmed to you.

How great is the role of the love of our Father in Heaven and of His Only Begotten Son. How unfathomable is the extent of the blessings, peace, and happiness that flow from that love. Should we not constantly emulate it as we are able in our own lives?

I know of the indescribable depth of the love of Jesus Christ, of how it communicates confidence in time of need, peace in periods of turmoil, and boundless happiness to overcome loneliness and sadness. May our Lord and Master bless you for your faith in Him with an undeniable confirmation of His pure love. May the power of love fill your life with peace and happiness.

CHAPTER 26

THE POWER OF A
PERSONAL TESTIMONY

As WE APPROACH THE end of our time together, there is one more principle I am anxious to discuss with you. I realize that very little of what I have shared in these pages will have any lasting benefit unless you believe the doctrines we've talked about. It is necessary that you have or acquire a personal testimony of their truthfulness. For that reason I have reserved that vital subject until now. In the following paragraphs I will present principles and suggestions intended to strengthen your personal testimony of God, our Eternal Father, His Precious Son Jesus Christ, the Holy Ghost, and the eternal truths They have provided for your everlasting benefit.

For enduring peace and security, at some time in life, in quiet moments of reflection, if you have not already done so, you must come to know with a surety that there is a God in heaven who loves you, that He is in control, and that He will help you. That conviction is the core of a strong testimony.

In this uncertain world, some things will never change: the perfect love of our Heavenly Father for each of us; the assurance that He is there and will always hear us; the existence of absolute, unchanging truths; the fact that there is a plan of happiness; the assurance that success in life is attained through faith in Jesus Christ and obedience to His teachings because of the redemptive power of His Atonement; the certainty of life after death; the reality that our condition there is set by how we live here.

Whether one does or does not accept these truths does not alter their reality. They are the fundamental building blocks of a living testimony. A strong testimony is the unshakable foundation of a secure, meaningful life where peace, confidence, happiness, and love can flourish. When we consistently obey the teachings of the Savior, we develop a testimony that provides the conviction that life will be purposeful. Such a testimony also helps us have the capacity to overcome the challenges that arise in life. A testimony grows from understanding truth, confirmed by prayer and the pondering of scriptural doctrine. It is nurtured by living those truths in faith and the secure confidence that the promised results will be obtained. It is anchored in a conviction that an all-knowing God is in command of His work. He will not fail. He will keep His promises.

Some never gain a testimony because they cast away truth when it differs from their own convictions. If you know of any individuals like that, counsel them to begin by accepting that the principle in question could be true. Then encourage them to believe that they can have a confirmation of the truth in doubt by consistently living it. That trial of their faith will in time result in a confirming witness.[1]

A strong testimony is the sustaining power of a successful life. It is centered in an understanding of the divine attributes of God our Father, Jesus Christ, and the Holy Ghost. It is secured by a willing reliance upon Them. A powerful testimony is grounded in the personal assurance that the Holy Ghost can guide and inspire your daily acts for good.

A testimony is fortified by spiritual impressions that confirm to you the truthfulness of a principle or a righteous act—or that give warning of pending danger. Such impressions can teach you things you did not know but very much need. Often such guidance will be accompanied by powerful emotions that make it difficult for you to speak and that bring tears to your eyes. But a testimony is not emotion. It is the very essence of righteous character. Your testimony will deepen and be strengthened by correct choices made with trusting faith in things that are believed and, at least initially, are not seen.[2]

A strong testimony has sustained prophets throughout the ages and fortified them to act with courage and determination in times of difficulty. A powerful testimony can do the same for you. As you reinforce your own personal testimony, you will have power to make correct choices so that you can stand unwaveringly against the pressures of an increasingly vicious world. Your personal security and happiness depend on the strength of your testimony, for it will guide your actions in times of temptations, trial, or weakness.

Honestly evaluate your personal life. How strong is your own testimony? Is it truly a sustaining power in your life, or is it more a hope that what you have learned is true? Is it a vague belief that worthwhile concepts and patterns of life seem to be reasonable and logical? Such mere mental assent will not help you much when you face the serious challenges that will inevitably come to you. Does your testimony guide you to correct decisions? To do so, fundamental truths must become part of the very fiber of your character. They must be an essential part of your being, more treasured than all material possessions. If an honest assessment of your own testimony confirms that it is not as strong as it should be, how can it be strengthened?

Recognize that the Lord wants you to understand and prove through personal experience the truthfulness of His teachings. He will confirm the certainty that His laws will produce the promised results as you willingly obey them. Your willing obedience of those laws, with your exercise of faith that they are true, will convert your wavering belief into a rock-solid, vibrant testimony of their truthfulness.

Your testimony will be fortified as you exercise faith in Jesus Christ, in His teachings, and in His limitless power to accomplish what He has promised.[3] The key words are "exercise faith." True faith has enormous power, but you must follow correct principles to unleash that power. Moroni taught, "Faith is things which are hoped for and not seen; wherefore, dispute not because ye see not, for ye receive no witness until after the trial of your faith."[4] That means you must practice the truth or principle you have faith in or feel that you should have faith in. As you live it consistently, you will receive a witness of its truthfulness through the power of the Holy Ghost. That confirmation often comes as a feeling of peace. It can also be manifest as a stirring within you. It might be evidenced by opening doors to other truths. As you patiently look for a confirmation, it will come. The Lord will give you the capacity to understand and prove through personal experience the truthfulness of His teachings.

There are many ways to strengthen your testimony. Perhaps setting goals is one way that can help you. Another can be establishing a method to report to a trusted friend your progress toward those goals. If you have not done so already, you will discover that an even stronger way to build a firm testimony is to study, ponder, and distill truths from the doctrines of the Church as the very foundation of your life. Doctrine, understood and applied, is a mighty, sustaining, supporting force for good. It is the certain foundation of a strong testimony.

A powerful testimony grows from quiet moments of prayer and pondering as you recognize the impressions that accompany such effort. Humble, trusting prayer brings consolation, solace, comfort, direction, and peace the unworthy can never know.

Some truths regarding prayer may help you energize your personal testimony. The Lord will hear your prayers in time of need. He will invariably answer them. However, His answers will generally not come while you are on your knees praying, even when you may plead for an immediate response. There is a pattern that must be followed. You are asked to *look* for an answer to your prayers.[5] Obey His counsel to "study it out in your mind."[6] Often you will think of a solution. Then seek confirmation that your answer is right. This help can come from prayer and from pondering the scriptures, by the intervention of others,[7] or from your own efforts, through the guidance of the Holy Spirit.

At times the Lord will want you to proceed with trust before you receive a confirming answer. His answer generally comes as small packets of help. As each piece is followed in faith, it will unite with others to give you the whole answer. This pattern requires you to exercise faith in His capacity to respond. While sometimes very hard, it results in significant personal growth. On occasion, the Lord will give you an answer before you ask. This can occur when you are unaware of a danger or may be doing the wrong thing, mistakenly trusting that it is correct.

The confirming witness that comes in answer to sincere prayer and appropriate fasting will fortify your testimony. Anchor your life in the bedrock of truth by understanding and applying eternal principles. A true principle makes decisions clear even under the most compelling temptations to violate truth and even in confusing circumstances that would otherwise make choices difficult.

President Marion G. Romney taught of the testimony-strengthening power of scriptures with this personal example: "I urge you to get acquainted with [the Book of Mormon]. Read it to your children; they are not too young to understand it. I remember reading it with one of my lads when he was very young. . . . I lay in the lower bunk and he in the upper bunk. We were each reading aloud alternate paragraphs of those last three marvelous chapters of Second Nephi. I heard his voice breaking and thought he had a cold. . . . As we finished he said . . . , 'Daddy, do you ever cry when you read the Book of Mormon?' 'Yes, Son. . . . Sometimes the Spirit of the Lord so witnesses to my soul that the Book of Mormon is true that I do cry.' 'Well,' he said, 'that is what happened to me tonight.'"[8]

Service to others will enhance your testimony when that service is freely given. Such service can result from formal callings to Church positions or missionary assignments. Another form of valuable service is through willing obedience to the law of tithing and fast offerings. Such obedience refines the spirit and engenders gratitude for the richness of the Lord's blessings. It also provides the means to administer relief and establish a financial base to extend the work of the kingdom throughout the world. I feel that the Lord expresses gratitude for such service by increasing your capacity to love and lift others around you.

As your testimony is fortified, Satan will try harder to tempt you. Resist his efforts. You will become stronger and his influence on you weaker.[9] Satan's increasing impact in the world is allowed to provide an atmosphere in which we can prove ourselves. While he causes havoc today, Satan's final destiny of total failure was fixed by Jesus Christ through His Atonement and Resurrection. The fate of Satan was sealed forever as Jesus, our Master, was resurrected from the dead and took His place by His Holy Father, to rule and reign forever.

The devil will not triumph. He must operate within bounds set by the Lord. He cannot take away any blessing you have earned. He cannot alter character that has been forged from righteous decisions. He has no power to destroy the eternal bonds established through the sealing power in a holy temple between a husband, wife, and children. He cannot quench true faith. He cannot take away your testimony. Yes, these things can be lost by succumbing to his temptations. But he has no power in and of himself to destroy them. The law of justice assures such protection.

These and other truths are certainties. However, your conviction of their reality must come from your own understanding of truth, from your own application of divine law and your willingness to seek the confirming witness of the Spirit. Your testimony may begin from acknowledgment that the teachings of the Lord seem reasonable. But it must grow by applying those laws. Then your own experience will attest to their validity and yield the results promised. That confirmation will not all come at once. A strong testimony comes line upon line, precept upon precept. It requires faith, time, consistent obedience, and a willingness to sacrifice.

A strong testimony cannot be built upon a weak foundation. Therefore, don't pretend you believe something when you are not sure of it. Seek to receive a ratifying witness of the matter in question. Wrestle in mighty prayer, live righteously, and ask for a spiritual confirmation. The beauty of the teachings of the Lord is that they are absolutely true and that you can confirm that for yourself. Hone your spiritual susceptibility by being constantly alert to the guidance that will come through the still, small voice of the Spirit. In humble prayer, let your Father in Heaven know of your feelings, your needs, your concerns, your hopes and aspirations. Speak to Him with total confidence, knowing that He will hear and respond. Then patiently go forth in your life doing those things you trust are correct, walking with confidence born of faith and righteousness. Then patiently wait for the confirming response that will come in the manner and at the time the Lord considers most appropriate.[10]

Why was Joseph Smith able to do that which was beyond his personal capacity? It was because of his powerful testimony. That conviction led to his obedience, his faith in the Master, and his unwavering determination to do His will. I testify that as your testimony grows in strength, you can enjoy inspiration when needed and earned, to know what to do and, when necessary, divine power or capacity to accomplish it.[11] Joseph Smith perfected his ability to follow the guidance of the Lord by practiced personal discipline. He did not let his own desires, convenience, or the persuasions of men interfere with that compliance. Follow his example.

Humbly pray to your Father in Heaven for guidance and strength in combating temptation. Your security is in Him and His Beloved Son, Jesus Christ. I know that the Savior loves you. He will confirm your efforts to strengthen your testimony so that it becomes a consummate power for good in your life, a power that will sustain you in every period of need and give you peace and assurance in these times of uncertainty.

As you pray for a stronger testimony, you may feel the need for a vigorous spiritual housecleaning, not just a rearrangement of prejudices or brushing off of accumulated convictions. It may require a deep introspective scouring, a cleansing away of inappropriate thoughts and acts, and a casting out of any debilitating habits or friends—in short, a spiritual rejuvenation. Such renewal is generally not self-initiated. It can arise from spiritual prompting occasioned by profound experiences, disquieting thoughts, or the recognition of divine guidance. Should such an impression come, give it full freedom. Respond quickly and decisively. The transient discomfort that accompanies spiritual stretching is compensated manyfold by increased capacity to feel and to interpret, through the Holy Ghost, the will of your Father in Heaven in your life.

Your determination to always choose the right will strengthen your growing testimony. Your use of the gift of the Holy Ghost provides the ability to develop a powerfully sensitive capacity to make the right choices. Cultivate that gift. As the Lord has said, that is accomplished by consistent, righteous living. As you enhance your capacity to sense the direction of that infallible influence you will avoid disappointment, discouragement, and even tragedy.

An invincible resolve to live worthily and be consistent in obedience is fundamental to developing a strong testimony. I have used extremely potent motivating influences to live such a life, influences that perhaps you might employ. These include the love of a cherished, eternal companion and a compelling desire not to disappoint her. Combined with that is the powerful motivating force of the love of children and parents. I have another compelling, motivating influence. It is the profound love of Father in Heaven and His Beloved Son, Jesus Christ, and of the Holy Ghost. This divine Godhead is the very foundation of all we can experience and enjoy for good. Our Father's plan of happiness provides the way. The love our Savior has for us and His capacities earned from His willing Atonement give us the power to overcome mistakes and grow. Their direction, through the Holy Ghost, leads us to make the right choices and warn us of dangers in our path. These personages provide the basis upon which you can strengthen your testimony and thus build a secure life. They are absolutely trustworthy, perfect in love and compassion, and want your success more than you yourself can ever desire.

With all the capacity I possess, I counsel you to strengthen continually your testimony that there is in very deed a Heavenly Father who is in control. Come to really know more of God through the scriptures, prayer, and the testimonies of His chosen servants. Then He can guide you in every circumstance. And in times of trouble and difficulty, peace will settle upon your mind and heart as you understand your true, total dependence upon the Lord and exercise faith in His perfect love and limitless power.

One may say, "I don't have all the blessings of an ideal family and full Church experience." Neither did I enjoy all of those advantages as my personal testimony of truth was founded, nor did some other members of the Quorum of the Twelve. Compensate by obtaining your own unwavering testimony of truth. Obtain a personal conviction that the Church of Jesus Christ has been restored to earth and that His doctrines are true. There are different paths to that treasured gift. A flickering flame of faith can die if not nurtured. But that tiny flame can grow into a brilliant, unquenchable fire through sincere prayer and consistent study of the Book of Mormon and other scriptures. Such faith will be sustained as you live the principles you learn. It will solidify your testimony.

My desire is that your heart has been touched, your imagination stirred, and your determination fortified to live a better life as a result of the messages in this book. Possibly you have been motivated to improve your life to make your actions more consistent with your goals and dreams. You may have been prompted to abandon a debilitating part of your current life, or to set in order an unwholesome habit that has begun to take root only to later produce bitter fruit if it is not overcome. You may be someone who has resolved to repent of serious mistakes and return to the refreshing renewal of righteousness. All such impressions to improve come from the Savior through the Holy Ghost. As you seek His help, He will guide you through the feelings communicated by the Spirit.

My own testimony was very weak when I went into the mission field. I didn't realize that fact at first. What I thought was a testimony was really an accumulation of facts in my mind that through missionary service the Lord helped convert into a strong conviction of His truth. Through the years, in a multiplicity of ways, some supernal, that fledgling beginning has been nurtured to become a heart-centered, deep, abiding, unquenchable testimony that now provides stability, strength, and confidence to everything I undertake to do in the name of the Lord.

I would bear that testimony of Him. Since thoughts of the Savior invoke in me tender feelings, I will first quote a few of His own declarations and then that of one of His prophets.

> I am the way, the truth, and the life: no man cometh unto the Father, but by me.[12]

> Behold, I am Jesus Christ, whom the prophets testified shall come into the world. And behold, I am the light and the life of the world; and I have drunk out of

that bitter cup which the Father hath given me, and have glorified the Father in taking upon me the sins of the world, in the which I have suffered the will of the Father in all things from the beginning. . . . Arise and come forth unto me, that ye may thrust your hands into my side, and also that ye may feel the prints of the nails in my hands and in my feet, that ye may know that I am the God of Israel, and the God of the whole earth, and have been slain for the sins of the world.[13]

[Jesus] stood in the midst, and saith unto them, Peace be unto you. And when he had so said, he shewed unto them his hands and his side. . . . As my Father hath sent me, even so send I you. And when he had said this, he breathed on them, and saith unto them, Receive ye the Holy Ghost.[14]

"Listen to the voice of Jesus Christ, your Redeemer, the Great I AM, whose arm of mercy hath atoned for your sins; who will gather his people even as a hen gathereth her chickens under her wings, even as many as will hearken to my voice and humble themselves before me, and call upon me in mighty prayer.[15]

Behold, I come unto my own, to fulfil all things which I have made known unto the children of men from the foundation of the world, and to do the will, both of the Father and of the Son.[16]

For I will reveal myself from heaven with power and great glory, with all the hosts thereof, and dwell in righteousness with men on earth a thousand years, and the wicked shall not stand.[17]

I quote from Alma's testimony as if it were my own, for I have that same conviction:

> I speak in the energy of my soul. . . . For I am called to speak after this manner, according to the holy order of God, which is in Christ Jesus; yea, I am commanded to stand and testify . . . that I do know that these things whereof I have spoken are true. . . . They are made known unto me by the Holy Spirit of God. . . . I have fasted and prayed many days that I might know these things of myself. And now I do know of myself that they are true; for the Lord God hath made them manifest unto me by his Holy Spirit.[18]

I solemnly testify that I know of the reality of the following declarations:

> To some it is given by the Holy Ghost to know that Jesus Christ is the Son of God, and that he was crucified for the sins of the world. To others it is given to believe on their words, that they also might have eternal life if they continue faithful.[19]

> Neither have angels ceased to minister unto the children of men. For behold, they are subject unto him, to minister according to the word of his command, showing themselves unto them of strong faith and a firm mind in every form of godliness. And the office of their ministry is to call men unto repentance . . . and to do the work of the covenants of the Father, which he hath made unto the children of men, to prepare the way among the children of men, by declaring the word of Christ unto the chosen vessels of the Lord, that they may bear testimony of him. And by so doing, the Lord God prepareth the way that the residue of

men may have faith in Christ, that the Holy Ghost may have place in their hearts . . . ; and after this manner bringeth to pass the Father, the covenants which he hath made unto the children of men.[20]

I know that someday I will be judged by how well I testified of my certain knowledge of Jesus Christ. Therefore, as one of His Apostles, authorized to bear witness of Him, I solemnly testify that I have an absolute witness that the Savior lives, that He is a resurrected, glorified personage of perfect love. I solemnly testify that this Being we refer to as our Master and Redeemer has an incomparable capacity to express love. I know of His perfect love. I witness that He gave His life that we by qualifying can live with Him eternally. He is the Prince of Peace, our Hope, our Mediator, our Savior. I solemnly witness that because of His Atonement our Father's plan of happiness will succeed, and Satan's horrible plan of compulsion and slavery is doomed to failure.

I know that when He began the excruciating experience that culminated in the Atonement, He knew that there would be no guaranteed outcome. Yet, He understood perfectly, as only a God could, that He must make no mistake or fall short in the most minimal degree. With our mortal minds we can only inadequately imagine what a tremendous weight of responsibility He felt on His shoulders, knowing that if He in any detail did not fulfill the expectations of His Father, every one of us would have been lost to the eternal torment of Satan. We will never know in mortality, for it is beyond our power of comprehension, what He endured in the trial of Gethsemane. He did fulfill His Father's expectations perfectly. He paid the price in full. He yielded His life in death to break the bonds of death. I know that He is now a glorified, resurrected being.

No mortal mind can adequately conceive, nor human tongue properly express the complete significance of all that Jesus Christ has done for the children of Father in Heaven through His incomparable Atonement.

I know that in describing Him we can use the terms *omniscient, omnipotent, omnipresent.* Those concepts are difficult for me to thoroughly comprehend, but I understand His love. I know something of His compassion. I know He appreciates how weak and how ill-prepared each of us who love Him feel. I have the certain confidence that He will strengthen you and bless you as you walk in faith, acting with trust. He will give you the strength you need to fulfill to the fullest measure everything our Father's plan for your happiness anticipates. The Prince of Peace will help you have great joy and happiness as you live worthy of that help.

I know this Church is the true restored Church of Jesus Christ. I positively know it. I know that it is presided over by a prophet of God. I know he is a prophet. I know that Jesus Christ directs the work and loves each of us personally. I witness that when we qualify by obedience and the proper exercise of moral agency, He helps us in direct and positive ways so that this experience in life is enriched, our capacity to serve is strengthened, and our joy and happiness are made full.

I solemnly witness that God our Father lives, that His plan of happiness is perfect. I bear testimony that as you raise your voice in prayer, those prayers are heard. They can best be answered when they come from a broken heart and a contrite spirit. I solemnly witness with every capacity that I possess that He knows you and that He loves you and will bless and guide your life through His Only Begotten Son, Our Master and Redeemer.

I adore our Savior Jesus Christ, and I solemnly bear witness that I know He lives. I accept total responsibility before our Father in Heaven for that witness, for it is true. The Master watches over His Church personally. He knows and loves you. As you seek to know and obey His will He will guide you, through the Holy Ghost, to enduring peace, consummate happiness, and periods of overwhelming joy.

NOTES

NOTES TO CHAPTER 1:
PURPOSE: TO FIND PEACE WITH HAPPINESS AND JOY

1. John 14:27.
2. D&C 19:23.
3. See Alma 36:20–22.
4. See Alma 42:16.
5. See Mosiah 4:2–3.
6. Topical Guide, s.v. "Light of Christ."
7. D&C 88:6–12.
8. D&C 88:13.
9. John 3:19–21; Moroni 7:19; D&C 84:46–47; 93:28.
10. Moroni 7:16.
11. D&C 84:46–47.
12. Mosiah 4:3.

NOTES TO CHAPTER 2:
THE PLAN OF HAPPINESS AND EXALTATION

1. Moses 1:39.
2. See Moses 6:36.
3. See D&C 98:12.
4. See Job 23:10–13; D&C 58:2–4; 101:4–5, 7–8.
5. Abraham 3:24–26.
6. Mosiah 3:19.
7. Mosiah 23:21–22.
8. James 1:3–4.
9. Acts 14:22; James 1:3–4; Ether 12:6.
10. See D&C 58:2–3.
11. See D&C 58:4.
12. John 3:16–17.
13. 2 Nephi 2:27.
14. 2 Timothy 3:12.
15. Topical Guide, s.v. "Salvation, Plan of."

16. D&C 58:26–29.
17. 2 Nephi 2:25; Abraham 3:24–26.
18. See D&C 132:3–6, 19–22.
19. Alma 42:24–25.
20. Alma 34:16.

NOTES TO CHAPTER 3:
TO LIVE THE FAMILY-CENTERED GREAT PLAN OF HAPPINESS

1. Moses 2:27. See also Moses 2:28; 3:5; James R. Clark, comp., *Messages of the First Presidency of The Church of Jesus Christ of Latter-day Saints,* 6 vols. (Salt Lake City: Bookcraft, 1965–75), 4:200–206; James E. Talmage, *Millennial Star,* August 1922, 539.
2. 2 Nephi 9:13.
3. Alma 42:15.
4. 2 Nephi 11:5.
5. Moses 6:62.
6. Alma 42:8.
7. See Alma 12:32.
8. "The Family: A Proclamation to the World," *Ensign,* November 1995, 102.
9. See "The Family: A Proclamation to the World," 102.
10. See "The Family: A Proclamation to the World," 102.
11. See 2 Nephi 2:15–16, 27.
12. See D&C 29:36–39.
13. See D&C 10:12, 23.
14. Moses 4:17.
15. Moses 4:18.
16. Moses 4:19.
17. Moses 4:19.
18. Moses 5:10; emphasis added.
19. Moses 5:11; emphasis added.
20. See Moses 5:1.
21. See Moses 5:2.
22. Moses 5:6.
23. Moses 5:7–8.
24. Moses 5:12.
25. Moses 5:16.
26. See Spencer W. Kimball, San Antonio Fireside, 3 December 1977, 9–10; see also "The Family: A Proclamation to the World," 102.
27. See Ezra Taft Benson, Fireside for Parents, February 22, 1987.
28. See 2 Nephi 9:13.
29. Joseph Fielding Smith, *Doctrines of Salvation,* 3 vols., ed. Bruce R. McConkie (Salt Lake City: Bookcraft, 1954–56), 2:76.
30. See "The Family: A Proclamation to the World," 102.
31. Jeanene W. Scott, BYU Women's Conference, 6 April 1989, 1.

NOTES TO CHAPTER 4:
FULL CONVERSION BRINGS PEACE WITH HAPPINESS

1. See Matthew 17:1–3.
2. Luke 22:31–33.
3. Mark 14:27–31.
4. Luke 22:56–62.
5. Acts 3:2–10.
6. Acts 4:31.
7. Marion G. Romney, in Guatemala Area Conference, 1977, 8.
8. See Romans 10:17; Joseph F. Smith, *Gospel Doctrine* (Salt Lake City: Deseret Book, 1939), 99.
9. See Ether 12:6.
10. Mark 4:14–15.
11. Mark 4:16–17.
12. Mark 4:18–19.
13. Mark 4:20.
14. Helaman 3:35.
15. 3 Nephi 9:13–14.

NOTES TO CHAPTER 5:
TO UNDERSTAND SPIRITUAL GUIDANCE

1. D&C 43:15–16.
2. 1 Nephi 3:7.
3. Edward L. Kimball, *Lengthen Your Stride: The Presidency of Spencer W. Kimball* (Salt Lake City: Deseret Book, 2005), 216.
4. D&C 8:2–3.
5. D&C 50:13–14.
6. D&C 50:17–20.
7. D&C 50:21–22; emphasis added.
8. See Helaman 9:19–20.
9. See Helaman 9:25–36.
10. Helaman 10:2–5.
11. Helaman 10:5.
12. Ether 2:13.
13. Ether 2:14.
14. Ether 2:15.
15. Ether 3:9.
16. Ether 3:11–13.
17. D&C 9:7–8.
18. D&C 8:2–3; emphasis added.
19. D&C 9:9.
20. D&C 9:8.
21. D&C 6:23.

22. David O. McKay, in Conference Report, April 1969, 153.
23. David O. McKay, in Conference Report, October 1968, 85–86.
24. McKay, in Conference Report, October 1968, 86.

NOTES TO CHAPTER 6:
TO OBTAIN SPIRITUAL GUIDANCE

1. Alma 26:22; emphasis added on this and the following scriptures.
2. D&C 93:1.
3. Enos 1:3–8.
4. 3 Nephi 14:7–8.
5. Enos 1:10.
6. Psalm 25:9.
7. D&C 42:61.
8. D&C 45:57.
9. Alma 17:2–3.
10. D&C 88:67.
11. Alma 5:46.
12. Ether 4:7.
13. Joseph F. Smith, *Gospel Doctrine* (Salt Lake City: Deseret Book, 1939), 3–4.
14. D&C 50:24.
15. Psalm 119:105.
16. D&C 11:13–14.
17. Wilford Woodruff, in *Teachings of Presidents of the Church: Wilford Woodruff* (Salt Lake City: The Church of Jesus Christ of Latter-day Saints, 2004), 49.
18. Wilford Woodruff, *The Discourses of Wilford Woodruff*, ed. G. Homer Durham (Salt Lake City: Bookcraft, 1946), 290; see also page 289.
19. Woodruff, *Discourses of Wilford Woodruff*, 288.
20. John Taylor, in *Teachings of Presidents of the Church: John Taylor* (Salt Lake City: The Church of Jesus Christ of Latter-day Saints, 2001), 153.
21. J. Reuben Clark Jr., in Conference Report, April 1934, 94.
22. Private communication.
23. D&C 1:28.
24. See Alma 26:22.
25. See D&C 43:16.
26. See 2 Nephi 25:23.
27. 1 Corinthians 2:11, 14.
28. Ether 12:27.
29. Alma 26:10–12.
30. Moroni 7:33.
31. Mosiah 4:3.
32. Helaman 3:35.
33. Ether 12:6.
34. Hugh B. Brown, in Conference Report, October 1969, 105.
35. Joseph Smith, *Lectures on Faith* (Salt Lake City: Deseret Book, 1985), 72.

36. James E. Faust, "A Personal Relationship with the Savior," *Ensign,* November 1976, 59.

37. Helaman 10:4.

38. D&C 43:16.

39. Personal communication. See also Harold B. Lee, *Decisions for Successful Living* (Salt Lake City: Deseret Book, 1973), 232–33.

40. D&C 50:19–22.

41. D&C 8:2.

42. D&C 84:43–47.

43. Joseph Fielding Smith, in Conference Report, October 1958, 22.

44. Alma 26:22.

45. D&C 9:8–9.

46. Marion G. Romney, "Seek the Spirit," *Improvement Era* 64 (December 1961): 947.

47. D&C 88:63–64.

48. John 14:16–18, 25–27.

49. Lee, *Stand Ye in Holy Places,* 245–46.

50. Gordon B. Hinckley, *Teachings of Gordon B. Hinckley* (Salt Lake City: Deseret Book, 1997), 556.

51. D&C 58:26–28; see also verses 29–33.

52. D&C 3:4.

53. David O. McKay, in Conference Report, April 1967, 84.

54. Argentine North Mission (now Argentina Cordoba Mission), November 1966.

55. McKay, in Conference Report, April 1967, 133.

56. D&C 59:21.

57. Personal communication.

58. D&C 78:19.

59. Spencer W. Kimball, "Spoken from Their Hearts," *Ensign,* November 1975, 111.

60. Brigham Young, *Discourses of Brigham Young,* ed. John A. Widtsoe (Salt Lake City: Bookcraft, 1998), 10.

61. Joseph Smith, *History of the Church of Jesus Christ of Latter-day Saints,* 7 vols., ed. by B. H. Roberts, 2d. ed. rev. (Salt Lake City: The Church of Jesus Christ of Latter-day Saints, 1932–51), 2:199.

NOTES TO CHAPTER 7:
TRUST IN THE LORD

1. See 2 Nephi 2:7.

2. See Proverbs 3:11–12; Hebrews 12:5–9.

3. See D&C 11:12–13; Alma 36:3.

4. See Proverbs 3:5–7.

5. Matthew 26:39.

6. Matthew 26:42; see also verse 44.

7. Matthew 26:42.

8. 3 Nephi 27:29.

9. D&C 50:5.
10. D&C 58:2–4.

NOTES TO CHAPTER 8:
TO MAKE AND KEEP THE RIGHT DECISIONS

1. See Moroni 7:12–17.
2. See D&C 64:34.

NOTES TO CHAPTER 9:
DIVINE CURRENTS

1. Spencer W. Kimball, "Ocean Currents and Family Influences," *Ensign,* November 1974, 110–11.
2. D&C 1:31–32.
3. D&C 8:2; see also verse 8:3.
4. D&C 42:14.
5. D&C 19:38.
6. D&C 11:12–14.
7. See D&C 43:15–16.
8. D&C 101:16.
9. D&C 3:1–3.
10. Psalm 23:1–6.
11. Jacob 4:10.
12. Psalm 55:22.
13. D&C 61:18; 82:5; 92:1; 93:49.
14. 1 Nephi 19:23.
15. D&C 46:7.
16. D&C 6:36–37.
17. Joseph Smith, *History of the Church of Jesus Christ of Latter-day Saints,* 7 vols., ed. B. H. Roberts, 2d. ed. rev. (Salt Lake City: The Church of Jesus Christ of Latter-day Saints, 1932–51), 2:170; emphasis in original.
18. See D&C 43:15–16.
19. D&C 59:21.

NOTES TO CHAPTER 10:
THE ATONEMENT CAN SECURE YOUR PEACE AND HAPPINESS

1. Moses 7:53.
2. See James 5:16; Alma 5:45–46; D&C 112:10.
3. See D&C 133:50, 52–53.
4. 2 Nephi 2:8; emphasis added.
5. 2 Nephi 25:23.

NOTES

NOTES TO CHAPTER 11:
FORGIVE TO BE FORGIVEN

1. Matthew 6:14–15.
2. Gordon B. Hinckley, *Faith, the Essence of True Religion* (Salt Lake City: Deseret Book, 1989), 89–90.
3. D&C 64:9–10; see also Matthew 18:21–22; D&C 98:40.
4. Mosiah 26:30–31; see also 3 Nephi 13:14; D&C 82:1.
5. Truman Madsen, *Joseph Smith the Prophet* (Salt Lake City: Bookcraft, 1989), 87–88. See also *Journal of Abraham H. Cannon,* 9 April 1890.
6. Mark 11:25–26.
7. See Ephesians 4:32; Colossians 3:13.
8. See Boyd K. Packer, "Balm of Gilead," *Ensign,* November 1987, 17–18.
9. Joseph Smith, *History of the Church of Jesus Christ of Latter-day Saints,* 7 vols., ed. by B. H. Roberts, 2d. ed. rev. (Salt Lake City: The Church of Jesus Christ of Latter-day Saints, 1932–51), 4:141, 142.
10. Smith, *History of the Church,* 4:162–64.
11. Smith, *History of the Church,* 2:338.
12. Smith, *History of the Church,* 2:338.
13. Smith, *History of the Church,* 2:339.
14. Smith, *History of the Church,* 2:342–43.
15. Smith, *History of the Church,* 2:343–44.
16. Joseph Smith, *The Personal Writings of Joseph Smith,* comp. and ed. Dean C. Jessee (Salt Lake City: Deseret Book, 2002), 143–44. See also Lawrence R. Flake, *Prophets and Apostles of the Last Dispensation* (Provo, Utah: Religious Studies Center, 2001), 367–69.
17. Mark 11:25.

NOTES TO CHAPTER 12:
THE BENEFIT OF REPENTANCE

1. D&C 133:46–50.
2. See Mosiah 5:10–13; 2 Nephi 25:20.
3. See 2 Nephi 2:10; 9:22.
4. See 2 Nephi 9:7–9.
5. See 2 Nephi 2:5–8.
6. See Alma 42:15.
7. See 2 Nephi 9.
8. See Helaman 5:9; Alma 34:8–13; 42:11–30.
9. Helaman 5:9, 11; emphasis added.
10. D&C 58:42.
11. Matthew 6:12; see also 18:23–35; 3 Nephi 13:14–15.
12. Matthew 6:14–15; see also Ephesians 4:32.
13. D&C 1:31–33.

14. Spencer W. Kimball, *The Miracle of Forgiveness* (Salt Lake City: Bookcraft, 1969), 149.
15. Joseph F. Smith, *Gospel Doctrine* (Salt Lake City: Deseret Book, 1939), 100–101.
16. Alma 42:27; emphasis added.
17. Helaman 3:35.

NOTES TO CHAPTER 13:
HOW TO REPENT

1. Alma 42:24.
2. Howard W. Hunter, "'Exceeding Great and Precious Promises,'" *Ensign,* November 1994, 8.
3. 3 Nephi 9:22.
4. 3 Nephi 9:13–15.
5. Spencer W. Kimball, *The Miracle of Forgiveness* (Salt Lake City: Deseret Book, 1969), 353.
6. Spencer W. Kimball, *Faith Precedes the Miracle* (Salt Lake City: Deseret Book, 1972), 181.
7. From J. Reuben Clark Jr., "As Ye Sow . . . ," Brigham Young University Speeches of the Year, May 3, 1955, 7.
8. Moroni 6:8.
9. Helaman 5:12.
10. D&C 58:42.
11. Proverbs 28:13.
12. Joseph Smith, *Teachings of the Prophet Joseph Smith,* comp. Joseph Fielding Smith (Salt Lake City: Deseret Book, 1976), 148.
13. D&C 58:42.
14. D&C 82:7.
15. D&C 82:10.
16. See Leviticus 6:4; Numbers 5:7.
17. D&C 1:31–32; emphasis added.
18. Alma 34:15–16; emphasis added.
19. Alma 38:8.
20. Harold B. Lee, "'Stand Ye in Holy Places,'" *Ensign,* July 1973, 122–23.

NOTES TO CHAPTER 14:
TO FIND MORE PEACE AND JOY IN LIFE

1. 2 Nephi 2:25.
2. D&C 98:1.
3. D&C 78:19.
4. Sir Winston Churchill, *Painting As a Pastime* (London: Odhams Press, 1948), 7, 18–19.
5. See D&C 78:17.
6. 2 Nephi 2:25.

7. 1 Nephi 3:7.
8. 1 Nephi 3:15; 4:6–7.
9. See D&C 78:17–19; 82:10.
10. See D&C 130:20–21.
11. See James 1:2–4; 5:11.
12. Mosiah 24:14–15.
13. Spencer W. Kimball, *The Teachings of Spencer W. Kimball,* ed. Edward L. Kimball (Salt Lake City: Bookcraft, 1982), 252.
14. D&C 24:8.
15. See 2 Nephi 2:22–25.
16. Isaiah 40:31.
17. Alma 41:10.
18. Psalm 128:1–2.
19. 2 Nephi 2:15–16; Alma 12:24.
20. See D&C 29:42–43.

NOTES TO CHAPTER 15:
TO LIVE WELL AMID INCREASING EVIL

1. Gordon B. Hinckley, "Standing Strong and Immovable," Worldwide Leadership Training Meeting, January 10, 2004, 20.
2. Gordon B. Hinckley, "The State of the Church," *Ensign,* November 2003, 4, 7.
3. D&C 64:32–34.
4. Joshua 24:15.
5. Romans 12:21.
6. D&C 6:33–34.
7. D&C 75:16.
8. Moroni 10:32.
9. Alma 41:10.

NOTES TO CHAPTER 16:
TO OVERCOME LONELINESS AND WORRY TO FIND PEACE AND HAPPINESS

1. Personal communication from Mary Lee Call.
2. David O. McKay, in Conference Report, April 1969, 150.
3. Moroni 7:45–47.
4. Alma 41:10.
5. Ether 12:27.
6. Orson F. Whitney, quoted by Spencer W. Kimball, *Faith Precedes the Miracle* (Salt Lake City: Deseret Book, 1972), 98.
7. N. Eldon Tanner, quoted by Richard G. Scott, "To the Lonely and Misunderstood," in *Hope* (Salt Lake City: Deseret Book, 1988), 168.
8. D&C 58:42–43.
9. D&C 101:16.

10. See Jacob 4:13–14.
11. See 2 Nephi 28:21.
12. Moses 1:39.
13. Moroni 7:16–17.

NOTES TO CHAPTER 17:
"I CAN'T DO IT." "YES, YOU CAN."

1. Moroni 7:19–20, 25.
2. Moroni 7:26, 33.
3. Spencer W. Kimball, "The Family Influence," *Ensign,* July 1973, 17.
4. D&C 88:67–68.
5. Mosiah 4:27.
6. Spencer W. Kimball, *The Teachings of Spencer W. Kimball,* ed. Edward L. Kimball (Salt Lake City: Bookcraft, 1982), 530.
7. D&C 43:16.
8. D&C 43:9.

NOTES TO CHAPTER 18:
TO COPE WITH WHAT IS UNFAIR

1. In Boyd K. Packer, *Let Not Your Heart Be Troubled* (Salt Lake City: Bookcraft, 1991), 250.
2. See "Bishop John Wells: His Life and Labors," Harold B. Lee Library, Brigham Young University, typescript, 15.

NOTES TO CHAPTER 19:
TO COPE WITH MAJOR CHALLENGES THAT ARE COMPLETELY UNFAIR

1. See James 1:6; Enos 1:15; Moroni 7:26; D&C 8:10; 18:18.
2. Joseph Smith, *Teachings of the Prophet Joseph Smith,* comp. Joseph Fielding Smith (Salt Lake City: Deseret Book, 1976), 364.
3. 3 Nephi 17:7–8.
4. See D&C 122:7.
5. See D&C 138:1–4.
6. See Articles of Faith 1:3.
7. Matthew 18:6.
8. See D&C 64:10.
9. 3 Nephi 12:44.
10. See Mormon 9:27; Moroni 7:26, 33.

NOTES TO CHAPTER 20:
THE SUSTAINING POWER OF FAITH AND CHARACTER

1. See D&C 50:40–43; 58:26–28.
2. Helaman 12:1; see also Proverbs 3:5–6.

3. Ether 12:6; emphasis added.
4. Revelation 3:19.
5. Brigham Young, in *Journal of Discourses,* 26 vols. (London: Latter-day Saints' Book Depot, 1854–86), 3:205–6.
6. See D&C 89:3; 136:31–33.
7. See Ether 12:6.
8. James 1:3–4.
9. See Helaman 10:3–4.
10. Helaman 10:5.

NOTES TO CHAPTER 21:
FORTIFY YOUR RESOLVE TO DO BETTER

1. See 1 Nephi 3:7; 2 Nephi 2:27; D&C 50:21–22, 41–42, 44; 82:18.
2. See 2 Nephi 31:19–21.
3. D&C 6:36–37.
4. D&C 58:26–28.
5. Alma 37:37.
6. Demosthenes, "Third Olynthiac Oration."
7. David O. McKay, "'Let Virtue Garnish Thy Thoughts,'" *Improvement Era* 72 (June 1969): 28.
8. D&C 82:10.
9. Proverbs 23:7.

NOTES TO CHAPTER 22:
THE POWER TO OVERCOME

1. 3 Nephi 18:20.
2. Proverbs 3:5.

NOTES TO CHAPTER 23:
TO FIND PEACE AND DIRECTION FROM THE
SCRIPTURES AND PROPHETS

1. See the official Church conference reports, conference and other messages in the *Ensign* and *Liahona,* many digital compilations of General Authority talks, and so forth.
2. D&C 84:43–47.
3. 3 Nephi 9:22.
4. John 14:16–18, 25–26.
5. Ether 4:12.
6. John 14:27.
7. D&C 88:63–64.
8. Ether 12:27.
9. D&C 88:67–68.

10. D&C 46:7.
11. D&C 11:12–14.
12. D&C 64:32–34.
13. Psalm 119:105.
14. Proverbs 3:11–12.
15. Proverbs 3:5–7.
16. Romans 12:21.
17. 2 Timothy 3:16.
18. 1 Nephi 19:23.
19. Joseph Smith, *History of the Church of Jesus Christ of Latter-day Saints,* 7 vols., ed. B. H. Roberts, 2d. ed. rev. (Salt Lake City: The Church of Jesus Christ of Latter-day Saints, 1932–51), 1:282–83.
20. Joseph Fielding Smith, in Conference Report, October 1963, 22.
21. Ezra Taft Benson, "Godly Characteristics of the Master," *Ensign,* November 1986, 47.
22. Marion G. Romney, in CES Coordinators Convention, April 13, 1973.
23. Romney, in CES Coordinators Convention, April 13, 1973.
24. Gordon B. Hinckley, "The Power of the Book of Mormon," *Ensign,* June 1988, 6. See also, Gordon B. Hinckley "A Testimony Vibrant and True," *Ensign,* August 2005, 6.
25. Gordon B. Hinckley, *Discourses of President Gordon B. Hinckley, Volume 1: 1995–1999* (Salt Lake City: Deseret Book, 2005), 271–72.
26. Spencer W. Kimball, *The Teachings of Spencer W. Kimball,* ed. Edward L. Kimball (Salt Lake City: Bookcraft, 1982), 134.
27. Kimball, *Teachings of Spencer W. Kimball,* 135.
28. Spencer W. Kimball, "Planning for a Full and Abundant Life," *Ensign,* May 1974, 88.
29. Enos 1:3–4.
30. Enos 1:8.
31. Enos 1:10.
32. Helaman 10:3–4.
33. Helaman 10:3–4.
34. Helaman 10:3–4.
35. Helaman 10:3–4.
36. Helaman 10:3–4.
37. D&C 25:14–15.
38. D&C 25:16.
39. Psalm 23:1–6.
40. D&C 101:16.

NOTES TO CHAPTER 24:
THE PEACE AND HAPPINESS TEMPLE ORDINANCES CAN PROVIDE

1. D&C 132:5.
2. D&C 132:15–17.

3. D&C 132:19–21.
4. D&C 131:1–4.
5. D&C 128:9.
6. D&C 128:22–23.
7. Personal communication from one who was present.
8. Ezra Taft Benson, "The Book of Mormon and the Doctrine and Covenants," *Ensign,* May 1987, 85.
9. See Sheri L. Dew, *Ezra Taft Benson, A Biography* (Salt Lake City: Deseret Book, 1987), 511.
10. D&C 124:39.

NOTES TO CHAPTER 25:
THE ROLE OF LOVE

1. John 3:14–17.
2. Proverbs 3:11–12.
3. Matthew 5:46, 48.
4. 4 Nephi 1:15–18.
5. Psalm 97:10.
6. Deuteronomy 11:13–15.
7. 2 Nephi 31:20.
8. John 15:9–14.
9. Deuteronomy 6:5.
10. Matthew 22:36–39.
11. John 13:34–35.
12. D&C 88:123.
13. D&C 42:29.
14. John 21:15–17.
15. Parley P. Pratt, ed., *Autobiography of Parley P. Pratt* (Salt Lake City: Deseret Book, 1985), 259–60.
16. 2 Nephi 2:27; 9:8–9.
17. Moroni 7:45–47.

NOTES TO CHAPTER 26:
THE POWER OF A PERSONAL TESTIMONY

1. See Ether 12:6.
2. See Ether 12:6; Hebrews 11:1.
3. See Alma 26:22; D&C 3:1–10; 82:10.
4. Ether 12:6.
5. See D&C 6:23, 36; 8:2–3, 10; 9:9.
6. D&C 9:8.
7. See Spencer W. Kimball, *The Teachings of Spencer W. Kimball,* ed. Edward L. Kimball (Salt Lake City: Bookcraft, 1982), 252.
8. Marion G. Romney, in Conference Report, April 1949, 41.

9. See David O. McKay, "Let Virtue Garnish Thy Thoughts," *Improvement Era* 72 (June 1969): 28.
10. See David O. McKay, "The Times Call for Courageous Youth and True Manhood," *Improvement Era* 72 (June 1969): 117.
11. See D&C 43:16.
12. John 14:6.
13. 3 Nephi 11:10–11, 14.
14. John 20:19–22.
15. D&C 29:1–2.
16. 3 Nephi 1:14.
17. D&C 29:11.
18. Alma 5:43–46.
19. D&C 46:13–14.
20. Moroni 7:29–32.

INDEX